HOW TO PICK A PERFECT PRIVATE SCHOOL

Harlow G. Unger

Facts On File

How to Pick a Perfect Private School
Copyright © 1993 by Harlow G. Unger

Facts On File, Inc.
460 Park Avenue South
New York, NY 10016
USA

Library of Congress Cataloging-in-Publication Data
Unger, Harlow G., 1931–
  How to pick a perfect private school / Harlow G. Unger.
     p.   cm.
  Includes index.
  ISBN 0–8160–2753–6.—ISBN 0–8160–2887–7 (pb)
    1. Private Schools—United States.   2. School, Choice of—United States.
I. Title.
LC49.U54   1993
371′.02′0973—dc20   92–24176

A British CIP catalogue record for this book is available from the British Library.

Facts On File books are available at special discounts when purchased in bulk quantities for businesses, associations, institutions or sales promotions. Please call our Special Sales Department in New York at 212/683-2244 (dial 800/322-8755 except in NY, AK or HI).

Text design by Ron Monteleone
Jacket design by Ellie Nigretto
Composition by Facts On File, Inc.
Manufactured by the Maple-Vail Book Manufacturing Group
Printed in the United States of America

10 9 8 7 6 5 4 3 2 1
This book is printed on acid-free paper.

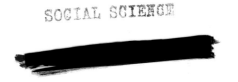

ABOUT THE AUTHOR

Harlow G. Unger has written three other books on education, *"What Did You Learn in School Today?"*, *A Student's Guide to College Admissions— Everything Your Guidance Counselor Has No Time to Tell You*, and *But What If I Don't Want to Go to College?*, all published by Facts On File. A veteran journalist and former adjunct professor at two New York–area colleges, he was educated in private schools, graduating from Horace Mann Lower School in New York and The Taft School, in Watertown, Connecticut, before getting his B.A. at Yale University and M.A. at California State University. His son Richard also attended private schools and is a graduate of Hackley School, in Tarrytown, New York, and Yale.

To Harold and Caryl
Dear cousins, dearest friends

SPECIAL DEDICATION

To Peter and Carol Gibbon
Walter Schneller
Raymond Mitton
John Van Leer

and the faculty and staff of Hackley School
for the deep, unflagging devotion and perfect education
they so generously give to all their students.

—Harlow G. Unger
—Richard Unger, '83

CONTENTS

ACKNOWLEDGMENTS

The author wishes to express his thanks to those whose knowledge, experience and counsel helped make this book possible: Dr. Peter Gibbon, Headmaster, Hackley School, Tarrytown, New York; Mr. Archibald A. Smith III, Headmaster, Trinity-Pawling School, Pawling, New York; Mr. Ronald D. Potier, Director of Admissions, Elizabethtown College, Elizabethtown, Pennsylvania; Mr. Richard Everett III, Educational Financial Consultant, Gloucester, Massachusetts, and former Business Manager, Groton School; the following members of the administration of Hackley School: Ms. Pamela Wetherill, Director of Admissions; Mr. David P. Bridges, Assistant Headmaster, and Mr. Daniel F. DiVirgilio, Director, Lower School; the following members of the administration and faculty of Trinity-Pawling School: Mr. Christopher G. Kelly Jr., Director of Admissions, and Ms. Carol C. Kneeland, Director of Language Retraining; Brother James Bonilla, Principal, Bishop Loughlin High School, Brooklyn, New York; Ms. Kathy Ishizuka, Associate Editor, Facts On File, New York, New York.

CHAPTER 1

PRIVATE VS. PUBLIC . . . IN CASE YOU'RE UNDECIDED

With annual tuition at some private day schools approaching $15,000 and some boarding schools charging more than $20,000 a year for tuition, room and board, many parents question whether they can afford private schools for their children. After all, the total cost of sending a child to private school, from kindergarten through 12th grade could, with inflation, easily exceed $150,000 in the next few years—not including the school taxes you'll have to continue paying to cover costs of public schools your child is *not* attending.

Add to that the annual cost of $25,000 to $30,000 for attending the most costly private colleges such as Yale, Harvard or Princeton (or up to $10,000 a year for attending public universities), and it means that you'll have to be prepared to spend as much as $300,000 or more to provide each of your children with a private-school education. If you've got three kids, count on spending a million dollars or more. And the costs could easily double if your children decide to go to graduate school.

Obviously, average-income parents cannot afford to spend so much, and, even if they can, many may not want to. For, aside from costs, many parents believe that the choice of public versus private schools involves an ethical question—i.e., that public schools represent a training ground for the "real world" where their children will eventually have to live as adults—as opposed to the elitist world of the wealthy, which, they believe, is symbolized by private country day schools and prep schools.

Now you may already have resolved these questions, but in case you haven't, let's take a brief look at what kind of education is available in the "real world" of today's public schools.

The sad truth, according to the U.S. Department of Education, is that 90% of 13-year-olds in U.S. public schools are "not adept at reading and are unable to understand complex information." The department found that public school "students at all grade levels are deficient in higher-order thinking skills" and that more than half the 17-year-olds in the United States cannot read or write adequately. More than 25% of all youngsters who graduate from public high schools are too illiterate to hold the most menial jobs, let alone go to college.

As for public-school teachers, most "come from the lower half of their college classes," according to the Carnegie Foundation for the Advancement of Teaching. What's more, many usually don't have or are not required to have degrees in the subjects they teach. They can major in modern dance at college and go on to teach history or math or anything else. Twenty percent of American public school teachers admit they have been assigned to teach subjects they are not qualified to teach.

A U.S. government study in 1983 found that one-half of the math, science and English teachers hired at the time were not qualified to teach those subjects, and that less than one-third of U.S. public high-school physics courses were taught by qualified teachers. Yet, those teachers now have almost 10 years' tenure in public schools across the country.

Making matters worse is the lack of national standards in education. Each state, and often each school district, has different standards—usually set by politicians, not educators. Unfortunately, American public-school education is controlled by a citizen democracy—elected school boards— that determines what children can and cannot learn in school. There are no literacy standards one must meet to run for and win school board membership, and, across America, thousands of school board members are elected and serve only to promote non-educational issues such as prayer in school, the banning of books they dislike, or imposition of such discredited subjects as "creation science." Promotion of better education—reading, writing and calculating skills—is not on the agenda of many school boards, and the quality of the schools they control invariably reflects their "know-nothing" approach to education.

The result is an educational hodgepodge that cripples tens of thousands of American children each year, leaving them unable to read, write or calculate adequately to attend college or even hold a job. Indeed, according to statistics from the most recent U.S. Department of Education publication, *Digest of Education Statistics,* the public school systems in nine states—Mississippi, Oklahoma, South Dakota, Alabama, Idaho, Tennessee, Utah, Hawaii and Louisiana—are substandard and rank 20% or more below national averages for school quality, while school systems in 16 other states, including California, Florida, Texas and Vermont, rank 10% to 20% below national averages. Only seven states have above-average public school systems and only one state in the entire United States—Connecticut—has a superior public school system. That means the chances of your child's obtaining even an average education in almost any public school are poor, at best, and almost nonexistent in most areas of the nation.

"If an unfriendly foreign power had attempted to impose on America the mediocre educational performance that exists (in public schools) today," the National Commission on Excellence in Education warned a decade ago, "we might well have viewed it as an act of war." The situation has deteriorated badly since that warning was issued.

In addition to abysmally poor education, many public schools seethe with social problems—poor discipline and supervision, fighting in hallways and school yards, assaults on students and teachers and open sale and use of drugs and alcohol. The brightest, academically gifted children and even many average children who would like to concentrate on academics often face humiliation or, worse, physical danger in some public schools. The problem of student and teacher safety in public schools is so great that some schools must now use metal detectors to screen students for weapons.

Social and academic problems are not limited to schools in low-income neighborhoods. According to the U.S. Department of Education, serious academic deficiencies are evident among students in about half the public schools in the United States. Even schools in affluent suburbs that once provided education equal to some of the finest private schools are graduating scores of children incapable of writing an intelligible letter or communicating thoughts more complex than "Like, ya know . . . well, like . . . it was cool, ya know."

Such gibberish doesn't just reflect an adolescent phase that children will outgrow. It reflects a basic inability to communicate and is a direct result of poor education. But that, unfortunately, is the frightening, disgraceful reality of "the real world" of public schools, and that is why millions of American parents turn to private schools to educate their children.

SUPERIOR PUBLIC SCHOOLS

Although the U.S. Department of Education deemed most American public school *systems* substandard, it did find many individual public schools that ranked well above national averages for various factors that measure school quality. So, if you're lucky enough to live near such a school, you should, quite obviously, give it serious consideration before laying out tens of thousands of dollars for private school.

In some communities, such as Lake Forest, Illinois, or Chappaqua, New York, as many as 85% of all high-school graduates go on to attend college.

3

Every year, such academically renowned public high schools as Philadelphia's Central, New York's Stuyvesant, and the Chicago area's New Trier and Lake Forest high schools send their top students to the most prestigious, academically demanding colleges and universities in the United States, including Duke, Harvard, Princeton, Rice, Stanford, University of Chicago, University of Michigan, Yale and many others. Indeed, thousands of other far less academically demanding public high schools can also boast that they too have sent students to an Ivy League or Ivy League-equivalent college or university.

And if you are sure that your children will thrive in such schools, by all means consider sending them there. But by thriving, I don't mean just having a good time. Just because kids are "happy" at school doesn't make that school a good one. By thriving, I mean getting the best possible education, and that means working and functioning at one's maximum abilities.

In public school, that means finishing in the top 20% of the class and emerging with almost straight As and Bs for all four, or certainly the last three, high-school years. To do less, given the level of instruction at most public schools, is essentially to fail.

In addition to a high grade point average, success at public school also means getting a combined score of at least 1000 or better on the Scholastic Aptitude Tests, scores of 600 or higher on each of three College Board Achievement Tests, and 4s or 5s on two or three Advanced Placement Examinations.

Success at public school also means participation and leadership in two or three major extracurricular activities such as the high-school newspaper, student political organizations and one or more major sports. If you are certain your child will compile that kind of record in your local public school system, then you may have no reason to consider private school. Such a youngster will probably win admission to almost any top college or university with little difficulty.

Indeed, the child I've described can probably get a good education at even the most mediocre public school, because that type of student is not only intellectually gifted, but motivated enough to reach out and seize every available intellectual, academic and social opportunity.

Most children, however, are obviously more average, and, left in even some of the best American public schools, they can easily emerge "deficient in higher-order thinking skills" and unable to read, write or calculate adequately. Here's why:

Most educators agree that few schools have much difficulty educating the top 25%, or top quartile, of any student body. Most teachers not only enjoy working with such bright, eager students, they go out of their way to help and encourage them as much as possible. Even the questions of intellectually curious children command teacher attention—often more than their share. Teachers tend to call on them in class more often than they call on other children—for two reasons. They know the brightest students will probably know the correct answers—and that means the class will move along more rapidly. Secondly, teachers hope that, by answering in "kid talk," the bright students will, indirectly, help teach slower students, who understand the language of their peers better than the more formal language of adults.

But there's another group of children in public schools that also commands a great deal of teacher attention—again, more than its share. This group is in the bottom quartile. Some are disruptive, badly behaved and unruly. Others simply need special help, but, because of budgetary considerations, are thrown into the same classes as the rest of the school population.

Unlike private schools, public schools are required by law to accept *all* children in the school district, and a teacher has no choice but to admit them into the classroom. There, such children necessarily interfere with the ability of the teacher and the rest of the students to concentrate on learning. Even one or two unruly children in a class, for example, can literally steal teacher attention and deprive other students of learning opportunities. An astonishingly high 41% of public-school students say that "disruptions by other students interfere with my learning," according to a 1989 U.S. Department of Education survey.

Remember, though, that most kids in the top quartile—those eager, motivated, academically gifted kids—probably have the ability to ignore interruptions by unruly children. Along with intellectual gifts, many gifted children also have the ability to concentrate and shut out the world around them. So unruly classmates may not necessarily destroy the learning opportunities of the top quartile, although poor teaching and a lack of homework for honing writing skills can hurt even these kids.

But that's not true of the two middle quartiles—the children who are closer to "average." Let's take a close look at those average children for a moment and see how closely they resemble our own kids—or ourselves when we were young.

They're normal in every respect—physically, intellectually, emotionally. We love them dearly, and they love us just as dearly and want to please us by succeeding in school. They have the ability to succeed. When they were smaller—and even now—their intellectual curiosity was evident in their incessant "why's" and in their demands to understand every new phenomenon we exposed them to.

They may never become straight-A students, but we know they have it in them to be solid B students or even B-plus if the schools they attend and their teachers help them be "the best they can be," to paraphrase a slogan popularized by U.S. Army recruitment commercials. Unfortunately, if ignored, they also have it in them to be C, C-minus or even D students, and in a public school, with 20 or more students in many classrooms (the national average is 17.6) the students in the second and third quartile may indeed be ignored and left on their own.

They lack both the intellectual gifts to ask the penetratingly insightful questions of gifted students and the academic aggressiveness to snap their hands in the air with answers to the toughest questions. And without the rude upbringing or emotional problems that get attention by disruptive behavior, such average students—our children—usually wind up getting less teacher attention than they need for maximum success. They are often the forgotten majority of students in American public schools and are truly "at risk" academically, socially and emotionally.

For these average children simply tend to drift through school, year after year, sitting quietly in class, listening, trying to understand as much as they can without probing aggressively for the in-depth explanations gifted children invariably demand. In effect, they plod through academic life, earning Cs and Ds from sympathetic teachers who grade them as much for their passive, nondisruptive classroom behavior as for their actual academic performances. Neither they nor their parents demand better education. So the schools gradually adjust standards downward to allow such children to pass through the system and graduate with precious little learning.

Their parents, unfortunately, often don't know they can do better, and their teachers don't give them much of a chance. They are the 90% of American 13-year-olds the U.S. Department of Education found to be "not adept at reading and . . . unable to understand complex information." They're nice kids, but many are uneducated and ill-equipped to succeed in or govern, let alone lead, the world they'll inherit.

For the average parent of such kids, there are only two choices. One, of course, is to provide at home the motivation and education the school is not providing—to supplement school and teacher efforts. But half the school children in America now live in single-parent homes and many of the rest live in homes where both parents work and have little time or energy to take on a second job as part-time teacher when they return from work. Moreover, many parents lack the skills to teach their children formal subjects such as mathematics or chemistry.

In any case, most children won't adapt easily or happily to repeating classroom routine at home each evening after a long day at school. Resentment will build as their friends go off to Little League practice and other after-school recreation, while they're forced to come home to lessons with their parents. Remember, too, that the average public school gives its children less than one hour of homework per night. (Many give less than one hour of homework per week.) So most public school children grow up finding the idea of studying after school quite alien.

That does not, however, mean that you, as a parent, cannot supplement an otherwise average public-school education to ensure that your child grows up well educated and cultured, with every opportunity to gain admittance to, and succeed at, the most academically demanding colleges and universities. The odds are high against this, however, if your child falls into the "average" category—the middle two quartiles—described above.

THE PRIVATE SCHOOL OPTION

The other option you have to help your children thrive academically is private school. Instead of about 18 students per teacher, as in public schools, private schools assign only about a dozen students to each teacher (9.3 in independent schools that are unaffiliated with any church or government agency), thus guaranteeing the individual attention each child needs to thrive intellectually, socially and emotionally, and indeed to function at levels he or she—and you, as a parent—may never have dreamed possible. There are many reasons to explain the success of private schools.

Private schools try not to admit disturbed, unruly children who so monopolize teacher attention in public schools. The handful that slip through are summarily expelled as soon as they begin to disrupt school routine or the lives of other children. Private-school teachers are thus free to devote all their time to teaching instead of dealing with disciplinary problems, and their students can, therefore, concentrate on learning.

In addition, academic achievement is the primary goal in most good private schools. Social rebels are scorned by their peers, and academic achievers are usually the most honored youngsters in school—honored by teachers, by parents and by other students. So *every* student tries to do his or her academic best, and, as a result, all students accomplish more than they would in a school environment where they are allowed to drift, or where brawn is more admired than brains.

And finally, students are always expected to adjust upwards to the school's academic and social standards, rather than standards being lowered to adjust to unwilling students. The result is a calm, disciplined, scholastic atmosphere in which educators determine what students must learn and how they must behave—and not the other way around. Private schools prevent "drifting" by requiring each child to participate in all academic activities and a wide variety of extracurricular activities. Children are not given the wide choice of electives and noncredit courses available in the academic cafeterias of public schools, where learning to cook or drive a car count as much towards graduation as studying mathematics does.

Private schools require all children to take a core curriculum of English, mathematics, history, science, foreign language, music and art, from kindergarten through high school. Electives at the high-school level are limited to additional courses in those disciplines, and children are not given any choice to veer away from the educational building blocks of civilization. It is one of the great failings of American public schools that educators and parents acceded, beginning with the student rebellions of the 1960s, to student demands for greater freedom in selecting their courses. Adolescents are often incapable of choosing the right foods to eat to help their bodies grow properly, let alone the right subjects to study to help their minds grow.

The results of student freedom of academic choice are evident in the more than 40% of American public high-school students now enrolled in so-called general studies, where they fill their classroom hours with "personal improvement" courses instead of learning how to read, write, calculate and govern themselves, their communities and their nation. Almost two-thirds of the students in general studies drop out before graduating— more than 2 million kids a year. And while they're in school, they provoke the majority of the daily disruptions that poison the atmosphere in so many public schools.

The atmosphere of a private school is far different. A good private school is a large family, with every member eager to contribute to the good of every other member and the good of the whole community.

After you visit a few outstanding private schools, you'll see how much joy of learning they provide the children lucky enough to be there. You'll marvel at the education gap between private and public schools. You may also shake your head in disbelief at the ease with which private schools provide the most average children with superior education and the tragic failure of public schools to do the same—often with equal or greater funding.

That, of course, is one of the ironies of the failure of American public schools. Many often spend more to educate each child *inadequately* than private schools spend to provide superior education. In St. Louis, for example, Cardinal Ritter College Prep, run by the Catholic diocese, educates its inner-city children at a cost of only about $3,500 a year per pupil. The school has a 100% graduation rate and all of its seniors go on to college. In contrast, the average cost per student at Northwest High, a nearby public school, is $7,800 a year (all from taxes), and only slightly more than half its students even graduate. Northwest High has a disgracefully high 45% drop-out rate. Only 15% of its students ever go on to college.

Who Goes to Private Schools?

Of the more than 45 million school children in America, more than 5 million, or nearly 12%, attend private schools. The term "private" school, however, can be somewhat misleading. Of the 110,000 schools in America, 27,700, or about 25%, are private. The vast majority of these, however, are operated by religious organizations and churches. Only 1,500 private schools are "independent," or unaffiliated with any church or state agency. Although there are, as you'll see later, some outstanding religiously affiliated schools, "independent" schools tend to be the strongest, most academically demanding of the private schools.

A recent national study of 8th graders by the U.S. Department of Education found that 68% of independent-school students achieve at the highest level of reading proficiency, compared with only 50% of 8th graders in all other private schools, 44% of 8th graders in Roman Catholic schools and a mere 32% of public-school 8th graders. About 63% of 8th graders in independent schools achieved at the highest level of mathematics proficiency, compared with only 34% in all other private schools, 19% in Roman Catholic schools and 18% in public schools.

Now those results are not because private schools get the brightest kids, but because the kids they get are forced to work harder. According to the same study, independent-school students do an average of 10.7 hours of homework per week, compared with 6.4 hours in other private schools, 6.3 hours in Roman Catholic schools and only 5.4 hours in public schools.

Private-school students as a group do 2.2 hours of outside, nonschool reading per week, compared to only 1.8 hours for public school kids, and they watch only 14.1 hours of television a week, compared with 21.7 hours for the average public-school child. Students at independent boarding schools seldom watch more than two hours of television per week, unless it's a special program related to their studies.

So private-school students concentrate on their studies more than public-school students do, and they work much, much harder. They also have better school facilities. Nearly half the 8th graders in private schools, for example, are enrolled in science courses *with* laboratory work, compared to only 21.5% in public schools. And, according to the U.S. Department of Education, private schools spend $36.54 per pupil for library facilities—more than double the disgracefully low $17.58 spent per pupil in public schools.

The results of these advantages are amply evident in the successes scored by private-school students when they reach college age and, later on, when they go to work. Although students from private schools represent only 12% of all school children in the United States, they fill 40% of the seats at the most selective, academically demanding colleges. As they become adults, they fill as disproportionately large a number of leadership positions in business, finance and government. More than 10% of the chief executives of America's 1,000 largest corporations, for example, graduated from just four universities—Yale, Harvard, Princeton and Stanford.

Again, those successes are not the result of private-school kids being brighter than public school kids. They are the result of growing up in peer groups with youngsters who, along with their families, value and admire academic achievement. They are the result of growing up in an atmosphere where discipline governs and scholarship is the primary goal. They are also the result of growing up with better teachers.

Independent schools believe strongly that a person who majored in a subject at college—biology, for example, or mathematics—knows far more about, and is better equipped to teach, that subject than someone who majored in education and may have taken one or two biology or mathematics courses. Private schools, in other words, look for depth of knowledge rather than a state teaching certificate as the major qualification for teaching—especially at the high-school level.

Aside from being more motivated and harder working, students at private schools generally tend to be healthier both emotionally and physically. Unlike public schools, private schools do not have to try to be all things to all people. They do not have to deal with profound social problems. The law does not force them to accept troubled youngsters from troubled families. They can, in other words, refuse to assume responsibilities that they feel properly belong to parents, social workers, psychiatric therapists or the courts. Children that do not obey school rules can be expelled. Unlike public schools, private schools can pick the kids they want from families they know will support school goals.

Now that may sound elitist to some, and it is in one sense. Most private schools limit their enrollment to good kids who are well behaved, are able to accept discipline and are eager to learn. They try to limit their enrollment to kids from families who value education, and that's an elitism that private schools rightfully boast about.

Private-School Kids Are Average

But contrary to public opinion, the most selective, academically respected private schools are far from elitist in the social or economic sense. An average of 18% of the students attending independent schools receive some financial aid, and some schools offer as many as 40% of their students financial aid. About 36% of families with children in private schools have incomes below $50,000 a year, while 21% have annual incomes between $50,000 to $75,000, according to the National Association of Independent Schools (NAIS). In other words, more than half the families who send their kids to private schools are solid, middle-income families who believe that, next to love, a good education is the most important gift they can give their children—and they're willing to sacrifice to make that gift.

Of course, there are a lot of private school children from extremely wealthy families. About 31% come from families with annual incomes of more than $100,000, but their presence does not make private-school education "elite." Those kids have no more privileges than other students. They must conform to the same high academic standards, the same rules of conduct and the same moral and ethical codes as their schoolmates. And that, by the way, is another "subject" that's taught in private schools, but seldom discussed in public schools: morality and ethics. Good private schools all teach their students proper behavior and respect for others as well as for themselves.

As for social elitism, 13% of the kids at private schools in America are students of color, including African American, Hispanic American, Asian American and Native American students. Foreign students make up an additional 2% of the student population at independent schools.

The top private schools, in other words, have a greater racial, ethnic and religious mix of students than the vast majority of public schools. That's simply because most public schools draw their students from racially homogeneous neighborhoods and towns. The small New York City suburban community where my son attended public-school kindergarten had no Hispanic or African American families and, therefore, no Hispanic or African American children in school. That was true of most of the surrounding communities. So much for the "real world" of public schools.

In sharp contrast, the prestigious Hackley School, in Tarrytown, New York, another New York suburb, reaches outside the community to draw children of many races, religions and nationalities. Its student body includes children from more than 20 nations. And in Lakeville, Connecticut, at The Hotchkiss School, the famed preparatory school that sends about one-third of its graduates to Ivy League colleges every year, more than 20% of the student body is nonwhite and 10% are foreign nationals.

Most other private day schools and boarding schools have similarly diverse student bodies, thus offering their students—American and foreign, white, African American and Asian—an unequaled opportunity to work and play together, to learn to understand each other and, above all, to emerge as close, lifelong friends.

So there's nothing "elite" about private schools in the social or financial sense. And in the global, cosmopolitan sense, their student bodies reflect the racial, ethnic and economic mix of the real world far more than most public schools do.

What does make a typical private school elite, however, is the unanimity with which the entire school "family"—faculty, parents and students—seeks the best in education and conduct. Those who do not, need not apply. They're not wanted. And that's *not* elitist; that's simply goal oriented, and the goals are good education and mature behavior.

So, if you share those goals and want your children to have the very best opportunities for education and social development, begin now looking for the perfect private school for your kids.

Gifted Children

All schools have their share of intellectually gifted kids, and such children usually make up a higher percentage of the student body in private schools than in most public schools. There's a good reason for that, of course. Like you, the parents of gifted children want their kids to have the best opportunity to succeed intellectually and socially, without the distractions created by undisciplined, unruly social rebels.

They also want their kids to have the individual attention that private schools offer, along with the vast array of academic, social, cultural and recreational opportunities described later in this book. Just to list a few, they include frequent student trips to museums, theater and opera; trips to historic cities such as Boston, Washington and New York; on-campus performances and lectures by renowned artists and scholars; day-to-day contact with teachers who have advanced degrees from America's finest universities; and access to the finest, most advanced classroom equipment and extensive library facilities that money can buy. Recreational opportunities at private schools include facilities for *all* children at the intramural as well as interscholastic levels in football, soccer, field hockey, basketball, wrestling, ice hockey, skating, gymnastics, swimming, tennis, baseball, softball, lacrosse and many other sports.

It's little wonder that academically gifted children thrive in such schools. One boy in my son's private high school was a world-class pianist who performed for the First Family and their guests in the White House when he was only 16 years old and is now one of America's premier concert pianists.

Far from being intimidating, however, the presence of, and deep friendships formed with, such exceptional boys and girls encourage all the other children in school to excel and to display their own individual talents. Most of the other children are not world-class musicians, scholars or athletes. Indeed, 20 of the 43 members in a recent graduating class at one of America's finest private day schools only scored in the 500–600 range in the verbal SATs—well below the 800 maximum possible score. But all those students have individual strengths and talents, and the strength of a private school is its ability to give all the students the individual attention they need to reach their potential—to help each student become a "star" and an important member of the school community. And, indeed, those kids with the average SAT scores in the 500–600 range are now attending such colleges as Duke, University of Pennsylvania and Swarthmore.

When to Enroll

Learning is organized in specific groupings. Kindergarten is one such grouping. Others, depending on the particular school, may be 1st through 3rd grade; 4th through 6th; 7th and 8th; and 9th through 12th. The groupings may vary by a grade or two at different schools, but the important thing to remember is that it can be extremely difficult to adjust academically if a child has to transfer from one school to another, especially from an academically inferior public school to a fast-paced private school, in the middle of such a grouping—in 2nd grade, for example, or 11th. Many children can make that adjustment, but many find it quite difficult, because such in-between years don't have beginning-of-the-year review periods during which students who have transferred from an inferior school are given an opportunity to catch up to their new classmates.

Every academic year begins with a bit of a review for the first few days, but the first year of each of the groupings mentioned incorporates an extended two-week or even three-week period of extensive review of the knowledge that should have been acquired during the previous grouping. That allows transfer students to catch up with regulars, and all can then get off to the same start when they attack new material.

If your child is only about to begin school, in preschool or kindergarten, he or she won't have to face this problem. But if your child is older, waiting until the beginning of one of the grouping periods mentioned can make the transition easier. Ask the admissions department at each school you consider about the appropriate year for your child to enroll.

In addition to the academic transition your children will have to face moving from public to private school, there will also be a social transition that can be even more difficult. Again, preschoolers, kindergartners and probably even 1st graders won't have much difficulty, but a 5th, 6th or 9th grader may well balk at the idea of transferring and having to part with close friends.

The Problems of Changing Schools

There are two critical elements to this separation. One is the child's feeling of having failed somehow in public school and having thus provoked your decision to force a transfer. The second element is the prospect of permanently losing old friends and the fear of not being able to replace them with new ones.

It is essential that you make it clear that your child has *not* failed in any way. At the same time, it's just as essential to make it clear that the school has not failed your child either (even if it has). It can be destructive for your child to go to school and tell other children that their school is failing them.

When discussing the transfer to private school, assure your child that he or she has not failed—that you truly like the old school and that it's a terrific school for a lot of children. But you believe that he or she has the ability to work at a different, much higher level than is possible at public school; that you want your child to study subjects unavailable at public school (and you'll have to explain what they are); and that you want him or her to have cultural and recreational opportunities not always available at public school—and here you can mention the sports and extracurricular opportunities, the trips to other cities, etc. Show your child catalogs of private schools; leave them around the house for your child to look through on his or her own, and take your child on trips to visit the schools you are considering.

Parting with friends is difficult to explain to any child's satisfaction. You can say, of course, that your child will still be able to get together with old friends, but both of you will know that's unlikely. Indeed, one common reason for transferring is to put your child in a new peer group, and even if that's not the primary reason, that's what's going to happen. Children's friendships quickly disintegrate when they no longer share their daily school lives and have little or nothing in common to chatter about—how much they hate (or love) a particular teacher, for example, or classmate or course or extracurricular activity.

It's best, therefore, to admit the probability that your child may indeed see less of old friends. Don't deny the obvious. Assure your child, however, that there will be lots of new and interesting friends to make—and prove it when you take your child to visit the schools you're seriously considering. Chances are that you and your child will be amazed and excited by the magnificent facilities at most good private schools. They're far better than at most public schools—better even than at many colleges. Your child may indeed meet new friends on such visits, because many private schools arrange to have one or more students host your child while you're busy interviewing the head of the school and the admissions director. That can give your child an opportunity to ask questions of other children, who may help relieve some anxieties.

So, remember that while you know a move to private school may be the absolutely best gift you can give your child and some children may actually be eager and excited about it, some children may feel hurt, depressed or angry, and it will be up to you to help your child feel good about the change. A year later, of course, your child will have adapted completely and forgotten any temporary unhappiness, and 10 or 20 years later your child will bless you for having selected a private school—as my son now blesses me.

Affording Private School

The biggest problem for many parents who are considering private school for their children is, of course, cost. Private school can often double or even triple the cost of educating your children. That's because sending kids to private school doesn't excuse you from paying the costs of local public schools. In other words, you'll have to continue to pay taxes to cover the costs of the public school your child is *not* attending as well as the costs of the private school your child *is* attending.

A few communities in the United States are experimenting with so-called voucher systems that allow parents to use some of the school taxes they pay for public schools to help them pay for private schools. But this is a controversial program that has yet to be tested in court and is only in effect in a handful of communities. So, in all probability, you'll be paying the costs of two schools by sending your child to private school.

Is it worth it—especially if doing so may mean that you may not be able to afford the costs of a private college?

Even state universities can often cost upwards of $5,000 per year for in-state students and $10,000 a year for out-of-staters. Many private colleges such as Yale or Harvard now cost more than $25,000 a year—more than $100,000 for a four-year college education. Add to that the $100,000 to $150,000 required for private school, from kindergarten through 12th grade, and you come up with a sum that is beyond the reach of all but a handful of extremely wealthy families—especially families with more than one child to educate.

For such families, the question then becomes whether to spend their available savings on private elementary or secondary schools, or let nearby public schools educate their children and reserve their savings to pay for college.

Given a choice between the two, few educators would not choose the former—i.e., they would urge you to spend the money on private elementary and secondary schools.

There are several reasons for this. In the first place, all real, basic education takes place long before college. Almost all vital educational, social and intellectual skills children will need in college and adult life are learned in elementary, middle and secondary school. College and university merely provide the "icing" on the educational cake. The cake itself must be prepared and "baked" in elementary and secondary schools. It's true that college and university may provide the stepping stones to professional life, but a child who emerges semiliterate from high school, unable to read, write and calculate adequately, may not ever get into college and certainly will never graduate or ever hold a responsible professional position in the adult world.

Moreover, the differences in educational quality between colleges and universities are far less pronounced than the differences in educational quality between most public and private schools. Syracuse University, for example, a private university whose costs for tuition, room and board are now around $20,000 a year, offers no better education, say, than the State University of New York in Albany or many of New York's 28 other four-year, state-run colleges, where total costs amount to about $6,000 a year for New York State residents and no more than $10,000 for out-of-state students. And a future doctor or lawyer learns no more medicine or law at Yale or Harvard than at many far less costly private or state university schools of medicine or law.

In other words, the same knowledge is there for the taking at any accredited college or university in America. It's up to the student to take it. No college or university—private or public—will spoon-feed its students. That's not the case, however, in elementary and secondary schools, where most students need good teachers to teach them how to learn as well as what to learn.

And there's still another reason why, given the choice, you'd be better off spending your savings on your child's private elementary- and secondary-school education than on college. That's because there is far more money available for scholarships at college than at private elementary and secondary schools.

It's true that as many as 40% of the children at some private schools receive some scholarship aid, but that aid is usually based on *available funds* rather than the *needs* of applicants. The sums granted are often as little as token stipends of $100 or $250 dollars, simply because the schools have no more to give. Yet that's hardly enough to provide much help for an average middle-income family whose child simply won't be admitted if it cannot afford to pay the thousands of dollars in remaining costs.

Remember, too, that there are heavy extra costs at private school—clothes, because many private schools have dress codes, and textbooks, which can often add $250 to $500 a year to total costs. Public schools lend textbooks free of charge to students and provide free bus transportation, and kids can usually dress in very casual clothes. You may have to pay for private transportation for your child to travel to and from a private day school if it's out of state or out of your school district. Few private schools have scholarship funds available to cover all those expenses.

Colleges and universities, on the other hand, have enormous sums available for scholarships. In addition, the U.S. government and most state governments supplement those funds with their own grants. Moreover, there are a host of low-cost, government-guaranteed loans to help students pay for college costs. In other words, it's not difficult to put together a financial aid package to cover the costs of sending your child through even the most expensive colleges and universities.

Remember, too, that some private colleges admit their students on what's called a "need-blind" basis. They don't know or care whether an applicant can afford to attend—only whether he or she is qualified. Once admitted, the colleges then look over the Financial Aid Form that a student has filled out and help that student put together a financial aid package that will cover *all* costs of attending, including clothes. Selective colleges admit only students they most want, and once they've selected those students, they do everything—including providing enough scholarship aid and access to loans—to ensure that those students can attend.

In other words, it's fair to say that if you ensure your child's getting the finest elementary- and secondary-school education you can afford, the college admissions process and college costs will take care of themselves. Indeed, top scholarship performance at a top private school will almost guarantee your child's admission to a top college, which in turn will help you find means to afford your child's attendance.

As mentioned earlier, the question should not be whether you can afford to send your children to private school, but whether you can afford *not* to. Few colleges or universities can compensate for the inferior education of most public elementary and secondary schools. Nor will any superior college or university admit a student with inferior elementary- or secondary-school education.

17

On the other hand, a superior elementary- and secondary-school education, will virtually assure any student of getting a superior college and university education—and the costs of the latter are easily covered by available institutional and government scholarship grants and low-cost student loans.

Financial Aid

If, of course, your family truly cannot afford a private school, there are remedies. As mentioned, most private schools offer a variety of scholarships to eligible applicants—almost always based on need, although a handful of merit scholarships are awarded to students who have demonstrated excellence in academics, the arts, athletics or some other area.

Need scholarships are based on a combination of factors including family income, net assets (real estate, investments, bank accounts, etc., less indebtedness), number of dependents and other elements of the family's financial condition as shown in the family's income tax forms. In addition, the school weighs such factors as parents' marital status and occupations, value of the family's motor and recreational vehicles, cost of summer camps, vacations, day care and club memberships, and annual rent or mortgage payments.

Although some schools have their own financial aid forms for parents to fill out, most independent secondary schools use the School and Student Service for Financial Aid (SSS), of Princeton, New Jersey, to analyze family financial conditions. If you indicate on your child's application for admission that you need financial aid, the school will send you a Parents' Financial Statement to fill out, disclosing all the material facts of your financial circumstances. Aid from private schools is, however, limited and awarded on a first-come first-served basis. Nor is aid automatically renewed each year. Several years of recession and declining enrollments have reduced the available aid at many schools. So, get your aid application papers filed as quickly and as early as you possibly can.

Besides the schools themselves, there are other sources of financial aid worth investigating. Some companies, for example, provide scholarships for employees' children. Some professional associations, trade associations and labor unions do the same for their members' children.

In addition to outright grants, many private schools make it easier to cover costs through tuition payment plans and tuition loan programs that allow you to pay annual tuition on a monthly basis over an extended period of time. Appendix C describes eight tuition payment plans and five tuition loan programs. Tuition payment plans let you pay current tuition in 10 or 12 equal monthly installments *at no out-of-pocket interest* costs, although there usually are modest application and annual service fees. Payments usually begin three to four months before your child enrolls in school each year so that each semester's tuition is paid in full at the beginning of the semester.

Although some plans have been around a long time, others have come and gone. Remember that, in turning over money to a tuition payment plan, you are, in effect, lending them your money, and there is a risk involved if the operators of the plan should fail. So investigate the financial condition of the plan you select to be sure your money will be in safe hands, and compare each plan's terms with those of all the others.

Besides tuition payment plans, creditworthy parents can also pay for private schools through so-called extended payment plans, which are nothing more than unsecured personal loans—usually at exorbitantly high interest rates. Many banks offer similar programs called Educational Credit Lines, which, again, are simply costly, unsecured personal loans.

Remember, though: Interest on educational loans is *not* tax deductible. So, if you must borrow to pay for your child's education and you own your own home or apartment, it is far less costly to obtain a mortgage, refinance an existing mortgage or get a home equity loan (second mortgage). Not only are interest rates lower, they are fully deductible from current income taxes, even when you use the funds for educational purposes.

Alternatively, you can use a low-interest broker loan against securities to pay for your child's education by selling enough stock (or taxable bonds) to cover school costs and then buying it back on margin (i.e., with a loan from the broker). If the stock is sold at a loss, you can deduct some of the loss from current income taxes. You can also deduct the interest on the broker loan to repurchase the securities, because interest on broker loans *for investment purposes* is tax deductible. The interest is *not* deductible if you simply borrow money against your securities to pay for your child's education. On paper, at least, the loan must be for investment purposes.

In addition to tuition payment plans and loans, which are available to families of children at almost *all* private schools, some private schools offer special parent loan plans that are partially underwritten or guaranteed by various education foundations such as the Independence Foundation or the Clarence Manger and Audrey Cordero Pitt Trust Fund. Not all schools offer this option, but those that do allow parents to make monthly payments of principal, interest and insurance over a total of 12 years. During the four years following high-school graduation, while the child attends college, parents are excused from paying any part of the principal and only pay interest and insurance costs. Interest rates are usually low—well below prime.

Different programs have different requirements. Some only grant loans on the basis of need; others limit the amount of money they lend. Ask each school you apply to whether it is affiliated with a low-cost parent loan program or whether it has its own loan program or tuition payment program that might make it easier for you to pay for your child's education.

You'll find lists of private schools that offer financial assistance and loans to parents in *Peterson's Guide to Independent Secondary Schools,* which is an indispensable directory available in many bookstores and is discussed in detail later. It's important to get a copy of that directory as early as possible in your search for private schools. Verify any information you find in *Peterson's,* of course, with each school to be certain the school still offers financial assistance and that it will have what you require if it admits your child.

Regardless of the payment plan you choose, however, none will leave you free of financial strain. Private-school education is extremely expensive, and before deciding whether you think it's worth it, you should spend as much time looking at private schools as you would looking at new homes.

At a possible $100,000 to $150,000, your child's education will certainly be the second biggest investment you'll ever make, and may well be the biggest. Don't just "kick the tires" as you might with a new car. Spend at least as much time "buying" a school as you would a car or home. Examine every alternative carefully.

By all means take a close look at available public schools—especially so-called "magnet" schools, if there are any in your area. Magnet schools are highly selective public schools designed for gifted children and to which any student in the area or state may apply. Some specialize in the arts or sciences; others offer broader curricula. Check with the state superintendent of schools or board of education in your district to see if the city, county or state where you live has such schools. Many are absolutely wonderful.

For purposes of assessing educational quality at nearby public schools, use the handy checklists in my book, "*What Did You Learn in School Today?*", which is designed as a parent's guide for evaluating public schools. Then use the guidelines in the following chapters of this book, along with the School Evaluation Form in Appendix A, to evaluate private schools before deciding which schools you want your children to attend.

These won't be easy decisions. I know. I went through the process myself with my own son—which is why I wrote this book: to help you avoid the pitfalls many parents face trying to pick perfect private schools for their children.

And good luck!

CHAPTER 2

DEFINING YOUR CHILDREN'S NEEDS

*F*ar more than public schools, private schools are designed to meet the *individual* needs of each student. So, before trying to select a school for your children, it's important to identify and define their needs as well as to identify and define *your own needs* and *your own motives* for sending your child to private school. Unfortunately, many parents select schools not because of what's best for their children but, as one headmaster put it, for the prestige of the school decals on the rear windows of their station wagons. Status and snob appeal, in other words, are all too often the motives of some parents who send their children to private school.

There are, however, many appropriate reasons for wanting to send your child to a private school, and every private school admissions officer will want to know those reasons. Remember: There are other children competing for your child's seat in most good private schools, and the job of the admissions officer is to serve as a friendly, helpful "gatekeeper" to make certain the right student enters that particular school—to "make a good match," as one admissions director put it. So prepare now to develop some insight and to be able to answer questions about yourself, your family and your child.

The first question almost every admissions officer will ask is why you want your child to attend private school. If your reasons are all negative, some schools may not consider your child's application. Most private schools cannot restore a troubled, unruly child to emotional health or turn an unmotivated D student into a scholar—or teach a rude, badly behaved child good manners! Although there are a few schools that do help children with behavioral difficulties, most do not. Nor do they want to. Only a therapist is equipped to deal with emotional problems, and it is the job of parents to control their children's behavior and motivate them academically.

So your motives for sending your child to a private school should be positive. First and foremost, you should be considering private school for its academic benefits and advantages over public school, including improved chances for eventually getting into an academically superior college. In addition to better teachers, more discipline and a broader, more rigorous academic program, private schools offer far more cultural experiences, with constant exposure to music, art, philosophy and the other foundation stones of civilization. Art, music and other cultural programs are usually the first to be eliminated in cash-strapped public schools, most of which have become cultural wastelands.

Because they can afford to offer far smaller classes than public schools can, private schools also guarantee your child the individual attention needed to assure understanding, learning and academic and social growth. Independent private schools—which, as mentioned earlier, represent the most academically demanding of all private schools—have an average student–teacher ratio of 9.3, or one teacher for every nine students. In sharp contrast, the average public school has a student–teacher ratio of 17.6—almost double.

And that's why many parents send their children to private schools—especially independent private schools. These parents are convinced that lack of individual attention in public school has left their children functioning below their potential. Many such children are obviously gifted—but bored because of the failure of public-school teachers to challenge them. Others are simply bright kids who just aren't doing well or no longer seem to be trying. A child with an IQ of 130, for example, should not be doing C work in school, and no child who gets Bs in elementary school should drop to a C average in middle school.

The smaller classes and individual teaching attention of a private school can often help stimulate such children to do the A or B work of which they are obviously capable.

Even at the kindergarten level, private schools offer enormous academic advantages over public schools. The latter tend to treat kindergarten as a bridge between the home and learning environments. That's because 35% of the children entering public-school kindergartens are still not ready to learn, according to a study by the Carnegie Foundation for the Advancement of Teaching. The result is that most public-school kindergartens have to concentrate on teaching children social, rather than academic, skills—i.e., getting along and sharing with other children, self-control, etc.

In contrast, children admitted to private-school kindergartens are already prepared for learning. Indeed, private-school kindergartens expect preschools to have taught most children the social skills and self-discipline they'll need in a school environment.

Most good private-school kindergartens are academically oriented. They are pre-1st grades, where kids learn the basics of reading, writing, counting and computing, reasoning and problem solving, along with recognition of geometric shapes and a wide variety of natural phenomena in the world around them. Kindergarten, in other words, is the first year of *school* in a private school. It's not an extended child-care service. So if your child is not ready to learn, consider repeating a year in a preschool—but be certain it's a good one. Be certain it's not just a play group.

Safety

In addition to academic and cultural advantages, private schools ensure your child's safety—physical, moral and ethical. Lower student-faculty ratios permit teachers to supervise every child almost all the time. There is seldom an opportunity for groups of unsupervised children to get into mischief. In private school you'll see none of the between-class chaos and corridor mob scenes of public school. Private school rules are usually strict. Violations lead to instant correction and, if warranted, penalties. Serious violations lead to suspension or expulsion.

The result is that your child can spend his or her childhood relaxed, in a warm, caring atmosphere, where he or she can grow up more slowly than in public school and concentrate on doing what children should be doing—being children and learning.

Behavioral Controls

Making that task easier for them is the near unanimity of values in the world in which they'll be living. The entire faculty and most of the parents whose children attend independent schools value good education, culture and good behavior. In addition, their peers will share those values, and that will become increasingly important as your children grow older and peer influence begins to supersede parental influence. Consciously or unconsciously, every parent realizes that peer pressures will eventually outweigh parental pressures in the minds of their children. The best way to prevent those peer pressures from pushing your child down danger-laden pathways is to select in advance, as carefully as possible, a private school that teaches ethical and moral values similar to your own.

The Negatives of Private Schools

Now that doesn't mean there are no negatives to private school. There are many—for both you and your child—and it's best to recognize them in advance. The huge costs of tuition, school fees, books, dress clothes for your child and, often, transportation can mean enormous sacrifices for many parents. Depending on where you live, private school can mean a long, tiring trip for your child (and you, if you have to do the driving!) to and from school each day. It will also mean your child's having to dress up every morning if there's a dress code.

For children, going to private school may mean the loss of neighborhood friends and even possible resentment by neighborhood public-school kids. Private school will also produce unimaginably heavy work loads in comparison to public schools. Make no mistake about it: Schoolwork at most good private schools is *hard work*, requiring a level of maturity and self-discipline that most American kids today seem unwilling or unable to display. The heavy burden of homework will mean less time for fun and a loss of freedom to do as one pleases on weekends and weekday evenings. While neighborhood kids go off to neighborhood baseball games and other outings, your child may have to stay home to write a report or prepare for a major exam.

And if your child goes away to boarding school, not only will you miss each other, you'll miss many of the joys of watching your child grow and mature.

So there are some negatives to private school. The question you and your child must decide is whether a superior education and a more certain, brighter future for your child are worth your financial sacrifice and your child's deferral of the immediate, short-lived pleasures that are available to public-school children.

Practical Considerations

In addition to the more general reasons for wanting to send your child to private school, almost all school officials will want to know how or why you selected and are considering their school. Your reasons may well depend on your child's or your family's needs.

Obviously, proximity of the school to your home may be one valid reason for choosing a particular school. Another may be school hours. For working parents, private-school kindergartens are a blessing, because they run the full school day, five days a week. Fiscal restraints have forced public schools in thousands of communities to put kindergartens on half-day schedules, sometimes only four days a week, thus affording children no real opportunity to learn. By the time most five-year-olds get their coats and overshoes off and put away and settle into their seats, almost a quarter of a two-hour morning session can evaporate.

In addition to offering standard, six-hour school days, many private schools also have after-school programs lasting until 6:00 P.M. each workday evening.

Another practical consideration in looking for private schools is whether you want a school to combine academics with religious instruction. Devout followers of a particular faith may simply not want their children exposed at a young, impressionable age to conflicting religious or ethical beliefs.

A practical reason for looking at boarding schools, on the other hand, might center around an impending or actual family breakup that you may consider too traumatic for your child to witness. Or it may be that you live in an isolated area with no private schools, and the only way you can assure your child a good education is to send him or her away to boarding school. A boarding school can also be a good choice for a child who is suddenly left alone at home much of the time because older siblings have left and both parents now work full time. There may also be a variety of psychological reasons for which a child needs to be separated from parents.

Still another valid reason for selecting a particular school may be family tradition. Many older private schools—especially boarding schools—have often educated three, four or even more generations of children from families that consider attending such schools an integral part of growing up. If you attended a private school as a child or your family has sent several generations of children to a school and helped support it with generous financial contributions, the school will undoubtedly welcome your child warmly.

So there may be many practical reasons for sending your child to a particular private school. Above and beyond those, however, the most important reason should be fulfillment of your child's own, individual needs, and every admissions director will ask you as a parent, "Tell me about your child."

How Well Do You Know Your Child?

Of course, you'll respond with a litany of his or her accomplishments as well as a list of the personality characteristics you most cherish in your child. That's a normal response for most parents. But remember: Unless your child is exceptionally gifted and accomplished, he or she probably won't be much different from most other children applying to the school—at least superficially.

So it's a good idea to ask yourself in advance of any interviews with private-school admissions representatives how well you really know your child. To answer the question properly, you'll need to compile a list of all your child's social, intellectual and emotional qualities and needs. Does he or she get along better in big groups or small? Is he or she a loner? Rough and tumble or gentle? An avid reader or audio-visual in orientation? There are dozens of important characteristics you'll need to define before considering any school.

You should know your child's weaknesses as well as strengths. In that way you will be able to describe how you think private school will help your child build on strengths or acquire new skills that will compensate for, or overcome, weaknesses. For example, the individual attention of a skilled kindergarten teacher can often teach a shy "loner" the joys of working in teams and sharing with others. Similarly, the same teacher—again, because of small class sizes—can help convert various interests (drawing, for example) into outstanding skills.

So, get to know and begin listing your child's strengths and weaknesses and do so by *observing* him or her in a new way—starting now. Don't try to recall what you *think* your child's strengths and weaknesses are. And don't depend on your child to report his strengths and weaknesses accurately or honestly. Most kids tell us parents what they know we want to hear. One 10-year-old I knew told his working parents he was starring in Little League. One afternoon, they returned home early, hoping to surprise him at practice—only to find him sitting alone atop the grandstand, watching. He had never even made the team, but never dared tell his parents.

Most parents tend to see and remember only what they want to see and remember about their children. So don't write anything down from memory. Start *watching* your child for the first time and write down everything he or she does at the time it happens.

How long is his or her attention span? Does your child enjoy working in a group or prefer working alone—or both? Does your child enjoy puzzles? Building and making things? Listening to you read aloud?

What's your family life like? Is yours a one- or two-parent home? How does that affect your child and how can the school help compensate for the lack of one parent? If not, do you and your spouse both work? Who is raising your child? Does a housekeeper or governess serve as a surrogate parent? Is your child left alone a lot of the time? Do you take many family trips? Do you read to your child? How often? What kinds of stories or books? What kinds of rules do you have at home? What kinds of things do you do together with your child: picnics? sports? concerts? museum visits? Where does your child fit into relationships at home, with brothers, sisters

26

or other family members living there? Family dynamics and family structure are important influences on your child and will affect your child's school life enormously.

How does your child relate to other children? It's important to observe your child carefully during interactions with other children and to take copious notes. Does your child share easily or does he snatch what he wants from others—or let them snatch what is his? Does your child listen and absorb what others say—both adults and other children? Or does your child interrupt incessantly and demand to be heard? It's important to be as objective as you possibly can, because what you consider cute may actually be immature behavior. The son Dad describes as a boy who "doesn't let others push him around" may be an extremely disturbed, hostile, aggressive child. Similarly, a youngster whose lapses of memory parents ignore or excuse because he or she "is thinking about more important things" may actually have a learning disorder that needs immediate remediation.

So that's why, if you can, you should try to describe your child's actual, observed behavior as it happens by taking careful, complete, accurate notes that can't be embellished later with wishful interpretations. It's difficult to misinterpret as something cute and appropriate three objective notations such as "hits Johnny in the face" in the course of 20 minutes. Nor can six or eight entries each day beginning "Forgot to. . ." be ignored as the behavior of an absentminded scholar. And a 3rd grader still drawing stick figures while others are adding volume to their drawings does not simply lack an "aptitude" for drawing. That child should be tested by a learning-disability specialist.

Most parents who love their children tend to overlook or excuse a lot of behavior they don't like and remember the good things their children do. So, for purposes of evaluating and getting to know how your child is doing, taking a few pages of objective notes while watching your child interact with the family and with other children may provide a completely different picture from the one you've selectively stored in your fantasies.

And when you reread those notes, don't try to hide or ignore the obvious from yourself and your spouse. Those notes could be the most essential tool in guiding you to the right private school for your child.

Special Needs

Every child should be tested for learning disorders, regardless of IQ or achievement test scores. Some authorities on the subject estimate that one of every two children has some form of learning disability, and that many brilliant children are often deprived of reaching their full potential because of correctable learning disorders that went ignored or undiagnosed. The earlier you spot such a disorder, the easier it is to treat. Any child prone to ear infections throughout infancy is particularly prone to developing learning disorders.

Most of us, however, grow up believing that what is really a learning disability is just an example of poor aptitude—that we've never been good at math, for example. Other learning disabilities are so mild and so specific that it's easy to work around them by avoiding the type of academic course at school, or activity at play or at work that would bring the learning disorder into focus.

For example, one child I knew had what seemed to be a poor aptitude for foreign languages, and he simply avoided his problem by fulfilling his course requirements over eight long years, but never again spoke a word in the language he had studied—even when traveling in countries where that language was spoken.

"Let them speak English," he insisted.

But it turned out he might have done quite well in his studies had a few sensitive teachers diagnosed his problem as a minor and quite specific learning disorder. Quite simply, he knew, understood and could easily use in a French sentence the spoken or written word *chaise* and snap out the English translation *chair*. But, faced with an actual chair or a picture of a chair, he could not recall the word *chaise*. The same held true for other words, and this is an example of a minor learning disorder that was ignored because it had little or no effect on the child's functioning at school and in later life. Had he been retrained, however—had his learning disorder been treated—he might have gotten As in French instead of Cs, and he might have learned to love foreign languages and foreign travel.

There are, of course, far more serious learning disorders that no one can ignore. Some can be crippling unless treated as soon as they're detected. And still others disappear as mysteriously as they first appeared. Some children simply outgrow them.

The key point to remember, however, is that learning disorders can and should be treated as early as possible. Often they can be treated relatively easily. Early, proper treatment can teach most learning-disabled children to be on their own and independent the rest of their lives.

There are now many schools and specialists who can teach—and that's the right word, *teach* not treat—all types of learning-disabled children. Moreover, there are many approaches to the treatment of learning disorders—and although none are perfect, all have benefits. So, it's hard to go wrong. If the first effort doesn't work, simply switch to another approach and try it.

Often it's difficult to spot a learning disorder without professional help. What some parents believe to be a learning disorder is often simply a developmental problem that a child will outgrow. He or she is simply lagging in one area of development, but will eventually catch up and be equal to or outperform peers at a later age.

Nevertheless, it's best not to guess. Take your child as early as practical to an educational consultant, as specialists in learning disorders are often called. And don't waste a day in doing so. Don't ignore even the smallest signal. Three- and four-year-olds *should* be able to associate and sound out many big words they see regularly on signs or packages—PIZZA, STOP, etc. There are other signals of possible learning disorders, such as difficulty in learning to read or an inability to communicate thoughts easily. When your child repeatedly says, "uh . . . uh . . . uh. . ." and is unable to "spit out" a thought—despite having a large vocabulary and an ability to read well—don't smile and say, "Well, perhaps you'll think of it later." Have your child tested.

Similarly, children who cannot write properly and have difficulties forming their letters may well be suffering from dysgraphia, and children who have difficulties reading because they see letters backwards or in reversed order may be suffering from dyslexia. Other symptoms of a learning disability may be excessive frustration attempting to do ordinary homework and endless surrenders to defeat by crumpling and discarding homework papers. And a child who gradually begins hating school and refuses to get on the school bus each day may also suffer from a learning disability.

All these disorders can be treated by a variety of methods based on the assumption that children with learning disorders are not *learning* the wrong way. They're learning the only way they can. Teachers, however, often *teach* them the wrong way, and their teaching methods must be adapted to meet such children's special needs. To put it another way, American children would have little success learning to read Hebrew if they attempted to read the characters as they do in English, from left to right. A teacher would have far more success by "retraining" them to read from right to left *or* by rearranging the Hebrew characters so that they could be read from left to right.

And that's what retraining learning-disabled children is all about, and the reason some private schools have such enormous advantages over public schools: Private schools are designed to adapt their teaching methods to meet each child's *individual* needs.

If you think your child may be learning disabled—or even if you don't, but feel you ought to make sure early on—talk to your child's pediatrician and ask for a reference to an educational specialist who can test your child for learning disorders. Be certain that any specialist you consult has the proper credentials and is a member of The Independent Educational Counselors Association (38 Cove Road, Forestdale, Massachusetts 02644.

Tel: [508] 477–2127). Another source of information is the Orton Dyslexia Society at 80 Fifth Avenue, New York, New York 10011 (Tel: [212] 691–1930). It's important to have your child evaluated as early as possible so that you can search for a private school that can help your child overcome and correct the problem as effectively as possible.

Setting Goals

Having identified your child's needs, it's important for you to determine your goals for your child—and again, write them down so that you can study them objectively and see if they are indeed appropriate. Don't use meaningless adjectives such as happy, successful or nice, as in "I want him (her) to be a nice person." And certainly don't let career goals enter your mind unless your child is obviously exceptionally gifted.

For purposes of selecting the right private school, it's important for you to write down specific goals. What is it you want your child to learn? Academics? Writing skills? Athletic skills? Concert piano? Extracurricular activities? Social behavior? Ethics? Religious values? Be specific and set your goals down on paper so you can match them to the stated goals of each private school you visit, and see whether that particular school can indeed help your child attain those goals.

Admission to Selective Colleges

If eventual admission to a selective college—Ivy League or Ivy League equivalent—is one of your goals, by all means list that also. But keep in mind that all too many parents mistakenly believe that a "top" college preparatory school will automatically ensure their child's eventual admission to a "top" college. For most, nothing could be farther from the truth, because of the enormous academic competition at most "top" private schools.

For example, a child who is a straight-A student and tops in the class at Smalltown Junior High (and almost certain to become valedictorian at Smalltown Senior High) may wind up only 40th or 60th in the class at a prestigious New England prep school and have virtually no chance for admission to an Ivy League college. Had that child remained in public school, he or she might not have received as sophisticated a high-school education, but might well have breezed into the Ivy League.

So be certain to think through carefully and write down your goals for your child, to be certain a private school can realistically help achieve them. And try to develop carefully thought-out answers to all the other questions we've discussed. It's certain to be difficult at first, but after a few days you'll get better at it. As your notes become more thorough, you may be amazed at how little you knew about your child. But those notes will not only give you a better idea of who your child is, you'll have a far greater appreciation and love of the entire person—not just the person you'd like your child to be. By getting to know your child better, you'll soon be able to figure out what kind of school will be of greatest benefit.

CHAPTER 3

DIFFERENT SCHOOLS FOR DIFFERENT KIDS

W hether your children are gifted with immeasurably high IQs and talents that rival those of most adults, or whether they need remediation or special care, there is a perfect private school for them—and for every other child. It may be secular or religious, a day or boarding school, a military school or a school for children with special needs. That's what's so exciting about private-school education—the freedom to choose the right school for your children. Let's take a look at the various categories of private schools to help you begin narrowing the list of schools that can best serve your children. Appendix B lists the more than 900 private schools of all categories that belong to the National Association of Independent Schools (NAIS), an important professional group that only admits the finest, accredited, independent private schools.

Nondenominational Day Schools

There are three basic types of nondenominational day schools: city, country (or suburban) and a variety of boarding schools. Most boarding schools now admit day students and are more appropriately called day/boarding or boarding/day schools, depending on whether the day students make up a majority or minority of the student body. Within each of these three categories of school, there is a choice of coeducational or single-sex schools for both boys and girls.

It's simple enough to envision the superficial differences between a city school and a country day school, but it's also important to understand some of the other, less evident advantages and disadvantages of each, especially if you're considering moving from a big city to the suburbs or country and education is a factor in your decision.

A key advantage of a city school over a country day school is accessibility. Until your child is 16 or 17 and able to drive, you or some adult may have to drive your child to and from a country or suburban school every day, unless a private bus service is available or state law mandates free public transportation for all school children.

Just as important a consideration, however, is your child's extracurricular life at school and social life at home. You will always be responsible for driving your child to and from after-school activities (sports, plays, etc.) at most country day schools and for driving your child to visit friends at their homes. Remember: Private schools are seldom neighborhood schools like public schools, which draw all their children from a district measured by a limited radius from the school. Your child's best friends could live 10, 15 or more miles away, and you and your child's friends' parents will have to drive that route almost every weekend and on many days during school vacations to allow the kids to visit each other.

And that's an important factor to keep in mind about private school. In all likelihood, your children will no longer draw their friends from the immediate neighborhood. No matter how compatible, children rarely remain good friends without the common bond of attending the same school and sharing the same friends, teachers, school activities and homework.

City Schools Vs. Country Schools

A private school in the city is usually far more accessible for its students than one in the country is for its students. City children can walk or take public transportation to and from school by themselves, if they're old enough and if it's a safe neighborhood, or in groups. And they can often walk or take public transportation to each other's homes. Moreover, city day schools have easy access and frequently take their children to all the cultural attractions a city offers: museums, theater, concerts, opera, special events and major universities that make their faculty and facilities available to local school children. This can be especially important for children with special gifts in music, for example, who require professional instruction from world-class teachers.

On the other hand, most city schools lack the boundless playing fields, huge gymnasiums and sprawling campuses of many country day schools and boarding schools. Children at country schools are out of doors each day, and, of course, they face fewer dangers to their personal safety than children on the streets of many major American cities.

Day Students at Boarding Schools

Now it may have surprised you to find boarding schools in a category devoted to day schools, but all but a handful of the nearly 250 accredited independent boarding schools in the United States frequently have a large proportion of day students from nearby communities. Indeed, day students constitute more than half the student bodies at more than one-quarter of America's independent boarding schools, while day students make up 20% or more of the student body at 50 others, including such highly selective schools as Choate, Lawrenceville, Taft and Phillips Academy at Andover, Massachusetts. At Groton, Deerfield and Phillips Exeter Academy, day students make up more than 10% of the student bodies.

Some day students live in the same town as the boarding school and can walk to school each day. Others must rely on their parents or some other form of transportation. Ironically, many century-old boarding schools built in then-rural areas 100 miles or more from the nearest cities now have as many as or more day students than boarders, because the cities and their surrounding suburbs expanded and engulfed the countryside surrounding the schools.

One disadvantage of being a day student at what is primarily a boarding school, however, is the lack of bonding with the majority of students, who socialize together at school in the dining halls, common rooms, corridors and living quarters after classroom hours, while day students often return home immediately after classes or afternoon sports activities. Despite efforts by many boarding schools to integrate day students into total boarding-school life, some day students find their social lives somewhat barren at school and at home, where they have little in common with neighborhood children attending local public schools. Indeed, it's not uncommon for envious neighborhood children to shun former friends in private schools as "snobs."

Nevertheless, boarding schools can serve as viable private day-school alternatives for children living in areas with only substandard public schools as educational alternatives. Boarding school for a day student can be particularly satisfying if several day students from a particular neighborhood attend together—in that way they have each other as a social core group. And, of course, another way to permit your child to overcome the possible social disadvantages of being a day student at a predominantly boarding school is to let him or her board there.

So, in broadest terms, those are the superficial advantages and disadvantages of city day schools, country day schools and boarding schools for day students. A few day schools, incidentally, have five-day boarding facilities for a limited number of students, who can thus experience life at a tradi-

34

tional boarding school without giving up home and family life entirely. Such boarding arrangements can be helpful for families who live too far away for their children to commute to school each weekday, but near enough to come home on weekends. Five-day boarding facilities can also be helpful for families with working parents who return home too late each night to provide a fulfilling home life for their child during the week. Five-day boarding is also a solution for a working parent who has transferred to an out-of-town job but can nevertheless return home on weekends. Families suffering some sort of trauma that might make it difficult for a child to concentrate on schoolwork at home also find five-day boarding helpful for their children. On-campus faculty and evening study halls at five-day boarding schools offer the supervision, structure and atmosphere for concentration on homework. The two dozen NAIS five-day boarding schools are listed in Part 3 of Appendix B.

Religious Day Schools

Each of the three types of day schools discussed may or may not be religiously affiliated. For devout members of any faith who want their children to be raised in the beliefs and rites of their faith, a private religious school—Catholic, Protestant, or Jewish—supplements the usual academic curriculum with required daily religious instruction, prayer and preparation for the rites of passage into the adult community of the particular religion (Communion, Bar or Bat Mitzvah, etc.).

There are, however, two basic types of religious school—parochial and independent. A parochial school is generally owned and operated by the church and clergy and subject to no outside interference by parents, state authorities or anyone else. The rules, regulations, curriculum and activities are determined unilaterally by the church, and students and their parents have only two choices—take it or leave it.

The Catholic church has two types of parochial schools. The first, usually at the elementary-school level, is literally parochial, serving children from the local church parish and operated by the priest of that parish. The second, usually a high school, is a diocesan school, which tends to serve a wider district and is operated by a board of clergy and an office of education serving the entire diocese. Teachers in parochial and diocesan schools may be members of the clergy or lay persons, with the latter usually, though not necessarily, being members of the Catholic faith.

Independent religious schools have no direct legal ties to the church or clergy. Like all independent schools, they are operated by an elected board of trustees, which may or may not include clergy, but usually is made up of members of a common religion whose goal may be the propagation of their beliefs. As in parochial schools, all students in independent religious schools, regardless of their own religion, are usually required to take religious instruction and attend services—sometimes daily.

So, it's important to know whether religious instruction is required before enrolling your child in a school—especially one that teaches a religion other than your own—and whether you want your child exposed to that religion. You usually will not be able to have your child excused from such religious instruction simply because it is not your own religion.

In general, independent religious schools are academically superior to parochial schools because the latter are run by clergy who may or may not be trained educators and who may put teaching and propagating the faith ahead of teaching academics. Indeed, there is often a danger that the clergy may distort history and science to conform with the teachings of their own religion.

Almost all academically selective prep schools—especially those in the Northeast—were founded as religious schools. Indeed, the first schools in what is now the United States were *all* religious schools, founded in the 1600s to teach children to read the Bible and learn enough "numbers" not to be cheated in the marketplace. Public nondenominational schools as we know them today did not emerge until the mid-19th century, with Horace Mann's advocacy of compulsory universal education for all American children in so-called free schools.

The vast majority of America's original religious schools, however, have now abandoned required religious instruction and student attendance at religious services. Only a few still maintain religious affiliations and even those have, for the most part, modified their services to make them nondenominational. Students are simply asked each day to pray together to a single, common God.

Of the nondemoninational schools, some require students to attend services of their own faith, while others make such attendance voluntary. Although each school's catalog usually describes the school's practices quite carefully, it's important to investigate what, if any, ties a school maintains to organized religion and how this may affect your child's life at school. A school catalog that states "Daily life revolves around the chapel" may also be indicating subtly that a child of a different faith may find life uncomfortable at that school. Don't wait to find out until after your child enrolls—and don't be subtle about asking questions about the role religion plays in the life of any school you consider.

In many areas of the United States—remote rural communities, for example, or inner city neighborhoods—many families send their children to religious schools of other faiths, not only because of the academic advantages such schools offer over local public schools, but also because of the safety, discipline and ethical and moral training they provide for their students. Like all private schools, religious schools try not to admit (or quickly expel) unruly, ill-behaved students, so that teachers and serious students can concentrate on academics in a quiet, safe environment. In some inner-city areas, as a result, many Catholic private schools have student bodies that are two-thirds non-Catholic!

Before selecting such schools, however, it's important to determine whether the academic advantages and the greater discipline and safety they offer are worth the price of having your child taught the beliefs and practices of another religion.

There is one other consideration to keep in mind about religious schools: *On average* they tend to be academically inferior to independent nonsectarian schools—usually because they do not have adequate funding to support a full range of academic programs. That does not mean *all* religious schools are inferior to independent schools. Indeed, there are some outstanding religiously affiliated schools. The Quaker-related Friends' schools are great examples of religiously oriented schools that are the academic equals of some of the finest nonsectarian independent schools. Graduating seniors from the Friends' Central School in Philadelphia go on to Harvard, Brown, University of Pennsylvania and other top universities. The same holds true for graduates of other religious schools. There are some great Jewish schools, for example, including The Frisch School in Paramus, New Jersey, which sends its graduates to Harvard and Columbia—as well as Yeshiva University. Iona Preparatory School, a Roman Catholic school in New Rochelle, New York, regularly sends graduates to Cornell, Georgetown, Notre Dame and Yale—as well as seminaries to train for the priesthood. And the outstanding Lutheran schools have equally impressive college placement successes.

So there are many outstanding religious schools. But *on average,* religious schools tend to be academically inferior to private nondenominational schools because of inadequate funding. In some cases, they may even be inferior to local public schools.

Beware especially of the private, so-called Christian academies in the South. They are among the worst schools of *any* kind in the United States—public or private. Founded to skirt federal court orders banning segregation, such schools not only censor, but actually rewrite, vast bodies of knowledge to conform with often backward religious and racial beliefs and prejudices. Students are forced to study "creation science," for example, to the exclusion of astronomy, anthropology, biology and other sciences. They are deprived of the opportunity to read many of the world's great literary works, including many plays by Shakespeare and important novels by such American authors as John Steinbeck. In many such schools, children are also taught racial, religious and ethnic bigotry.

Most such academies, in other words, are not schools of education but are schools of indoctrination, and their students seldom graduate having fulfilled the academic requirements for entrance into selective, academically superior colleges and universities. The Southern Association of Schools and Colleges refuses to accredit many Christian academies in the South, and, as you'll see later in the book, accreditation by a regional accreditation association is one of the key factors to consider before selecting any private school.

Roman Catholic Schools

Fortunately, most religious schools in the United States are far better than the Christian academies of the South. Indeed, the largest group of religious schools are Catholic, and, for the most part, they have a deservedly fine reputation. Some rank among America's finest schools academically, and almost all offer enormous advantages over public schools. About 2.5 million children attend the more than 7,000 elementary and nearly 1,300 Catholic high schools in America, and 12% of those kids are non-Catholic. The dropout rate at Catholic high schools is less than 4%, compared with a 27.4% national dropout rate at public schools. About 83% of Catholic-school children go on to college, compared with only 52% of public-school graduates.

In almost every category of academic achievement, students in Catholic schools score well above their counterparts in public schools: 11 percentage points higher in reading, 6 points higher in mathematics, 5 points higher in science, and 10 points higher in social studies. Moreover, those comparisons are true at every grade level—3rd, 7th, 11th, etc. Students at Catholic high schools average 21% higher scores than public-school students on Scholastic Aptitude Tests, which are used as college entrance examinations.

The comparisons are all the more startling in light of the fact that Catholic schools spend no more per pupil than public schools to obtain such dramatically better results. Both spend an average of about $4,000 per pupil per year.

There are many reasons, of course, for the better results in Catholic schools. For one thing, Catholic schools, like most private schools, refuse to admit unruly, deeply disturbed, disruptive children. Children found with drugs or alcohol, children prone to violence and children who don't obey the rules are expelled. Public schools must by law deal with all children, and, therefore, incur far higher costs handling disruptive, emotionally disturbed, physically handicapped or learning-disabled children.

A second reason Catholic schools do a better job than public schools is that they do not offer students the huge choice of often 200 or more frequently worthless electives found in "cafeteria-style" curricula at most public schools. Like all good private schools, Catholic schools stick to basics, limiting at least 75% of the curriculum to required courses—English, mathematics, science, foreign languages, social studies, music and art. Moreover, offerings are presented in a calm, quiet atmosphere, where discipline reigns. Children must be well groomed. Boys must wear slacks, shirts and ties, and girls must wear dresses, sleeved blouses and shoes— instead of T-shirts, jeans and sneakers. And they're expected to do seven or more hours of homework a week, instead of only 5.4 hours, which is the national average for public-school students.

For millions of children, therefore, the huge Catholic school system offers enormous advantages over public schools. For many families, they even have some advantages over independent private schools. The most obvious of these advantages is cost, which averages about $4,000 a year per student. As in most private schools, however, costs increase from grade to grade. Thus, Catholic elementary schools generally charge from $1,200 to $2,000 per year, while high-school costs can range as high as $7,500 per year or more.

Catholic schools, in other words, make private-school education affordable for many middle- and lower-income families who cannot afford the $10,000–plus annual cost of an independent day school. Moreover, for Catholic families, such schools combine good education with a grounding in the Catholic faith.

Like all good private schools, Catholic schools try to teach children self-discipline, reliability, honesty, respect for themselves and for others and love of family, of school and of country. Naturally, Catholic schools also teach love of God, of Christ and of the Catholic church. For Catholic children especially, education at a Catholic school makes growing up easier, because they are constantly immersed in an atmosphere of homogeneous values at school, at home and at play.

For non-Catholic children, however, attendance at a Catholic school can be a problem, because such children are invariably "outsiders." If you don't want your child immersed in the teachings of the Catholic church, you should not consider Catholic schools, because they invariably require all their students—non-Catholic and Catholic alike—to study Catholicism.

The "outsider" syndrome, of course, is true at all religious schools for children who are not members of the sponsoring religion. There are, however, other, far more important problems associated with Catholic schools. One is academic quality. Although far better than that of public schools, the academic quality of most Catholic schools—especially parochial schools—is far below that of most selective independent schools. Indeed, only 10% of Catholic children in America now attend parochial schools.

There are many reasons for poor-quality education in parochial schools. For one thing, the costs of Catholic schools are too low to ensure the best possible education. Obviously, when Catholic schools and all other religious schools were originally established in centuries past, their mission was to propagate religion. Reading and writing were taught not to help children get into top universities but to help them read the Bible. Teachers were unpaid clergy.

As the number of teaching brothers and sisters declined, Catholic schools were forced to hire—and pay—lay teachers. The latter have always been, and continue to be, badly underpaid—an average of $9,000 per year less than public school teachers. Nor can Catholic schools afford to pay more, because they must keep costs as low as possible to fulfill their mission to reach as many children as possible, no matter how poor. Indeed, no Catholic children are denied education at a Catholic school because their parents cannot afford to pay the tuition.

Although many lay teachers in Catholic schools are able and dedicated, the low salaries nevertheless attract many who are not able to get better-paying jobs at public schools or independent private schools, and the quality of academics necessarily suffers.

Catholic schools all teach the basics—reading, writing, mathematics, science, social studies, foreign languages, art and music, but most cannot afford to offer as wide a range of such courses as many independent schools can. Nor can they offer as broad a range of extra-curricular activities and athletics. In addition, they're forced to crowd more students into each classroom—an average of 23.9 in elementary school classrooms and 18.2 in secondary schools, compared to an average of 17.6 for public schools and 9.3 in independent private schools.

Making matters still more difficult is the fact that many Catholic schools draw a disproportionately large number of children from lower economic groups, and the average student is simply not on an academic par with the average student at the most selective independent schools. So, what this adds up to is that too many children with fewer cultural advantages tend to be crowded into classrooms with less-able teachers than in independent schools.

Although kids in many Catholic schools get a better education than they would in most public schools, the academic results of Catholic schools pale in comparison to those of independent schools.

Table 1.
Percentage of 8th graders scoring in top 25% of achievement tests.

Subject	Public Schools	Catholic Schools	Other Private Schools
Reading	23.0%	34.9%	47.2%
Math	23.8	29.7	45.7
Science	23.4	26.1	38.5
History	22.8	35.1	41.8

Source: U.S. Department of Education

As seen earlier, only 44% of 8th-grade students in Catholic schools achieve the highest level of reading proficiency. That's ahead of the 32% who achieve that level in public schools, but well below the 68% in independent private schools. The differences are even more dramatic in mathematics, where a mere 19% of 8th graders in Catholic schools achieve at the highest proficiency level—only one percentage point better than public-school students. In independent private schools, 63% of 8th graders function at the highest mathematics proficiency level.

In some subject areas, Catholic-school students not only get a poorer education than students in independent schools, they may even fare worse than students in public schools—again because of inadequate funding. For example, only 18.6% of 8th graders in Catholic schools are enrolled in laboratory sciences, compared with 21.5% of 8th graders in public schools and nearly half the 8th graders in independent private schools.

An astounding 87.8% of independent private-school students study a foreign language. Only 16.2% of Catholic-school students do the same, compared to 23.5% of students in public schools. Table 1 shows the percentage of 8th grade students from public, Catholic and private schools who scored in the top quartile of the same standardized tests in reading, mathematics, science and history.

As you can see, the students from Catholic schools consistently outscored public-school students, though not by much. However, Catholic-school 8th graders don't even come close to matching the performance of students from "other private schools."

So, *on average*, Catholic schools simply do not offer the academic quality of the vast majority of nondenominational independent schools. It's important to remember, however, that we're discussing *averages*, and that

41

many Catholic schools are in some of the most economically depressed areas of the United States. To their great credit, those schools and the Catholic Churches and parishioners supporting them are spending precious resources, with little or no state or federal government aid, to teach some of America's most culturally and materially deprived *non-Catholic* children. The latter necessarily lower the average academic scores of Catholic schools as a group. The "other private schools" in the table do not teach as many such children, and the public schools that do are doing such a bad job that it borders on criminal negligence.

So, it's important in examining the above table to keep in mind that many superior Catholic schools operate at academic levels far above the average for their group and even farther above the average of public schools. As mentioned earlier, many are the equal of some of the finest independent schools, and those not operated by the church are listed in Appendix B with other NAIS schools.

Boarding Schools
(and the Boarding-School Experience)

Many of America's older boarding schools were modeled on what the British call "public schools." Some were designed to prepare their students for particular colleges. When Horace Taft built The Taft School, in Watertown, Connecticut, more than 100 years ago, and when his Yale roommate Sherman Thacher started Thacher School in Ojai, California, they founded their schools as preparatory schools for Yale University. Such old exclusive schools as Phillips Andover Academy, Phillips Exeter, Taft, Hotchkiss, Groton, St. Paul's, Deerfield, Lawrenceville and others used to feed the majority of their students into Amherst, Dartmouth, Harvard, Princeton, Williams, Yale and other prestigious colleges and universities.

Students in the top half of their classes at such schools never even bothered with applications to a "second choice" of college because there was no need for a second choice. That's why they were at Lawrenceville—to go to Princeton; and at Hotchkiss or Taft—to go to Yale; and at Groton—to go to Harvard. Admission from such "feeder" schools into the associated colleges was automatic, and, from the moment a boy enrolled at 14, he knew which college he would attend four years later.

Until the 1960s and 1970s, all the students at such prep schools, and at the colleges with which they were associated, were males. There were a handful of comparably selective girls' boarding schools, just as there were a handful of selective girls' colleges—Barnard, Bryn Mawr, Mt. Holyoke, Radcliffe, Smith, Vassar, Wellesley, etc. But none of the selective private boarding schools or day schools turned coeducational until the colleges they fed did so.

Today, feeder schools as such have disappeared. On average, boarding-school boys and girls have no better chances of getting into academically selective colleges and universities than do students from comparable day schools. There are some exceptions, however. About a dozen of the most academically selective boarding schools of the Northeast, which tend to limit admission to the most highly motivated, academically gifted students, continue to send a disproportionately high number of their students to the most selective colleges and universities. And that, of course, is one reason many parents try to get their kids into such schools.

Of the most famous ones, for example, Phillips Academy, in Andover, Masschusetts (usually referred to simply as "Andover"), has a physical plant that is larger and more extensive than many colleges. More than 210 years old, Andover is also the academic equivalent—indeed the academic superior—of many, if not most, colleges, and it sends more than 40% of its graduating seniors to the most selective colleges and universities, including all the Ivy League colleges and such outstanding non-Ivy League colleges and universities as Bryn Mawr, MIT, Northwestern, Stanford, Swarthmore, Wesleyan and Williams. More than one-fourth of the typical graduating class goes to Ivy League colleges.

At the similarly outstanding Phillips Exeter Academy, in Exeter, New Hampshire, 62% of a recent graduating class scored more than 600 on the verbal SATs and an astounding 86% scored above 600 on their math SATs.

Quite obviously, Andover and Exeter, along with such prestigious boarding schools as Groton, Hotchkiss, St. Paul's and Deerfield and such academically demanding New York City day schools as Collegiate, Dalton and Horace Mann, place disproportionately large numbers of their graduating seniors in the most selective, academically demanding colleges and universities. But, as mentioned before, they draw and tend to admit a disproportionately large number of the most mature, academically gifted students who would excel no matter where they went to school.

Why, then, would parents of more average students want to consider sending their children to such schools? As mentioned earlier, practical reasons can often dictate choosing boarding schools in today's educational climate. There may be no adequate public schools and no private schools of any kind nearby, for example. Going off to an outstanding boarding school can be a thrilling academic, cultural and social adventure for the right youngster, and parents of any bright, motivated child who is not being fully challenged academically at available neighborhood schools should certainly consider sending that child to boarding school.

There are other practical reasons for selecting a boarding school. A family in the midst of an emotional upheaval (separation, divorce or death in the family) might well consider boarding school as a safe haven where their children can escape the traumas of family disintegration and concentrate on schoolwork in an atmosphere of social stability, among close friends and a caring adult faculty. A parent's job transfer to an isolated or overseas post might be another reason for sending a child to a boarding school.

Although the vast majority of the more than 240 NAIS member boarding schools in Appendix B are high schools, some do have middle-school boarding programs, and about 40 have junior boarding programs accommodating children as early as 4th grade. A few accept students as early as 1st grade. Schools with junior boarding programs are in both the general NAIS listing in Appendix B and in a separate sublisting for parents specifically seeking such schools.

In addition to family trauma and parent job transfers, there are a host of other reasons for sending children to boarding school. Loneliness is one, as in the case mentioned earlier of the child with few or no friends living nearby, whose older siblings have left home and whose parents spend long days at work. Four years of coming home to an empty house, often eating dinner alone with only a television set for a friend, can be a desperately lonely existence for an adolescent. There's no substitute for the attention of a loving family, but a boarding school filled with friends and a caring adult faculty can often come very close.

Tradition is another reason many families send their children to boarding school. The old, prestigious boarding schools have often welcomed five or more generations of the same families. Such families consider it part of their tradition to send all their sons and daughters to the same schools, and those schools not only welcome such children, they depend heavily on the generous, voluntary financial gifts that such families make to help the schools expand their facilities and endowments.

Another reason for considering a boarding school may be its facilities. Some boarding schools may excel in a particular activity that your children love and in which they exhibit exceptional talents—ice hockey, for example. Many boarding schools have their own indoor or covered rinks. Few country day schools or city schools can offer the equivalent. Many boarding schools sit on hundreds of acres of land with facilities comparable to, or better than, those at many colleges—including, in some cases, meteorological observatories.

Some boarding schools, such as the justly famed Trinity-Pawling School, in Pawling, New York, have extensive facilities and a trained, renowned faculty for dealing with specific learning disorders such as dyslexia. Day schools, which a child attends only seven or eight hours a day five days a week, simply cannot do as effective a job treating such disorders as a live-in faculty with a large corps of trained, caring teachers who are in contact with the children throughout their waking hours seven days a week. For that reason, many day schools simply will not accept children with learning disorders, and parents have no choice but to send their kids to boarding school if they want to combine effective treatment with a superior academic education such as that at Trinity-Pawling.

Another important reason for some parents to send their children to boarding school is to effect a healthy separation from each other. There can be many reasons for this, not the least of which may be to encourage a child's independence and self-reliance. In other cases, parents and children simply aren't getting along. The child is rebelling at home, associating with unacceptable peers and no longer functioning at his or her capacity in school or out. It's always best to consult a family therapist or counselor, of course, but in many cases it may prove better for both parents and children to separate and to let a skilled boarding-school faculty deal with the day-to-day problems of adolescence and growing up. Often, as any parent knows, other, unrelated adults can help our children solve problems that have us baffled, because an unrelated adult can often deal with our children more objectively than we can.

By sending a child to boarding school, a family can reserve most parent-child contacts for the good times—the family reunions at Thanksgiving, Christmas and Easter and carefree summer-vacation fishing or camping trips—thus converting what may have been an unpleasant parent-child relationship into an extremely happy one, filled with genuine joy and love.

Many parents feel—and often are—inadequate and just not up to the job of parenting their children through what can be the turbulent adolescent years. Such parents prefer turning over part of the job over to a boarding school, where their child can grow up in a warm, nurturing atmosphere, shielded from most of the tensions and dangers of life on many city and suburban streets.

Freed to travel when and where they want, to come and go as they please, with no day-to-day parental responsibilities, such parents find they can happily devote themselves entirely to enjoying their children and lavishing them with love during school vacations together; in such cases, both children and parents are delighted with having chosen a boarding school over a day school.

For the mature boy or girl, boarding school offers an opportunity to be independent within a framework of adult supervision that prevents, or at least limits, much of the self-destructive risk taking to which so many adolescents are prone. For the less mature youngster, boarding schools teach and encourage independence, self-reliance and personal responsibility in

45

ways that few parents can in a home setting, where a youngster can manipulate the environment more easily.

Life Away from Home

At a typical boarding school, youngsters can choose between single, double and even triple and quadruple rooms. The majority of first-year students usually share rooms with roommates selected by the school. Applicants usually fill out personality profile forms that help the school match children with compatible personalities. Students may select their own roommates in subsequent years—subject always, however, to approval by the youngster's immediate faculty supervisor or advisor.

Rooms are simple to start with—a desk, desk chair, lamp, bureau, bed and closet for each student—but youngsters quickly convert their quarters into "homes" that reflect their interests and personalities. They add sofas or comfortable chairs, stereos and a range of wall and floor decorations and other accessories, limited only by their individual imaginations and school rules governing good taste. Rules also usually require youngsters to make their beds and clean their rooms for daily inspections. Students may also help clean and maintain school hallways, classrooms and grounds at some boarding schools.

Rooms are normally clustered near the apartment of a faculty member who serves as surrogate parent, disciplinarian, trusted friend and wise counselor on everything from academics to personal problems. Usually, too, a common room, complete with television and stereo, serves a corridor or group of rooms. Occasionally, there's even a refrigerator filled with food and soft drinks.

A typical boarding school day starts at 7:00 A.M., with breakfast in a common dining hall. Dress codes vary widely. Some schools have none; others require ties, jackets, slacks and shoes for boys and equally formal dress for girls during classroom periods and at all meals. Rules for personal grooming also vary.

Some schools have denominational or nondenominational chapel services or simply an assembly for announcements before classes begin at 8:00 or 8:30 A.M. Classes last 45 or 50 minutes, with each student required to attend four to six classes daily, with an hour off for lunch, cafeteria-style, with free seating. Any other free period is used for study or conferences with teachers.

Afternoons are spent on playing fields or in gym in required intramural or interscholastic sports. These may include baseball, basketball, bicycling, cross-country running, diving, equestrian sports, field hockey, football, golf, gymnastics, ice hockey, lacrosse, martial arts, paddle tennis, sailing, skiing (cross-country and downhill), soccer, softball, squash, swimming, tennis, track and field, volleyball, wrestling and other sports.

As mentioned earlier, the vast acreages at some of the larger boarding schools may include a dozen or more playing fields, as many or more tennis courts and huge gymnasium complexes, with swimming and diving pools, a half-dozen or more basketball and squash courts, an indoor track, wrestling rooms, dance studios, weight-training rooms and large locker rooms with individual lockers for every student and, of course, large shower-room facilities for boys and girls. In every sense, they are luxurious facilities that few day schools can match. In addition, many boarding schools in northern climates have covered outdoor or indoor ice hockey arenas. Some have boathouses for crews if they're near a river or lake. Others have their own ski hills or ski trails and a few have their own nine- or 18-hole golf courses.

Most boarding schools serve dinner between 5:30 P.M. and 7:30 P.M., with seating often assigned at tables headed by faculty members and their families. From 8:00 to 10:00 or even later each evening, students study and do their homework. There's usually time before and after dinner, however, for involvement in extracurricular activities, which, like athletics, are many and varied and backed with extensive school facilities.

Most schools urge students as strongly as possible to participate in extracurricular activities. They can join a drama society (most schools have complete, professional theaters); glee clubs and choral and singing groups; the school orchestra or various chamber music and jazz groups; the daily newspaper, year book or literary monthly magazine; a professionally outfitted radio or television station that broadcasts in the school only. Other activities include photography clubs (most schools have professionally outfitted darkrooms), a political union to debate national and international issues, a student government organization to help run school activities. There are also many academic "clubs" that allow students to pursue academic interests in an informal setting without tests or homework requirements. There are also game clubs (chess, etc.), dance clubs and religious societies. And there are also community service groups. Many schools require students to engage in some form of community service—either in the school community (tutoring younger students, for example) or in the surrounding community.

And it's all these activities that make boarding school so different from day school. For a boarding school is a complete, independent, 24-hour community in every sense. As such, it can offer each community member far more time and opportunity to develop every talent. In academics, athletics and extracurricular activities, youngsters can devote all their waking hours to self-development, uninterrupted by a long commute home and undistracted by family problems and obligations or temptations to play.

Although a typical boarding school operates within a framework of rules and regulations established by adults, it is nevertheless a community of and for young people, who learn to govern themselves and assume responsibility for themselves and their community. Living together day and night in such close quarters, students in such schools often form deeper, longer-lasting friendships than those formed at day schools. Many last a lifetime.

At some schools, the students themselves are responsible for maintaining much of the discipline and order in school, and a student court punishes offenders. Elected student leaders serve as role models, peer supporters, dormitory leaders, members of disciplinary committees and student-faculty governing bodies. In theory, at least, students learn how to govern themselves and make democracy work.

Most youngsters emerge from such schools far more mature and self-reliant than their counterparts at day schools, where student life is more directed and governed by adults—parents at home and faculty at school.

A day-school student may often lead two separate and inconsistent lives—one at home, the other at school. Not so at boarding school, where a student's home life and school life are one, and behavior is under constant scrutiny by one's peers and the adult community. Faculty and students live together 24 hours a day, seven days a week and, as members of such a community, students are forced to learn self-discipline and respect for the laws that govern their community. Although free from parental involvement in day-to-day decision making, boarding-school students quickly learn that independence is not a license to take risks or to threaten the health, happiness or rights of others. At boarding school, perhaps more than at any other type of school, students learn the difference between a privilege and a right, and they learn to work daily and diligently to promote their own individual growth as well as the growth of their community.

A recent catalog from Phillips Academy at Andover put it beautifully:

> Trust and responsibility have many interpretations . . . but the ideas they embody—sensitivity to others, willingness to explore and respect differing points of view, charity and humility in expressing judgment, readiness to cherish friendship, to depend and be depended upon—are nonetheless fundamental (to) . . . the health and happiness of everyone in the community . . .

These are the values most boarding schools try to teach their students, and, unlike many day schools, they have the time and the attention of the students and faculty to do so.

On weekends, some boarding schools have Saturday morning classes; others do not. Saturday afternoons at schools where boarders predominate are usually reserved for interscholastic sports competitions involving varsity, junior varsity and other school teams. In addition, depending on their location, boarding schools try to arrange formal and informal trips to nearby cities. On-campus events may include dances, concerts, movies, plays and a variety of informal activities. Students also have access to darkrooms, art studios and music rooms to pursue individual interests during their free time. Sundays include required or optional religious services, free time for recreation and at least four hours of study.

Weekend life for boarders at schools where day students make up the majority can be somewhat less exciting, however—even a bit lonely. So it's important to ask about weekend life at any boarding school you consider. Where day students make up the majority of the student body, boarders can find themselves in an all-but-empty and eerily quiet building on weekends, with little to do but pine over thoughts of their day-student classmates enjoying themselves at home surrounded by family and friends. So be sure to check that any boarding school you consider fills the lives of its weekend residents with enjoyable activities.

Because the faculty at boarding school must serve as surrogate parents, dealing with personal problems of students is an important part of their work. Each student at boarding school has a faculty advisor to offer guidance and help at all times. Many schools have visiting therapists to help youngsters cope with more profound problems. And, of course, boarding schools have complete infirmaries staffed 24 hours a day by registered nurses and by at least one doctor who is on call 24 hours a day, seven days a week.

Disadvantages of Boarding Schools

For many, boarding schools represent an academic paradise for children. But like all schools, private and public, there are some disadvantages, which you should not overlook. The most obvious is cost, which is double that of even the most costly private day schools, and may be five times as much as a neighborhood parochial school. Added to the more than $20,000 you'll spend on tuition, room and board are the costs for the enormous wardrobe your child will need, the books and sports gear your child will have to buy, the much larger allowance your child will need for such things as snacks, weekend trips, etc., and the costs of transportation—perhaps by air—for long weekends, holidays and vacations. And those transportation (and possibly lodging) costs will work two ways—for your child to come home to visit you and for you and perhaps the rest of your family to visit your child.

In addition to costs, boarding school can mean a painful separation for the children who go away to school and for the parents and siblings who stay behind. Not all children or families adapt well to such a separation. Some kids are terribly lonely or homesick when they first go away. Most get over it, but some never quite do, although they manage to adapt. A handful ask to come home, and for them, the return represents a humiliating defeat. So be certain your child does indeed want and need to go before you consider boarding school.

And make certain, too, that you are willing to forego the joys (as well as the horrors!) of guiding your child through adolescence. The sudden absence of a bubbling 14-year-old at home can be devastating for many parents. So, before considering boarding school, consider whether you and your child *both* are ready to let go of each other. You'll both have to do so when your child reaches college age. The question is whether you're ready to do so now.

Military Schools

Once used as a threat against unruly rich boys, military schools were indeed institutions in which the troubled, often incorrigible sons of the wealthy were exiled. Today, they are simply boarding schools with a veneer of military "window dressing." Most are academically demanding, and they state quite clearly that they "have no capabilities for handling children with disciplinary problems." They refuse to admit youngsters sent in punishment for bad behavior at home.

The majority remain boys' schools, although there are a handful of co-educational military schools. There are no accredited all-girls military schools. Like other boarding schools, most military academies have a widely varying mix of day students and boarders. Like all private schools, each military school has its own "personality," which you'll have to examine at each school to see if it meets the needs of your child. Obviously, not every child will take to the discipline of a military school, and that is why there are relatively few of them. A handful are affiliated with the Roman Catholic church and combine the education of religious and military schools. At least one is affiliated with the Baptist church.

Graduates of military school go on to attend the same range of colleges and universities as graduates of other independent boarding schools and day schools, although a larger percentage of military-school graduates tend to apply to service academies.

The only substantial difference between military schools and other boarding schools is the military discipline and training required of students. The question you must ask yourself is whether your child will thrive and enjoy living in a quasi-military environment that will include wearing uniforms almost all the time, strict military bearing and conduct and instant obedience to orders issued by student superior officers as well as all adults. For many kids, military school is fun. Don't consider sending your child to one unless he feels the same.

In addition to the standard academic program of conventional boarding schools, military schools usually require studies of military and naval history and military and naval science, and they require membership in Junior Reserve Officers Training Corps and Naval Reserve Officers Training Corps. Most schools also offer a wide range of other courses needed by future officers, including aerospace science and navigation. Some schools teach sailing, others flying, and others offer equestrian activities. At least one school has its own airstrip, where boys 17 and older may earn their pilot's license. A list of 16 NAIS military schools may be found in Appendix B.

Special Schools

As mentioned earlier, no two children learn anything in precisely the same way. The great thing about private schools is the small teacher-student ratios that allow teachers and school administrators to adapt their teaching methods and school rules and regulations to the individual needs of each child. That's what tutoring children with learning disorders entails—adapting teaching methods to each child's needs so that he or she learns *the ability to learn*—at first with help, but eventually entirely independently. And after learning to learn by themselves, as with all children, their unique intelligence takes over. For most, there is no limit to what they can then do with their educational lives and eventual careers.

There are many great private schools—both day schools and boarding schools—with outstanding teachers and facilities for ensuring children with learning disorders a superlative education that is all but certain to lead them to college and a successful career. To try to force a child with a learning disorder to conceal that disorder, however, and to adapt to a school environment unable to cope with such a problem is certain to lead to failure and the destruction of your child's self-confidence.

Most educators believe every child should be tested for learning disorders as early as practicably possible and regardless of IQ or other intelligence or achievement test scores.

Many private schools won't handle learning disorders at all; others accept *only* children with learning disorders; still others accept a mixture of children. The latter treat learning disorders with special tutoring, but then "mainstream" those children in the same academic classes that all the other children in school attend. Some children with learning disorders can overcome their difficulties in a good day school; others accomplish more under the constant care and attention of a trained boarding-school faculty.

Trinity-Pawling School has one of America's most unique programs for learning-disabled boys. Set in the rolling hill country of Pawling, New York, about 70 miles north of New York City, Trinity-Pawling is a prestigious all-boys boarding school that sends its graduates to such colleges as Brown, Colgate and other highly selective universities. Each year, Trinity-Pawling admits a maximum of 55 dyslexic students—about 20% of the student body— into the 9th and 10th grades, where they participate in a two-year Language Retraining Program, while also studying basic history, mathematics and science courses. First-year students work in pairs with tutors studying such elements of language as phonetics, sequencing of ideas, handwriting, memorization techniques and other language skills. Second-year students join a language skills class and a tutorial class that meets four times a week. By the time they finish the language retraining program, most students are ready to join the rest of the Trinity-Pawling student body in the academic "mainstream"—i.e., the college-preparatory curriculum. Like all other students, they go on to study at some of America's finest colleges and universities.

There are, then, many approaches for teaching learning-disabled children. Every approach will have some benefits for every child, and none will be perfect. But some will be better for your child than others, and it's up to you to determine which. In evaluating each school, however, be certain that the school's program for children with special needs is well established. Unfortunately, in an effort to build enrollment, some financially shaky schools have simply added part-time specialists so they can advertise themselves as having special facilities for the learning disabled. If your child has even a slight learning disorder, it's important to enroll him or her in a school with a solid, well-established program. Check with the Orton Dyslexia Society at 80 Fifth Avenue, New York, New York 10011 (Tel: [212] 691–1930) or The Independent Educational Counselors Association (38 Cove Road, Forestdale, Massachusetts 02644. Tel: [508] 477– 2127).

Preprofessional Schools

One other type of special-needs school is the preprofessional school for youngsters with special gifts in the arts. The education of such prodigies is extremely complex, because parents have to try to balance the needs of a growing child with professional training whose demands are so great that they can easily deprive a child of a normal childhood.

Fortunately or unfortunately, parents of any prodigy must decide how to educate, train and raise their child early in their child's life—long before he or she can offer any feedback on the effects of those parental decisions. Such decisions should only be made after extensive consultations with professionals in the field in which the child is gifted, with one or more pediatricians and with former prodigies.

Before making such decisions about your child, keep in mind that there is no "only way" to raise and educate your child to assure him or her of the best professional training.

Some prodigies grow up in sociocultural vacuums, spending the vast majority of their time practicing and learning their art and getting only a minimum amount of conventional education—often from a private tutor. Although many grow into world-class artists, they often know little else but their art, and few do not regret as adults their lack of exposure to literature, history, philosophy and the other elements of education that form the pillars of civilization.

In sharp contrast, some parents insist that their children attend an academically demanding private school so that they get a good, well-rounded education. All the "spare" time of such children, however, is devoted to professional training. There is usually no time for sports, extracurricular activities or childhood fun.

A third path some children follow is attendance at a preprofessional school, where, with other gifted children, they are exposed to a fairly solid liberal arts education with extensive training in their particular art. The conventional education they get—in literature, math, history, etc.—is not as broad or profound as at standard prep schools, but it is more than adequate, and the somewhat reduced classroom time devoted to conventional school subjects can be added to the time spent in professional training. Moreover, children in such schools attend classes and socialize with other children with similar interests and needs. In other words, the rest of their friends don't go out to play baseball on sunny spring afternoons while they have to lock themselves in a music room to practice for four hours. All the children are doing the same things at the same time.

Many preprofessional day schools are public schools—"magnet" schools such as New York City's justly renowned Fiorello H. LaGuardia High School of Music and Art and Performing Arts, the school portrayed in the television show "Fame." Although such magnet schools are indeed public, the admission process is a grueling one and requires auditions or submission of works that clearly demonstrate that a child is exceptionally gifted. Fewer than 20% of all applicants are admitted. Magnet schools in some states such as North Carolina have boarding facilities to accommodate youngsters who live too far away to commute.

There are also some independent day and boarding schools that offer preprofessional training. The advantage of such schools is that students are immersed in an atmosphere that encourages professional growth without ignoring broader educational, social and emotional needs.

It's important for you as a parent, however, to investigate carefully the claims any private school makes about its special preprofessional training. Virtually every private school has music and art departments and some facilities for dramatic presentations. *That does not mean they are of pre-professional caliber.* Indeed, some private schools on the verge of bankruptcy actually mislead parents about the strengths of their music, art or dramatic arts programs in an effort to build enrollment. So if preprofessional training is important to you and your child, check with active professionals in the world of music, art, dance, theater, etc., to see if they know of and can genuinely recommend the schools you're considering. If you don't know anyone in those fields, call the admissions departments of some of the famous schools of music or art, such as the Juilliard School in New York, the Rhode Island School of Design in Providence, or the Yale Drama School in New Haven, Connecticut.

Coed vs. Single-sex Schools

The vast majority of independent schools (78%) are, of course, coeducational, and boys and girls share classes and all other educational opportunities equally. Coed schools, however, open up opportunities for teenage sexual activity and teenage pregnancies. That, of course, is no reason not to opt for a coeducational environment, which is certainly a more "normal" one for most boys and girls.

Within each category of private school however, there are still some single-sex schools, and many offer substantial advantages over their coeducational counterparts—especially for girls. In a study of higher education, the U.S. Department of Education found that all-women colleges accelerate the movement of women into traditional male fields such as science, mathematics, politics and business. The reason is they provide role models, a supportive environment and a chance for women to exercise the leadership that all but the most talented women tend to be denied in coeducational institutions. Men tend to dominate leadership positions in coed colleges, according to the department's study, and women often face overt or subtle, covert gender discrimination.

The department found that women attending women's colleges are three times as likely to earn bachelor's degrees in economics as those at coeducational colleges and one-and-a-half times as likely to major in science and mathematics. Moreover, the atmosphere at single-sex colleges is far different from coed schools. The tens of thousands of students and alumni who flock into a stadium or arena for a big event at a coeducational institution are usually not there to cheer women. They come to cheer men.

Now the same holds true for many coed schools at the elementary- and secondary-school levels. According to a recent study by the American Association of University Women Educational Foundation, elementary and secondary schools remain "places of unequal opportunity," where girls face discrimination from teachers, textbooks, tests and male classmates.

The report found that teachers in coed schools pay less attention to girls than boys, that girls lag in mathematics and science, that girls are often subject to sexual harassment, that tests tend to be biased against girls and that textbooks used in coeducational schools tend to ignore or stereotype women. The study applied primarily to public schools, and most selective private schools work hard at eliminating all the social evils inherent in public schools—especially discrimination of any kind on the basis of gender, race, religion and ethnicity.

Nevertheless, some gender bias creeps into the daily lives of even the finest coeducational schools. Boys' teams tend to lure more spectators and more prominent coverage by both school and local newspapers. In general, there are more athletic opportunities for boys than girls and, except in elementary schools, usually even more male than female teachers. So again, the question of adult role models for girls becomes important.

For both boys and girls, single-sex schools free students of most sexual distractions and leave them far more able to concentrate on their schoolwork during the week. It offers them strong role models of their own gender and frees them to pursue academic interests without the peer pressures that can distract boys and girls from pursuing academic excellence and that often force brilliant girls to suppress scientific or mathematical gifts.

On weekends, even the strictest single-sex boarding schools arrange for parties and dances with children of the opposite gender at nearby, comparable boarding schools. So a single-sex school does not deprive any child of normal weekend contacts with children of the opposite sex. It does, however, allow them to grow up a little more slowly than children faced with the temptations of experimentation that day-to-day heterosexual contacts produce in coeducational schools.

Like the other choices you'll have to make about private schools, deciding on the right environment for your child will depend largely on your child's own needs and how well you know those needs. But make certain your choice of school environment is indeed based on your child's needs—and not on your own.

Schools for Postgraduates

Many private high schools of all kinds—day, boarding, religious, military, etc.—admit children who have already graduated high school elsewhere, but, for whatever reasons, need to repeat their senior years to get the academic credentials to attend the colleges of their choice. In some cases, the schools they attended previously were academically inadequate; in other cases, the youngsters were not motivated enough to achieve their full academic potential. Regardless of the reasons, a wide variety of private secondary schools, including some of the most academically demanding, admit a limited number of such postgraduate students (PGs) to join the current senior class. The admissions process for PGs is no different from that of all other applicants.

CHAPTER 4

STANDARDS FOR EVALUATING SCHOOLS

*B*efore starting to narrow the list of schools to consider for your child, keep in mind that a school that's "perfect" for one child may not be perfect for another child, even in the same family. And that is one of the dangers of accepting, without personally verifying, the opinions of other parents or graduates of any school. There are no "best" schools—only schools that may be "best" for your child, and only you and your child can determine that.

Having identified your child's specific educational, social, emotional and other needs at school, and having identified such practical considerations as proximity, religious training, etc., you should now be ready to begin the process of evaluating schools to find those most likely to meet your child's and your family's needs. To do so, you'll need eight key educational standards with which to gauge each school and compare it to other schools: accreditation; educational philosophy (or educational goals); educational results; faculty quality; financial condition; academic strength; physical plant; and school "personality." Let's first take a look at each standard and its importance to your child.

Accreditation

The first standard any private school must meet to be worthy of your consideration is accreditation by the appropriate regional or state accreditation association. *Do not consider any school*—private or public—*that is not accredited by one of the regional or state accreditation associations listed below.*

Accreditation is *not* the same as certification—and don't let anyone try to confuse you by using the terms interchangeably. Every state requires every school—private as well as public—to be certified, which is nothing more than legal approval to operate. Depending on state laws, certification may only mean adherence to fire safety laws.

Accreditation, on the other hand, is the result of a complex examination conducted every one to ten years by the appropriate regional accreditation association in the list below. Each association puts together teams of respected educators from other schools in the region to visit a particular school and examine its educational goals and standards. Accreditation is voluntary and granted only to schools that meet the minimum standards of each regional association. These standards may differ slightly for public, independent and church-related schools, and the standards differ somewhat from region to region. All accreditation associations, however, demand that member schools clearly state their philosophies, or educational goals, the methods they use to achieve those goals and the success they've had achieving them. The goals may differ according to student community. The goals won't be the same at a religious school, for example, as at a school for the learning disabled, but whatever the goals are, accreditation will depend on a school's success in achieving them.

In addition, accreditation associations study faculty quality and set degree requirements for teachers and school administrators. They may also specify the minimum number of books and periodicals each library must have. They list acceptable student–teacher ratios, minimum acceptable student achievement levels, minimum number of subjects and courses a school must teach in each grade, and the acceptable materials it must provide for those courses.

The associations are not connected with any government agencies, although some states (Connecticut, for example) refuse to certify a school that has not gained accreditation. The associations are privately operated and run by leading educators from member schools dedicated to improving quality of education in the United States. They welcome inquiries from parents, and if you have any doubt about a school's accreditation, you should call the appropriate association.

Parents in the South should be especially careful about checking the accreditation of the many private "Christian academies" discussed earlier. As mentioned, many were designed solely to bypass integration. Most are *not* accredited and indeed offer education inferior to that of many public schools in the South.

All good private schools, however, seek and obtain accreditation—and proudly proclaim that fact in their brochures. If you're still debating whether to send your child to a public or private school, check on accreditation. The startling fact about public-school education in the United States is that only about 40% of elementary schools and 60% of high schools are accredited. In some areas, as few as 10% of public schools are accredited, which, in most cases, means they cannot or *will not* meet even the minimum standards of good education established by the regional accreditation associations.

If your local public school is not accredited, do not postpone sending your child to a private school that is. Any school—public or private—that refuses to adopt the standards of the regional accreditation associations obviously does not care about educational excellence for its students.

Here are the regional school accreditation commissions:

New England Association of Schools and Colleges (Maine, New Hampshire, Vermont, Massachusetts, Rhode Island, Connecticut), The Sanborn House, 15 High Street, Winchester, Massachusetts 01890. Tel: (617) 729–6762.

Connecticut Association of Independent Schools, P.O. Box 159, Mystic, Connecticut 06355. Tel: (203) 572–2950.

Middle States Association of Colleges and Schools (New York, New Jersey, Pennsylvania, Delaware, Maryland, District of Columbia), 3624 Market Street, Philadelphia, Pennsylvania 19104. Tel: (215) 662–5600.

New York State Association of Independent Schools, 287 Pawling Avenue, Troy, New York 12180. Tel: (518) 274–0184.

Southern Association of Colleges and Schools (Kentucky, Virginia, Tennessee, North Carolina, South Carolina, Georgia, Florida, Alabama, Mississippi, Louisiana, Texas), 1866 Southern Lane, Decatur, Georgia 30033. Tel: (404) 329–6500.

North Central Association of Colleges and Schools (North Dakota, South Dakota, Minnesota, Wisconsin, Michigan, Ohio, West Virginia, Indiana, Illinois, Iowa, Nebraska, Wyoming, Colorado, Kansas, Missouri, Arkansas, Oklahoma, New Mexico, Arizona), 1540 30th Street, Boulder, Colorado 80306. Tel: (800) 525–9517.

Northwest Association of Schools and Colleges (Alaska, Washington, Oregon, Idaho, Montana, Nevada, Utah), Education Building No. 528, Boise State University, Boise, Idaho 83725. Tel: (208) 385–1596.

Western Association of Schools and Colleges (California, Hawaii, Guam, American Samoa), 1606 Rollins Road, Burlingame, California 94010. Tel: (415) 697–7711.

In addition to accreditation by one of the above associations, any school you consider that is *not* supported by church or tax monies—in other words, any school that calls itself an independent school—should also belong to the National Association of Independent Schools (1800 M Street, Suite 460 South, Washington, D.C. 20036. Tel: (202) 833–4757). Appendix B lists alphabetically by state and city the names and telephone numbers of the more than 900 NAIS schools to help you find those near you. Each listing also tells you the type of school (boarding, day, etc.), whether it's coed or single-sex and the grades taught.

Quite simply, NAIS schools are among the best private schools in the United States. NAIS is a voluntary membership organization of more than 900 schools with about 370,000 students. To be eligible for NAIS membership, a school must be "independent"—i.e., it cannot be supported by tax or church funds and must be governed independently by a board of trustees. That does not mean it cannot be a religious school and teach its students the practices of a particular church. Indeed, about one-quarter of NAIS schools have some religious ties. But such schools are not *owned* or *operated* by any church.

In addition, all NAIS schools must be non-profit, racially nondiscriminatory and be approved and accredited by one of the recognized evaluating bodies listed above.

Although there are about 110,000 schools in the United States, and 27,700 are private, only about 1,500 are independent, and only 904 of those belong to NAIS. About 21% of NAIS schools are in New England, 19% in the middle Atlantic states, 12% in the Southeast, 11% in the Midwest, 8% in the Southwest, 12.5% in the West and 0.5% in U.S. territories. About 15% of NAIS schools are in New York and New Jersey alone. There are also some NAIS schools overseas, and they, too, are listed in Appendix B.

NAIS membership includes the gamut of school types—day schools, boarding schools, combination day/boarding schools, military schools, religious schools, coed and single-sex schools, schools for postgraduates and schools with various special facilities described earlier. NAIS schools offer no vocational training and, with the exception of a school for the blind in Massachusetts, they have no facilities for rehabilitation or care for the emotionally or physically disabled.

NAIS sets high standards. Parents should accept no less for their children. If the private schools near you are not NAIS members, try to find out why. They may have a valid reason, such as an unwillingness or inability to incur the extra costs of membership. Under no circumstances, however, should you consider a school unaccredited by one of the regional accreditation associations. There is almost *no* reason for refusing to apply for accreditation other than an inability or unwillingness to provide children with a proper education.

Educational Philosophy and Goals

No school can gain accreditation without a clear statement of its educational philosophy and goals, and it's important for you to examine those goals carefully to see that they coincide with your own and how they differ from school to school—if indeed they do. They may not.

Preparation for college, for example, will likely be at least one of your own long-range educational goals, as well as the goal of most other readers of this book. Some parents will, in addition, include religious training among their educational goals—or development of musical talents or perhaps treatment of learning disorders.

All of the schools listed in Appendix B share two broad educational goals: to teach students the basic liberal arts and sciences that are the foundation of western civilization; and, eventually, to prepare each student for college. Obviously, religious and military schools, and special schools for the learning disabled and for underachievers, have additional goals. But many other schools will seem much the same. Almost all use the same terms: *college preparatory, traditional curriculum* and a host of other, often flowery phrases that mean the same thing and can leave you confused about differences between many schools.

Even schools with similar philosophies, however, often differ in subtle ways: in the teaching methods they use, for example, or the amount of individual support they give their students; the depth of education they offer; the type of student they are willing to teach; the behavioral controls (rules and regulations) they impose on students; the leadership training they offer; and the relative emphasis placed on academics, athletics, extracurricular activities and community service.

Teaching Methods

For years, the world of education has been debating the pros and cons of *child-centered* and *subject-centered* teaching. At one extreme, a child-centered classroom appears to be in chaos, with students unfettered by discipline, doing whatever they choose, while harried teachers try to channel every student's urge into a learning experience.

At the other extreme, a subject-centered setting sees silent, well-dressed, well-groomed youngsters listening intently and unquestioningly to their teacher and, if they're old enough, scribbling notes as quickly as they can. Not until the teacher calls for questions do students raise their hands to be called on. Violations of classroom rules are met with immediate rebuke and correction in early grades and, in later years, by dismissal from the room and instructions to report to the administration office. Repeated violations result in a call to parents and, eventually, suspension or expulsion.

Even at the kindergarten level, a subject-centered setting finds some teachers in complete control, with children quietly engaged in individual or group projects. Most talk is in whispers. When the teacher calls the class together, students raise their hands before talking. The emphasis is on discipline, self-control, listening.

If neither extreme sounds appealing, it's because they both are more concerned with student behavior than with learning, and it's questionable how much learning takes place in either setting or how much joy of learning is imparted to the children. Few good schools advocate either extreme. The best schools borrow the best of both teaching methods, and that's what you should look for—an appropriate mix of both methods. That mix, however, will vary from school to school, and the variance in one direction or the other reflects the school's philosophy. What you must determine is which proportion of each method will most help your child function at his or her best.

In general, emotionally healthy, younger children require more of the child-centered approach. They simply do not have the attention span for a purely subject-centered approach to education. That's for university lecture halls. It's important for children of all ages—but especially the youngest ones—to give free rein to their imaginations from time to time. The only question is how much, because it's also important for children to learn self-discipline and respect for others.

On the other hand, as youngsters approach and enter adolescence, a more subject-centered approach is required to teach certain academic concepts, and, by the time students are 15 or 16, they should have developed the self-discipline to sit in a classroom and concentrate on what a teacher has to say. Even at the high-school level, however, skilled teachers use many child-centered teaching methods—asking questions, provoking lively student discussions and leading students along the paths of discovery.

So, teaching methods are an important element of a school's educational philosophy. Some child-centered teaching is important, but so is the discipline of the subject-centered setting, and the mix should shift as children grow older. Little or no learning of much value takes place in the chaos of a classroom of screaming children hurling every object within reach—except, perhaps, learning how to duck and run for cover. Similarly, little learning takes place when tiny children are lined up like soldiers at attention, forbidden to express themselves. In evaluating each school, it's essential to determine where along the gradient between those two extremes a particular school's teaching methods lie. Then you'll have to decide which mix of teaching methods will best help your child function best.

Student Support

Every school offers varying degrees of adult support to its students, and, depending on your child's needs, it's important to find out what kind of support is available and to what extent the school is willing to give it. For reasons as mysterious to parents as is the process of maturation itself, even the most gifted children can and often will falter suddenly in one or more courses—often when they move from one grade to the next. Sometimes it's an emotional problem, other times it's social and often it's purely academic, involving new abstract concepts that some children grasp earlier than others.

The question for your child is how the school reacts to such missteps and what support it offers. Some schools expect children to stand or fall on their own—to be independent young gentlemen and ladies. Others expect children to reach out themselves for any support. And still others step in with massive, reactive support, including mandatory, one-on-one tutoring, required study halls and immediate contacts with parents and a faculty-wide "alert" to keep an eye on the particular youngster both in and out of class.

Again, the question you must answer is what kind of support your child might need along the scale between these two extremes. You then need to find out how many successive bad grades in a course it takes to provoke a teacher's response at a given school, and whether the response is the appropriate one for your child.

Depth of Education

This is an extremely subtle element of a school's educational philosophy, and often it is the result of the school's teaching methods and the type of student the school admits. Depth of education is the amount of learning that takes place in the typical school classroom, and you won't be able to determine this until you actually visit individual schools. Even then, depth of education is not something you can measure empirically.

The amount of learning that takes place in almost any classroom can often be seen by the joy and excitement on the faces of the children, regardless of their ages or the complexity of the subject matter. Real learning, according to one educator, only takes place as children learn to think critically and make discoveries. So, one sign of depth of education is student attentiveness. Another is student participation in the classroom process and responses to tough questions that make them use their minds.

The student, not the teacher, must be the most active participant in the learning process. The teacher is merely a leader, asking questions, provoking students to ask their own questions and guiding students to the right answers by getting them to look things up, to conduct experiments, to make observations and, finally, to reach conclusions. Regardless of age, students learn best by doing, and good teachers encourage even the youngest kindergartners to do things—to touch, handle, count and interrelate materials.

The more senses and faculties involved, the more learning takes place. When kindergarten children handle blocks and say aloud that three blocks are more than two, they are using four faculties—speaking, hearing, seeing and feeling. Moreover, they are unconsciously experiencing the interconnection between language skills and mathematics. Far more learning takes place than when a student watches a teacher handle the blocks or stares at a sheet of paper with pictures of blocks and a place to make a pencil mark to answer the question, which set is bigger?

Depth of education in the higher grades is reflected by the degree to which a school encourages independent discovery, advanced study and research. The number of class projects and, for older students, the number of independent research projects under way are often good measures of depth of education and the amount of real learning that's taking place.

In science, for example, students learn far more by measuring the speed of sound themselves than by simply memorizing the phrase, "Sound travels in air at 1090 feet per second at 0°C or 32°F. It travels 4.5 times faster in water and 15 times faster in steel."

Another measure of depth of education is the degree to which a school interconnects the knowledge from different disciplines, thus linking knowledge in one subject area to other subjects and making them all part of a deeply meaningful and interesting whole.

For example, a history teacher's presentation of Egyptian civilization to 7th graders should delve into mathematics (the geometry of pyramids and cubes), the physics of the wheel and of levers and pulleys, the significance of hieroglyphics in the development of writing and art, and, of course, the techniques of research and preparation of written and oral reports.

A group of 12–year-olds who build a small pyramid in the classroom, using levers and pulleys to move a miniaturized set of heavy blocks, learns and remembers far more than youngsters who are simply asked to memorize the isolated formula, *Weight x Distance = Weight x Distance*—and that is what is meant by depth of education.

Type of Student Admitted

The admissions process is an integral element of a school's educational philosophy because it determines exactly what kind of youngster will help make up the student body, and, therefore, the teaching methods and curriculum. Some schools have extremely homogeneous student bodies, others heterogeneous. Homogeneity is achieved by limiting admissions to a narrow range of intellectual and academic abilities—extremely gifted students, for example. Other schools may specialize in handling a particular type of youngster—underachievers, for example, or learning disabled. If you think your child will do better in a school group where most youngsters do not differ much from each other, then be certain in advance that your child matches the description of the typical child in such a school.

On the other hand, if you prefer a more heterogeneous student body, try to determine in advance where your child will fit in academically, socially and emotionally in such a school. It's important to pick a school whose students will provide a comfortable peer group for your child.

For example, an immature child who needs special, individual attention might find it frustrating and even traumatic to attend a school where the typical student is a mature self-starter, able—and expected—to work independently. Similarly, a mature, academically gifted child might find it equally frustrating to be placed in a school for unruly underachievers.

Behavioral Controls

Although allied to teaching methods, rules and regulations and other behavioral controls extend outside the classroom and, in many cases, outside the school. Many schools have strict dress and personal grooming codes that some parents may find stifling. Other parents believe such codes to be basic to the proper education of young ladies and gentlemen.

Student rules and regulations affect almost every moment and aspect of student life—the clothes they wear, the length of their hair, their behavior in and out of the classroom, their attendance and punctuality, their academic effort, their homework and their ethics and moral conduct. For your child to succeed at school academically, socially and emotionally, it's essential that your own rules and regulations coincide with those of the school.

Leadership Training

Many schools state unequivocally that they train their students to be this nation's leaders of tomorrow in government, industry, the professions and the arts and sciences. Leadership training is, therefore, an integral part of the education they offer, and you, as a parent, must decide whether such training is appropriate for your child. To learn to lead, a child needs self-discipline, maturity and an ability to make decisions that can affect the health and welfare of others. It involves assumption of responsibilities for which many children are simply not ready.

When Horace Taft founded The Taft School in Watertown, Connecticut, more than a century ago, he envisioned it as a school "where boys were to receive the physical, mental, moral and spiritual training for leadership." He believed in man's "educability for higher purpose." To this day, one out of every seven Taft students serves at some time in the elected student government.

For many parents, leadership training is an important element of the education they want for their children. Emphasis on participation in student government is one way of teaching children how to lead and govern themselves responsibly. Some schools have no student government; others have elected student governments but give it no authority; and still others, such as Taft, make it a major factor in student life.

In addition, many schools go out of their way to assure as great a diversity as possible in their student bodies. They recognize the multiracial, multiethnic makeup of our society and feel that preparation for leadership requires students of as many racial, religious and ethnic backgrounds as possible to learn how to live together and form deep and lasting friendships with each other.

Relative Emphasis on Academics, Athletics, Extracurricular Activities and Community Service

Almost every parent has the mistaken belief that top private schools at all levels, including colleges, seek and try to develop "well-rounded students," whom one admissions director facetiously likens to "goose eggs: smooth, wholesome and scarcely discernible." American public schools are filled with so-called well-rounded students who dabble in everything during 13 years of school and accomplish nothing of any lasting value.

Few good private schools seek such well-rounded students. What they seek are well-rounded student bodies, made up of a wide variety of unique individuals, each with unique talents and qualities that make that student stand out among the rest of the class—qualities that will enrich the rest of the class and school community. So ignore the myth of the well-rounded student. It is a myth spread by people who know little or nothing about private-school education.

Good private schools recognize that each youngster is unique, and that their role is to help each youngster develop and display those unique qualities rather than make the youngster like everyone else—in other words, "well-rounded."

That doesn't mean that such schools concentrate only on developing one or two qualities in each student. They do help all their students try to develop in every way possible—intellectually, physically, socially, emotionally, etc. But they also provide the skilled teaching and professional facilities to develop each child's unique qualities to the maximum.

Obviously, not every school can offer the best, world-class instruction to every child—the virtuoso musician, the Olympic-class athlete and the future Nobelist in chemistry. Few schools can be all things to all children, and the areas they emphasize reflect their philosophies of education.

The primary emphasis at most private schools is preparation for college. All, therefore, emphasize academics. Beyond that, however, many schools have, over the years, built up reputations for excellence in specific areas that serve a particular constituency whose talents and interest require special training. Thus, one school may have a particularly strong music department, with one or more world-class musicians as teachers or with access to such teachers because of its location in or near centers of music, such as New York or Boston or other major cities. Such a school naturally lures students with exceptional talents who, in turn, make it more interesting for great teachers to teach there. Other schools develop outstanding art, writing or drama programs, and many schools with outstanding academic programs build equally outstanding athletic programs.

Again, such programs develop in many ways. A retired world-class athlete may decide to teach and coach at one school, or an alumnus may contribute several million dollars to build an outstanding athletic plant. Regardless of how it originates, an outstanding program in any area automatically attracts students interested in that area and, therefore, affects the relative emphasis placed on academics, athletics or extracurricular activities and on specific areas within each of those categories.

And again, from your point of view as a parent, if your child has specific talents or interests, it's important to select a school that can help develop those talents.

In addition to the academic-athletic-extracurricular mix, another reflection of a school's educational philosophy is the emphasis it places on community service, social development and ethical and moral training. Although almost all good private schools try to teach students proper ethical behavior, some require students to devote part of their lives at school to helping others—either fellow students or the community outside the school. Once again, as a parent, you must decide whether this element of the school's philosophy coincides with your own.

As mentioned earlier, nothing can be more destructive than sending your child to a school whose educational philosophy does not coincide with your own. Throughout your child's education, it is important that you be *at one* with your child's school. To allow your child to be pulled in different directions by school authorities, on the one hand, the peer group on the other and by you in a third direction is to place your child at terrible risk—and to defeat the whole reason for sending your child to private school. The right private school should provide a comfortable, secure environment in which all who influence your child believe in the same educational goals and the same philosophy for achieving them.

Educational Results

Next to accreditation and educational philosophy, the most important, overall standard that any school you consider should meet is whether it does for its students what it promises to do in its statement of educational philosophy. If, for example, a school says it is designed as a college preparatory school and sends only 75% of its graduates to college, it is not fulfilling its mission. And if a school says it has a program designed to help students cope with learning disabilities, it should be able to demonstrate the before-and-after improvements of its students.

Any school you consider should be able to demonstrate educational results to parents of prospective students, and as you begin the evaluation process, you should always check to see that the school does what it says it does. Those results are measurable in many ways. The simplest and most visible are student scores on standardized tests—achievement tests of some sort in the lower grades and College Board SATs, Achievement Tests and AP tests at the high-school level.

Faculty Quality

As mentioned earlier, one of the reasons for the decline of America's public schools has been the decline in faculty quality. One-half of the math, science and English teachers hired during the past decade by public schools were not qualified to teach those subjects. So, it's important that, before paying the huge costs of private school, you ensure that your child will be taught by highly qualified teachers.

The number of teachers with master's degrees and doctorates in the subjects they teach are one indication of faculty quality. About half the faculty at academically superior schools have M.A.'s, and often 10% or more have doctorates. Many should be educated enough to teach at the college or university levels. They should also have majored in, or at least studied in great depth, the subjects they teach.

Average tenure is another measure of faculty quality. Unhappy teachers usually don't stay at a school very long, and they're not very effective while they're there. The happier the teachers, the longer they stay and the better many of them become at their jobs.

Salaries are another gauge of faculty quality, although this guage can be a tricky one, especially when comparing private-school and public-school salaries. The average annual salary for public-school teachers in the United States is about $30,000 and ranges from less than $20,000 in states with the worst public-school education to about $50,000 in states with the best public-school education.

Private-school teachers usually earn less—often far less, for far more hours per day. The long workdays are the result of the enormous number of homework papers and quiz papers teachers have to correct each day and their required participation in athletic and extracurricular activities.

But they work fewer days per year and often have such important and valuable fringe benefits as free on-campus housing and meals and free education for their children. Moreover, they work in far safer conditions with motivated, well-behaved students who provide far more job satisfaction. In the huge number of homework papers and tests they correct each day, they find the rewards of their skills as teachers in the growth of each student's knowledge and maturity. That's why many lay teachers willingly agree to work in many private religious schools for abysmally low pay.

Nevertheless, you'll want to check on faculty earnings at each school to compare them with salaries at other private schools to see whether the school you're considering is competing effectively for the best teachers.

Financial Condition

Another broad standard for determining school quality is financial stability. Regardless of a school's academics or size or beauty, regardless of the fame of its alumni or its age, a school threatened with bankruptcy is not one you should consider for your child. Next to the breakup of one's family, there is nothing quite as traumatic for children as watching their school close its doors forever. Home and school, remember, represent the most stable worlds in a child's universe, peopled by often revered authority figures who, especially during a child's early years, are seen as all-knowing, all-powerful and incapable of making the kind of errors that would let either of those worlds collapse.

Unfortunately, half the children in America are forced to watch their families collapse because of parental separation and divorce. There's no need to put a child in a situation where their school lives also disintegrate, and where they're forced to witness the failures of teachers and school administrators and, just as devastating, forced to part with close friends.

69

To avoid this possibility, you'll need to check the school's financial condition carefully. Chapters 5 and 6 will show you what to look for.

Academic Strength

When you begin evaluating individual schools, it will be important to determine each school's academic strength from two perspectives: one, in relationship to other schools; the other, in relationship to your child's abilities.

The first is easy to measure; simply examine the depth and breadth of its curriculum, the academic performance of the student body and the educational results. All these elements will be evident in the school's brochures. The second perspective will be evident from your child's admissions test scores. Almost every private school requires some sort of admissions test for its applicants—even applicants for kindergarten. The tests grow more formal as children get older.

Some schools administer their own admissions tests. Others prefer standardized tests such as the Secondary School Admission Test, used by more than 600 schools to evaluate applicants for grades six through twelve. The multiple-choice test is administered by the Secondary School Admission Test Board at more than 250 sites across the United States.

Another well-known admissions test is the Independent School Entrance Examination used by more than 50 schools in the New York City area and administered by the Educational Records Bureau (ERB) of the Independent Schools Admissions Association of Greater New York. ERB administers admissions tests on nine Saturdays during the school year at various schools in the New York City area. Applicants for admission into grades 6 to 8 take a Middle Level Test, and applicants to grades 9 through 12 take an Upper Level Test.

Regardless of the type of admissions test your child takes, it's important for your child's future educational health for you to accept the results. Those results will show you and the schools to which you apply exactly where your child ranks among his or her peers at the time of the test. And if the test scores place your child in, say, the 30th percentile of applicants, there is little point in attempting to send your child to a school whose students *all* rank in the 80th percentile or better. Many parents try to do just that, hoping the intellectual stimulation of brighter children in an academically superior school will help their child leap to the top of the academic ladder.

Anything is possible, of course, but the most likely scenario is that, even if accepted, such a child will languish at the bottom of the class and grow up with the distinct and devastating feeling of being a failure. It would be far better to place such a child in a school that has experience in helping children at that level reach their potential rather than in an academic environment where teachers may ignore him or her in favor of the students who are academically and intellectually more aggressive.

Unfortunately, some schools are now admitting academically weak candidates only because the schools are so strapped financially that they need *any* students whose parents can pay the full costs of tuition. It's up to you as a parent to avoid the possibly tragic consequences of sending your child to an inappropriately difficult school.

Physical Plant

Physical plant per se will not necessarily reflect quality of education or the financial strength of a private school, but it may be of great importance for you personally and for your child, depending on your own and your child's expectations, personal interests and priorities.

If, for example, you're the parent of a superb athlete—say a hockey player, swimmer or tennis player—you and your child may want to select a school that not only offers state-of-the-art facilities appropriate for those sports, but also exceptionally skilled teachers and coaches. As mentioned earlier, some independent schools have physical plants that not only match, but are better than, those at many colleges. Many have superb playing fields and gymnasiums; some have Olympic-sized swimming and diving pools; others have indoor ice hockey rinks.

On the academic level, some have meteorological observatories and science laboratories that are also better equipped than the observatories and labs at many colleges. Many have classrooms that offer every advanced type of teaching equipment imaginable, including computers for every student and audio-visual labs for teaching foreign languages. Still others have superbly equipped art studios, large music conservatories and professionally equipped theaters.

In short, if you've never visited a well-endowed independent school, you and your child and the rest of your family are in for an unimaginable treat. Some are truly educational paradises that public-school families cannot even begin to imagine.

One caution in viewing the physical plant of any private school: Be certain that a magnificent physical plant is always supported by an equally magnificent endowment yielding funds to maintain the plant. Many schools overexpanded during the student population explosion of the 1970s and 1980s and are now faced with enormous maintenance costs that a sharply decreased student population cannot cover with tuition payments alone.

Make certain, too, if you're concerned about your child's intellectual development, that a magnificent physical plant in non-academic sectors is matched by equally impressive academic facilities. Some private schools are nothing more than wonderful playgrounds for wealthy children whose parents are more concerned with their children's physical, social and emotional gratification than with their intellectual development.

School "Personality"

Like people, schools also have distinct personalities—and that's not surprising. A school, after all, is nothing more than a group of people. Nothing has less personality than an empty school building. Fill it with brilliant, motivated teachers and bright, eager children, and it takes on a life of its own. It's no coincidence that children are often rather easily identified as being "a typical Andover student" or "Taftie" (from The Taft School) or "Grottie" (from The Groton School). These and many other schools have marvelous personalities, and the vast majority of their kids emerge with equally marvelous personalities of their own—each with something in common with fellow schoolmates, but each with a distinct individuality.

So, it's essential that you, as a parent, determine the school's personality before enrolling your child. For your child's personality must be able to blend happily with the school's personality and still develop and grow as a distinct entity. It's much like what happens to children in any family situation: They are like their parents in many ways, but eventually become distinct individuals. And that's what should happen to your child in the right private school with the right personality.

Although selection aids and school brochures will be of some help, you probably won't get an accurate picture of any school's personality until you visit each school and spend the day meeting teachers and kids and seeing them in action. And it's a school's personality that will, in the end, help you decide which among two or three or ten otherwise equal schools you feel comes closest to being the perfect private school for your child.

CHAPTER 5

EVALUATING SCHOOLS "ON PAPER"

*U*sing the eight basic standards for evaluating schools, you can now begin reducing the list of more than 900 NAIS schools in Appendix B to the dozen or so most likely to be best for your child. There are three steps to the evaluation process: examination of school selection aids; careful study of printed materials and videocassettes from each school; and a personal visit. This chapter describes the first two steps, and the next will guide you through the personal visit.

SCHOOL SELECTION AIDS

The first, rather superficial phase of the evaluation process can be done at your leisure at home, using an authoritative selection aid to help you narrow the list of schools to consider to no more than a dozen. There are a number of books and directories with extensive lists of private schools. You only need two: this book and *Peterson's Guide to Independent Secondary Schools*.

As mentioned earlier, Appendix B lists the more than 900 member schools of the National Association of Independent Schools, which are the finest private schools in the United States not under the direct control of any church or state agency. Each listing in Appendix B will allow you to eliminate many schools on the basis of such practical considerations as geographic location, type of school (boarding, day etc.), grades taught and whether it's single sex or coed.

For more complete descriptions of those schools, you'll need *Peterson's Guide to Independent Secondary Schools*. It is the best handbook of its type sold in bookstores, although descriptions are limited to secondary schools, which themselves supply all the written material in *Peterson's*.

Figure 1. A profile of an independent secondary school listed in *Peterson's Independent Secondary Schools* can help you make superficial preliminary evaluations of schools to consider for your child. (Reprinted by permission of Peterson's Guides, Inc., Princeton, New Jersey, and Hackley School, Tarrytown, New York.)

HACKLEY SCHOOL
293 Benedict Avenue
Tarrytown, New York 10591

Head of School: Dr. Peter Gibbon

General Information Boys' boarding and coeducational day college-preparatory school. Boarding grades 7-12, day grades K-12. Founded 1899. Setting: suburban, 20 miles north of New York City; 113-acre campus. Accredited by MSACS. Member of National Association of Independent Schools and Secondary School Admission Test Board. Endowment: $6.5 million. Total enrollment: 736.

Upper School Student Profile Grade 9: 82 students (46 day boys, 10 boarding boys, 26 day girls); Grade 10: 85 students (32 day boys, 10 boarding boys, 43 day girls); Grade 11: 96 students (45 day boys, 9 boarding boys, 42 day girls); Grade 12: 87 students (43 day boys, 7 boarding boys, 37 day girls). Largest student group from New York and New Jersey. 85% of students come from the local area.

Faculty School total: 91. In upper school: 27 men, 28 women; 36 have master's, 4 have doctorates; 36 reside on campus.

Facilities Total buildings on campus: 25. Facilities include 6 classroom buildings, science building, chapel, gym/pool, computer terminals/PCs, Kaskel Library. Value of physical plant: $31 million.

Subjects Offered Algebra, American history, American literature, anthropology, art, art history, astronomy, biology, calculus, chemistry, computer science, creative writing, driver education, ecology, economics, English, English as a Second Language, English literature, environmental science, European history, French, geology, geometry, German, Greek, history, Latin, mathematics, music, physical education, physics, social studies, Spanish, trigonometry, world history.

Graduation Requirements Include study in the following areas: English, foreign language, mathematics, physical education, sciences, and social studies.

Special Academic Programs Advanced Placement preparation in 16 test areas, honors sections, independent study, study at local college for college credit; academic accommodation for the gifted, musically talented, artistically talented; English as a Second Language courses and program.

College Placement 85 students graduated in 1992. All planned to attend college. Two or more students are attending Barnard, Boston University, Brown, Bucknell, Cornell, Dartmouth, Gettysburg, Harvard, Princeton, Skidmore, Washington University of St. Louis, University of Vermont and Wesleyan. 32% scored over 600 on SAT verbal, 55% scored over 600 on SAT math, 46% scored over 1200 on combined SAT.

Student Life Upper grades have: specified standards of dress; student council; honor system. Discipline rests primarily with faculty.

Summer Program Established in 1980. Academic (remediation, enrichment) programs offered; held on campus; accepts boys and girls; open to students from other schools. 50 students usually enrolled. 1992 schedule: June 29 to August 7. Application deadline: June 29.

Tuition and Aid Day student tuition: $10,700-11,900. Boarding school tuition and room/board: $14,700-$15,900. Additional standard fees: $45. Tuition-installment plan (The Tuition Plan) and Academic Management Services. Need-based scholarships, need-based loans available. In 1992-93, 25% of upper-school students received aid; total scholarship money awarded: $1 million. Average scholarship award: $9,174.

Admissions Traditional secondary-level entrance grade is 9. New students entered upper-level grades as follows: Grade 9, 20; Grade 10, 11; Grade 11, 9. Deadline for receipt of applicaton materials: none; $45 fee. Interview required, on campus preferred.

Athletics Interscholastic: baseball/softball (Boys, Girls), basketball (B, G), cross-country running (B, G), fencing (B, G), field hockey (G), football (B), golf (B, G), lacrosse (B, G), soccer (B, G), squash (B), swimming (B, G), tennis (B, G), track and field (B, G), wrestling (B); organized activity: martial arts (B, G), squash (B, G), swimming (B, G), tennis (B, G), weight lifting (B, G). 27 faculty coaches, 7 part-time coaches and one full-time trainer handle Hackley's 54 teams.

Contact Pamela Wetherill, Director of Admissions. 914-631-0128. Fax: 914-631-9240.

ANNOUNCEMENT FROM THE SCHOOL Hackley offers a core curriculum enriched with tutorials and seminars. Highlights include 16 Advanced Placement courses, an upper-and-middle school computer curriculum, and over 30 extracurricular activities. In 1992, 108 students sat for 219 Advanced Placement exams; 88% scored 3 or higher. In the last four years Hackley has produced 18 National Merit Semifinalists and 46 National Merit Commended Students, and 2 Hispanic and Negro National Achievement Scholars.

Peterson's has no descriptions of elementary or middle schools except for 15 junior boarding schools for middle schoolers in grades 6 to 9. However, each high school description states whether the school has an elementary- or middle-school division, and it's safe to conclude that the academic and other standards for each high school also apply to its elementary- and middle-school divisions.

Peterson's has descriptions of all NAIS schools and then some. All schools cite preparation for college as their primary goal. Some offer religious instruction, others military training and still others treatment of learning disorders, but all are "primarily college preparatory . . . (and) free of undue religious or political influence." All are listed alphabetically, although a separate listing orders them by state.

Peterson's is divided into two main sections—profiles and descriptions. Each profile and description has the school's complete address, telephone number and person or persons to contact for more information. As you can see in Figure 1, each profile is a fact sheet listing such basics as the type of school and its location, the makeup of the student body and faculty, grade levels taught, a brief history and whether it is affiliated with NAIS and accredited by the state or regional accreditation association. So, right away, you can determine whether a school you're considering meets the first of the eight key educational standards described in the last chapter—namely, accreditation. If the profile of a school makes no mention of accreditation by the appropriate regional or state association, *cross it off your list and do not consider it.*

Peterson's profiles also state whether a school has an endowment or not. The profiles describe each school's physical plant, academic and athletic offerings and college placement record. The section entitled Student Life offers brief references to dress codes and other appropriate details. Finally, the profile gives admissions information, graduation requirements and costs and available financial aid—all of which should help you cross a few more names off your list.

In Figure 1, you can see that Hackley School is accredited by every respected educational accreditation body and has a healthy $6.5 million endowment fund. The profile says that nearly half the faculty has master's degrees and is, therefore, well qualified. The range of subjects taught is broad and demanding.

The school's academic strength is evident from the list of colleges that the school's graduates are now attending—and that's a key word: *attending.* As you comb through *Peterson's* descriptions of private schools, you'll find many that cite only the colleges to which its graduates were *accepted.* But if only two students in a class of 100 were each *accepted* to four different Ivy League colleges, such a school could say truthfully, "Among the colleges to which last year's graduates were *accepted* are Yale, Harvard, Princeton, Dartmouth, Columbia, Penn, Brown and Cornell." But obviously only two students are actually attending Ivy League colleges— and the rest of the graduating seniors may not be attending *any* college. So, it's important to read *Peterson's* descriptions carefully. Only the list of colleges that a school's graduates are *attending* is meaningful, as in the profile in Figure 1.

Average SAT scores are also meaningful. The mean SAT scores in the Figure 1 profile show that the top half of the previous year's graduating class ranked among the top 25% and top 20% in verbal and math skills, respectively, of all college-bound students in the nation. Table 2 shows the distribution of SAT scores for all U.S. college-bound students for 1992; it allows you to compare the SAT scores at any school that you are considering against the national averages. The distribution does not vary significantly from year to year.

The profile of the Hackley School in Figure 1 shows that 32% of the students scored above 600 on the SAT verbal and 52% scored over 600 on the SAT math, putting those groups in the top 7% and 17%, respectively, of the nation's college-bound students.

So the profile shows you clearly that Hackley School students are exceptionally bright, motivated, achieving students taking a demanding curriculum taught by a well-educated faculty.

But the profile—and the range of SAT scores—tell you something else about Hackley students, namely, that they represent a broad range of ac-

Table 2
Percent of College-Bound Seniors in each SAT* Scoring Category (1992)

SAT scores	Verbal	Math
	(%)	(%)
200 or more	100	100
250 or more	95	99
300 or more	87	94
350 or more	74	85
400 or more	58	73
450 or more	40	59
500 or more	24	44
550 or more	13	29
600 or more	6	18
650 or more	2	10
700 or more	1	4
750 or more	0	1

* 800 is a perfect score in the SAT and seldom achieved by more than a half-dozen students in the U.S.
Source: College Entrance Examination Board

ademic ability. Although there are obviously many gifted students, there are also many average students. Only half the students scored above the mean SAT test scores—529 in the verbal SATs and 597 in the math SATs. The other half scored below those levels, and that tells you something about the school's educational philosophy—i.e., that it works with a heterogeneous student body that includes many average students with a wide range of skills.

So, as you evaluate each school's academic results, remember that SAT scores can often be interpreted to reflect the range of student each school admits. Then, on the basis of your knowledge of your own child, you must try to evaluate whether your child would do better in an academically diversified student body or a more homogeneous student body whose academic performance won't differ much from your child's.

The profile also describes an exceptionally large, well-equipped physical plant of 25 buildings (five classroom buildings, one science building, etc.) on a 113–acre campus. The school offers more than 20 sports for both boys *and* girls. That's more than many colleges offer.

Although the school is expensive, its profile indicates that it offers financial aid, equal to about 80% of the costs of attending, to 21% of its upper schoolers. That's an important figure if you need financial aid, because it shows that your chances of getting financial aid at this school are about one in five. That's a fairly conservative financial aid policy, but, as you'll see later on in the section on school finances, conservative aid policies are often a good indication of a financially healthy and stable school. It means that many parents want to send their children to that school and are willing to pay "full fare" to do so. As you'll also see later on, some schools facing near bankruptcy are literally "buying" students with partial scholarships to keep their classrooms filled. So, a school with a liberal scholarship policy is not necessarily the best school for you to consider—regardless of your family's economic circumstances.

School Descriptions

The more complete, two-page descriptions in the second half of *Peterson's* offer far more details about the schools still on your list. As you can see in Figure 2, the first section of the description, entitled The School, gives the school's history and, in the second paragraph, clearly describes its educational philosophy: "Hackley offers a rigorous, traditional, and individualized college-preparatory education to students who are able and motivated and whose parents value education. Hackley is rigorous in that students can expect serious classes, ample homework, and an insistence on all-out effort. The school is traditional in that students dress and conduct themselves decorously and the campus is gracious and stately." The school teaches "the democratic ethic, the work ethic, and the Judeo-Christian ethic."

From the description, then, it should be clear to any parent that Hackley is a school for well-dressed, well-behaved, motivated youngsters who take school and schoolwork seriously.

But neither is it a sink-or-swim situation for academic sharks. The description says that students get personalized, individual attention and extra help if they need it, and that "teachers strive to maintain close contact with parents."

The description of the academic program indicates enormous emphasis on writing skills and cultural enrichment. The school arranges student trips to Washington, D.C., and other important areas.

Hackley also "offers a wide range of performing arts experiences. In addition to band, chorus, and orchestra," says the description, "there is a developed jazz program, a vocal and instrumental chamber music program, an extensive student recital series, courses in music listening and music theory. . . .music theater and dramatic performances, and a drama

Figure 2. The more detailed "descriptions" from *Peterson's Independent Secondary Schools* provide enough data on each school to eliminate all but those that seem "perfect" for your child. You should contact the latter directly for brochures, videocassettes, course catalogs and other descriptive materials. (Reprinted by permission of Peterson's Guides, Inc., Princeton, New Jersey, and Hackley School, Tarrytown, New York.)

HACKLEY SCHOOL

Tarrytown, New York

Type: Boys' boarding (five-day grades 7–12) and coeducational day college-preparatory school
Grades: K–12: Lower School, Kindergarten–5; Middle School, 6–8; Upper School, 9–12
Enrollment: School total: 736; Upper School: 350
Head of School: Dr. Peter H. Gibbon, Headmaster

THE SCHOOL

Hackley School was founded in 1899 by Mrs. Caleb Brewster Hackley as a liberal arts boarding school for boys. It continued in this tradition until the 1940s, when it began to admit boys as day students in increasing numbers. Day enrollment became predominant when girls were first admitted, as day students, in 1970.

Hackley offers a rigorous, traditional, and individualized college-preparatory education to students who are able and motivated and whose parents value education. Hackley is rigorous in that students can expect serious classes, ample homework, and an insistence on all-out effort. The school is traditional in that students dress and conduct themselves decorously and the campus is gracious and stately. More importantly though, Hackley exposes students to classic texts and traditional disciplines, maintains an informed skepticism of fads and innovations in education, and inculcates the more serious elements of American culture—the democratic ethic, and the Judeo-Christian ethic. Hackley is also personalized, offering small classes, special

help, frequent communication with parents, student-teacher interaction outside the classroom, a largely residential faculty, and a high level of participation in team sports.

The 113-acre campus, located on a wooded hill overlooking the Hudson River and the Tappan Zee Bridge, is about 25 miles north of New York City. The school is near enough to the city for faculty members and students to take advantage of its cultural resources and its important contacts; yet, at the same time, it is far enough from the urban scene to preserve a relaxed community atmosphere.

The school is a nonsectarian, nonprofit institution. It is managed by a Board of Trustees made up of parents, alumni, and friends. The school is financially sound, with an operating budget for the current school year exceeding $9-million. Its land, buildings, and equipment are valued at $31 million. Gifts to the school in 1991–92 amounted to $759,277, and the school's endowment portfolio is valued at about $6.5 million.

ACADEMIC PROGRAM

The school operates on a semester basis, beginning in early Septem-

ber and ending in early June, with breaks for Thanksgiving, winter, and spring vacations. Teachers strive to maintain close contact with parents; grades are issued and sent to parents four times annually, with interim reports as required.

The curriculum for kindergarten–grade 3 emphasizes reading and oral and written expression. Beginning in grade 3, students write a weekly theme and begin to work on research papers (two a year). Through the mathematics program, students learn the logical structure of the number system and practice computation. Also included in the program are science, art, music, swimming, and physical education. The curriculum for grades 4 and 5 includes English (focusing on grammar, oral expression, expository and creative writing, and literary analysis), American history (grade 4) and ancient history (grade 5), mathematics (emphasizing the four basic operations and probability, graphing, and statistics), and a popular experiential science program. In addition to many other activities, the Lower School publishes its own literary magazine and produces its own musical and a Medieval Festival every spring. Bank Street alumnus Daniel DiVirgilio is the Director of the Lower School.

The Middle School curriculum builds on the skills and enthusiasm nurtured in the Lower School. Students continue honing their skills in English, math, science (including IPS), and American history (grades 7 and 8) and begin the study of Far Eastern history (grade 6) and Latin, French, or Spanish. While preparing them for high school, the Middle School faculty strives to maintain their students' enthusiasm for learning. Grade 7 students spend several days in Massachusetts, traveling to sites that they have studied (Boston, Plimoth Plantation, Sturbridge Village); grade 8 takes a similar trip to Civil War battlefields and Washington, D.C. The Middle School publishes its own newspaper and, through special events and excursions, maintains its own identity. The Director of the Middle School is Philip Variano, a Vassar graduate and twelve-year veteran of Hackley.

The Upper School curriculum is quite varied, running the gamut from traditional offerings and course requirements to one-on-one tutorials and small seminars. To graduate, Upper School students must complete 4 years of English; 3 years of a foreign language; 3 years of a science, one of which must be a laboratory course; mathematics through algebra II; and anthropology, European history, and American history. The Director of the Upper School is David Faus, a graduate of Kenyon (B.A.) and the University of Pennsylvania (M.S.).

Specific course offerings include English 9–12 (required); French 1–6, German 1–6, Greek 1 and 2, Latin 1–5, and Spanish 1–5; anthropology and early ancient history, ancient and medieval history, modern European history, American history, and Selected Topics in 20th-Century History; algebra I, geometry, intermediate algebra with trigonometry, algebra II with trigonometry, Advanced Topics in Algebra and Trigonometry, calculus 1–3, computer science 1–3, and finite math; biology 1 and 2, natural history and ecology, chemistry 1 and 2, biochemistry, physics 1 and 2, geology 1 and 2, and astronomy; fine arts, photography, pottery, sculpture, and art history; and instrumental music, music theory, and Music in the Western World.

Advanced Placement study is available in English, history, French, German, Latin, biology, chemistry, physics, mathematics, and music. In 1992, 108 students sat for 219 AP exams; 88 percent of them received a grade of 3, 4, or 5.

Hackley offers a wide range of performing arts experiences. In addition to band, chorus, and orchestra, there is a developed jazz program, a vocal and instrumental chamber music program an extensive student recital series, courses in music listening and music theory (including those at the AP level), music theater and dramatic performances, and a drama literature course. There is a music conservatory on campus. Attention is given to the special needs of pre-professional students as well as to the need of less serious amateurs.

Students can arrange for tutorials in English, history, language, and science. In recent years, there have been tutorials and seminars in Russsian history, the Vietnam War, the history of the Holocaust, genetics, vertebrate zoology, Russian literature, the short story, and women in literature.

Hackley offers ESL students a wide spectrum of classes, according to their language needs. Students begin with individualized instruction, then continue in small classes to work on vocabulary, idiomatic expressions, and English grammar. Students take literature and composition in a sheltered English program. A two-year course in American history is also available.

Each spring vacation, Hackley sponsors Science Seminar in the Caribbean, as well as other trips abroad. Recent excursions have included trips to China and Hong Kong, Egypt, France and England, and the annual ski trip to Austria.

FACULTY AND ADVISERS

The full-time faculty, including administrators who teach, numbers 91—35 men and 56 women. Fifty-six percent of the faculty live on campus. Ninety-one of them hold baccalaureate degrees, and 58 above graduate degrees. Institutions attended by 2 or more faculty members include Brown, Bucknell, Columbia, Dartmouth, Fordham, Harvard, Middlebury, New York University, Swarthmore, Trinity, Williams, and Yale. Faculty benefits include health and life insurance, a retirement plan, and summer sabbaticals.

Arriving on campus twenty-one years ago as a young history teacher, Dr. Peter H. Gibbon eventually became Director of the Upper School before assuming his current post as Headmaster. A graduate of Harvard (A.B., 1964) and Teachers College of Columbia University (PhD., 1980), Dr. Gibbon teaches seminars at Hackley in the twentieth-century short story and Russian literature. In addition, he writes frequently for major newspapers and professional publications.

COLLEGE PLACEMENT

In 1992, all graduating seniors planned to attend college. All Ivy League schools will have at least one

Hackley representative. Two or more are attending Barnard, Boston University, Brown, Bucknell, Carnegie Mellon, Cornell, Dartmouth, Gettysburg, Harvard, Princeton, Skidmore, the University of Vermont, Washington Univeristy at St. Louis, and Wesleyan. Joan Danziger and Julie King are the Co-directors of College Counseling.

STUDENT BODY AND CONDUCT

In 1992–93, the Upper School enrolled 350 students as follows: 82 in grade 9, 85 in grade 10, 91 in grade 11, and 87 in grade 12. The total school enrollment is 736. Boarders hail from Brazil, Japan, Hong Kong, England, Jamaica, Haiti, Liberia, and Korea, as well as from Connecticut, New Jersey, and New York. Day students come from communities throughout the tristate area—including those in Westchester and Rockland counties, northern New Jersey, and New York City—and represent twenty-six countries, including the United States.

ACADEMIC FACILITIES

The original structures, built in the Tudor Renaissance style, date from 1900. New classroom facilities include the science building and the Lower School and its annex. The 20,000-volume library was completed in 1985.

BOARDING AND GENERAL FACILITIES

Boarders live in either single or double rooms in the main building complex. All the facilities of the school are available to them. Resident faculty members supervise the boarders, and some faculty members conduct cultural and academic enrichment programs that are exclusively for boarders.

A registered nurse is on campus during school hours; emergencies can also be handled at nearby Phelps Memorial Hospital.

ATHLETICS

Hackley fields forty-five teams. Varsity sports for both boys and girls include basketball, cross-country, fencing, golf, lacrosse, soccer, squash, swimming, tennis, and track and field. Boys also compete in baseball, football, and wrestling, while girls compete in field hockey and softball. A member of the Ivy League of the metropolitan area, Hackley competes against League members and public and parochial schools. The football team has been recognized as a perennial power in the county. Since 1986, teams have won league championships in boys' and girls' scoccer, field hockey, cross country, girls' basketball, swimming, boys' and girls' lacrosse, baseball, track and field, and softball. Since 1982, nine students have received All-American accolades—3 in lacrosse, 5 in swimming, and 1 in cross-country.

Athletics facilities include the Allen Pool (indoor), the Thomas E. Zetkov Athletic Center (with two basketball courts, three glass-backed squash courts, a wrestling room, a fitness center, and locker rooms), six tennis courts, and four playing fields.

EXTRACURRICULAR OPPORTUNITIES

There are frequent field trips to New York City, and the school often hosts guest speakers from the city. The Malcolm Forbes Speaker Series provides for an ongoing program of guest speakers on public affairs. Traditional annual events include Parents' Day, Class Day, Fall Homecoming, and the Mini-Marathon.

The Community Council, composed of student and faculty representatives from grades 6–12, organizes many social service activities. Upper School students publish their own newspaper (using desktop publishing), lilterary magazine, and yearbook. Other activities include Student Teachers (who assist in Lower School classrooms); Model United Nations and Model Congress; Community Service (which sponsors a variety of service-oriented activities); chorus, orchestra, band, and jazz band; and drama, French, and chess clubs.

DAILY LIFE

Lower School students (K–5) begin their day at 8:15 a.m. and end at 2:30 p.m. The day is divided into seven 40-minute class periods, recess, and lunch. A typical day in the Middle School and the Upper School begins with homeroom at 8:15 a.m. Classes begin at 8:30 and run until 2:45 or 3 p.m. Lunch is served, cafeteria-style, from 10:45 until 1:45, and students may eat during their free periods. Sports and extracurricular activities occupy the balance of the day. Buses for day students depart at 4:45 p.m. No classes are scheduled on Saturday.

SUMMER PROGRAMS

The Hackley Summer School offers enrichment programs in writing, history, and science, as well as review work for students needing help in basic subjects.

Students entering grades 5–12 are eligible for admission. They need not be attending Hackley. The Director of the Summer School is Anne Budlong.

COSTS AND FINANCIAL AID

In 1992–93, tuition ranges from $7,800 for kindergarten to $11,900 for grade 12. Boarders pay an extra $4000, which includes all meals. Other extras include lunch ($675 for day students), books and accident insurance ($45).

In 1992–93, a total of $1 million in financial aid was awarded to 109 students on the basis of need plus merit. School-funded loans, a tuition payment plan and tuition insurance are available. Hackley subscribes to the School and Student Service for Financial Aid.

ADMISSIONS INFORMATION

The abilities Hackley looks for in its candidates for admission are not defined by any battery of standardized texts. Unlike many other strong, academic schools, Hackley does not "peel them off the top" of lists of scores. Quickness of intellect, precision of memory, and resourcefulness in problem solving are desirable traits. But Hackley particularly values curiosity, love of truth, honesty, diligence of effort, and humor—and these are not multiple-choice traits.

Students are admitted on the basis of a personal interview, a day-long visit to the campus, two teacher recommendations, the transcript from the previous school, and the results of Hackley's own admissions test.

APPLICATION TIMETABLE

Inquiry may be made at any time. Appointments for interviews may be made after October 15. Applications are accepted and students are admitted as long as vacancies exist, but it is advisable to apply early. Parents are notified of the student's acceptance after February 1 and are expected to respond within thirty days, although extensions are granted upon request. There is a $45 application fee.

ADMISSIONS CORRESPONDENCE

Pamela Wetherill, Director of
   Admissions
Hackley School
293 Benedict Avenue
Tarrytown, New York 10591
Telephone: 914-631-0128
Fax: 914-631-9240

1992–93 CALENDAR

School opening: September 15, 1992
Thanksgiving recess: November 24–30, 1993
Winter vacation: December 18, 1992—January 4, 1993
Spring vacation: March 12–29, 1993
Commencement: June 12, 1993

ACCREDITATION AND MEMBERSHIPS

Hackley is registered by the New York State Board of Regents and accredited by the Middle States Association of Schools and Colleges. It holds memberships in the National Association of Independent Schools, the College Board, the Association of College Admissions Counselors,a nd the New York State Association of Independent Schools.

STUDENT COMMENTS

"Teachers at Hackley have outstanding personalities. Their caring for and involvement with the students have inspired many of us. They have taught us the most important lesson of all—the joy of learning."

"The students are competitive yet supportive, fun loving yet hardworking bright yet well rounded. The competitive spirit felt by the students creates an incentive to do well and to strive to be the best. The supportive atmosphere makes it easier to accept helping each other, explaining what went on in a missed class, or exchanging different ideas about a project. All this creates a feeling of camaraderie."

literature course. There is a music conservatory on campus. Attention is given to the special needs of preprofessional students as well as . . . less serious amateurs."

The description of athletic facilities indicates more than ample opportunity for play and athletic achievement, as well as academic achievement. The school says it fielded 45 teams, won seven championships and produced eight all-American athletes. Its six tennis courts, indoor pool and an athletic center with two basketball courts, three squash courts, a wrestling room and a fitness center show that the school considers athletics vital to its students' education.

Under Extracurricular Activities, the description emphasizes activities that reinforce academic pursuits: cultural enrichment ("frequent field trips to New York City" and "guest speakers"); writing skills (newspaper, literary magazine and yearbook); leadership skills ("Model United Nations" and "Model Congress"); community service (student teaching); musical activities (chorus, orchestra, band and jazz band); and special academic interests (drama club, French club, chess club).

In effect, the only element of school philosophy that remains to be discovered after reading the description in Figure 2 is the school's classroom teaching methods. Teaching methods, however, are seldom evident until you personally visit the school and sit in on a class or two during the third and final evaluation phase. As for leadership training, that's a good question to save until you interview the head of the school.

The description in Figure 2 also details Hackley School's educational results, the third of the eight key standards you need for evaluating a school. The profile in Figure 1 disclosed the school's average SAT scores, and the section called College Placement in the description shows that two or more members of the previous year's graduating seniors are now attending such selective colleges as Amherst, Colgate, Columbia, Cornell, Hamilton, Haverford, Mt. Holyoke, Princeton, Tulane, University of Chicago and Washington (St. Louis). Most of those colleges generally accept fewer than 10% of all applicants.

Peterson's description also expands the profile of faculty quality, financial condition, academic strength, physical plant and "personality." The school's finances appear strong, although it's important to find out whether any school you consider has experienced any operating deficits.

The *Peterson's* description of the academic program indicates enormous strength, which can be verified when you get the school's course catalog and, later, when you visit the school. Similarly, the description of the physical plant under Academic Facilities and Athletics is adequate for a preliminary evaluation that this is a well-equipped school worthy of further consideration if you agree with its educational philosophy.

Personality, the last of the eight key educational standards, is difficult to determine from *Peterson's* profiles and descriptions, although such phrases as "traditional," "students dress and conduct themselves decorously" and "the campus is gracious and stately" do paint an easy-to-imagine picture.

As you can see, *Peterson's* descriptions offer a quick, easy way to conduct superficial evaluations of almost any private secondary school. Use the Private School Evaluation Form in Appendix A of this book to organize data about each school so that you can compare it with others you're considering and narrow your list to those worth contacting directly for more information.

In addition to profiles and descriptions, *Peterson's* has all sorts of handy "directories" in the back of the book. There are lists of day schools and boarding schools by gender, schools with elementary divisions, religious schools and military schools. In other words, you can pick just about any category of secondary school and find a listing for it in the back of *Peterson's*. There's a directory of "barrier-free campuses for full access by the handicapped" and another of schools with special programs for the gifted and talented. Another directory lists schools for students with special needs, including deaf or blind students, students with various learning disabilities and students needing remedial work in particular areas. There's also a listing of schools offering various sorts of financial aid and loan programs.

Beware, however, of using all the *Peterson's* directories with blind faith. As stated earlier, many schools are on the verge of bankruptcy or simply facing declining enrollments. To avoid financial disaster, many are resorting to a variety of "marketing" tactics to swell enrollment—regardless of the kind of student such tactics may attract.

Many are recruiting wealthy foreign students. Others are simply lowering academic standards to whatever levels are necessary to fill their classrooms with American kids. Others are adding part-time, specialized teachers to handle gifted students or students with special needs—and then advertising themselves as having "special facilities" for the talented or learning disabled. So check to see that any such "special programs" are extensive and well established.

There are a few other drawbacks to *Peterson's*. One is that not every school in the profiles section is in the descriptions section. If that's the case with a school you're considering, you'll have to skip this part of your preliminary evaluation and write directly to such schools for all pertinent material.

As mentioned, *Peterson's* also has no profiles or descriptions of elementary or middle schools, except for 15 junior boarding schools for 6th, 7th and 8th graders, although it does provide lists of independent lower and middle schools and of secondary schools with elementary divisions. If you like the description of a particular secondary school with a middle and elementary division, simply call the school for more details. The telephone numbers of all NAIS elementary and middle schools, regardless of whether they are affiliated with any upper schools, are in Appendix B of this book. It's always possible, of course, that a school may have joined NAIS since this book was published. To find out, contact NAIS, 1800 M Street, N.W., Suite 460 South, Washington, DC 20036. Tel: (202) 833-4757.

There are two other things to keep in mind while studying *Peterson's*. One is that the profiles and descriptions are written by the schools themselves, rather than by objective authorities on education who can attest that the information is accurate and unexaggerated. Eventually, you'll have to check on the accuracy of each description by personally visiting each school, but in the meantime, it's important to check to see if a school that may seem perfect in *Peterson's* is listed as an NAIS member in Appendix B of this book or, if not, whether it's at least accredited by a regional accreditation association. If neither is the case, cross the school off your list.

The second thing to keep in mind as you study *Peterson's* is the limited space devoted to each school. Obviously, the profiles and descriptions are, at best, capsules, whose primary value is to help you narrow your list of original schools and eliminate those that are clearly not right for your children.

School Rankings

You may wonder why neither *Peterson's* nor the NAIS listing in Appendix B ranks private schools, and you may be tempted to buy one of the directories or handbooks that does. There is a great danger in relying on such rankings, however. First, they are based on personal opinions and bias rather than any objective measurement that a skilled educator would subscribe to. Indeed, most educators would agree that ranking accredited schools as good, better or best is not only unfair to many fine schools, it is unfair to their faculties, their students and students' families, to generations of their graduates and, above all, to you and your children.

For your own child's sake and educational future, beware of books that rank private schools. *Every NAIS school listed in Appendix B is "best" for most of the students who go there,* and all rankings you may find elsewhere are invalid except those that rank a school good, better or best for *your own child.* In the end, only you and the trained admissions people at each school you visit will be qualified to make that evaluation.

Remember always that the school that's best for one child may not be best for yours. So, use the guidelines in Chapter 4 and the Private School

Evaluation Form in Appendix A to do your own evaluation and your own rankings of schools as good, better or best for *your* child.

Why Rankings Are Dangerous

Let's take a look at one popular ranking system to see how invalid it is in terms of determining the proper kind of school for your child.

Difficulty of admission, for example, is one standard often used to rank private schools. It's widely used for colleges and universities, and is somewhat valid at that level. Colleges that admit only 10% of their applicants usually limit acceptances to students who graduated in the top 10% of their high-school classes and earned exceptionally high Scholastic Aptitude Test scores.

But students living anywhere can apply to any college they want across the country. That's not true for elementary and middle-school kids or for high-school students who want to attend a day school. They're limited to nearby schools. So, a private elementary school that accepts only 10% of its applicants may simply be reflecting population pressures. It could well be the only school in a town where the quality of public-school education is so low that every family wants to send its kids there—not because the school is academically demanding, but because it is slightly more so than the public school and provides more discipline. It could well be academically substandard in comparison with private schools in other areas.

Los Angeles, for example, has too few private schools to accommodate all the children trying to escape educationally substandard and unsafe public schools. But just because Los Angeles private schools are difficult to get into does not necessarily make them any good academically. Many are not NAIS member schools or even accredited.

Another common standard for ranking private high schools is the number of graduates admitted to Ivy League and Ivy League equivalent colleges each year. Well, that's only a valid standard if getting your child into an Ivy League college is your primary reason for sending your child to private school in the first place. But, beware! The number of graduates that a private school sends to the Ivy League each year could well be the *worst* standard for you to use in selecting a school for *your* child.

As mentioned earlier, a school with exceptionally gifted scholars, which sends one-third of its graduates to the Ivy League, for example, might be so demanding academically that your child might finish in the bottom half of the class and lose practically all chances for admission to the Ivy League. On the other hand, if your child finishes at the top of the class at a less demanding school that gets only 10% of its kids into the Ivy League, your child might well waltz in!

Actually, a youngster who finishes at the head of a public school class (valedictorian) often has a better chance of admission to Ivy League colleges than one who finishes in the bottom half of the class at even the most prestigious prep school. The public-school curriculum might not be as academically demanding, but the youngster's class ranking can improve the chances of admission to the Ivy League dramatically if he or she has managed to develop acceptable writing skills. Moreover, the chances of admission increase even more if the youngster comes from a school west of the Mississippi because of the efforts of eastern colleges to achieve geographic diversification of their student bodies.

So, if admission to the Ivy League is your only educational goal for your children, be certain they attend school where they'll consistently finish at the head of the class.

We could go on to show how almost any popular standard for ranking private schools is invalid as a guide for *your* child—because your child has particular needs, and only the schools that meet those needs should be ranked as "best." If the most prestigious and costly school in the country cannot meet those needs, then it ranks among the worst for your child, regardless of its success with other children.

So stick to the NAIS listings in Appendix B and to *Peterson's* as your selection aids in completing the first phase of your evaluation process. Ignore publications that "rank" schools.

SCHOOL BROCHURES AND VIDEOS

Having narrowed your list of schools to those that seem perfect or close to perfect, you're ready to begin the second phase of your school evaluation by writing or telephoning the director of admissions at every school on your list and asking for the following: all descriptive literature about the school, including a videocassette "tour," if they have one; a student profile; a list of the faculty; a course catalog; a set of school rules and regulations; and the admissions requirements along with a complete application package. Each of these materials will help you broaden your evaluation.

As mentioned earlier, it's not a good idea to involve younger children in any of the evaluation and decision-making process, but if your child is a preteen or teenager applying for admission to 4th grade or higher, by all means show him or her the brochures, or "viewbooks," for each of the schools you're considering and, of course, the videocassette, if you get one. Most children usually enjoy the magnificent photographs and exciting descriptions.

Student Profiles

The viewbooks usually also contain a student profile. As you can see in Figure 3, a student profile tells you more than the *Peterson's* descriptions do about a school's educational results, its academic strengths and the type of student who goes there. Profiles not only list average Scholastic Aptitude Test scores, they also list Achievement Test scores for each subject for the previous year's graduating seniors, as well as the number of seniors who took Advanced Placement Tests, and their scores. Only 9% of the nation's college-bound high-school juniors and seniors score 600 or more on the verbal SAT test, while 33% score above 600 on the math SAT test; 800 is a perfect score on each (see Table 2, page 000).

Similarly low numbers of students score above 600 on The College Board Achievement Tests, which are also given as part of the college entrance examination procedure. Achievement tests are given in virtually every high-school subject. Advanced Placement Tests are given to only those high-school students who have enrolled in Advanced Placement (AP) courses, which are college freshman-level courses for students who have completed the entire available high-school curriculum in those subjects. So these scores, along with the percentage of high-school juniors and seniors enrolled in AP courses, reflect the academic strength of the school and the academic achievement levels of the student body.

Faculty Listing

The list of the faculty is a condensed, yearbook-style brochure that usually includes photographs of each faculty member, and lists the college and university degrees he or she holds, subjects in which he or she majored and the subjects he or she now teaches. The number of advanced degrees, the caliber of colleges attended and whether or not a teacher now teaches a subject that he or she studied in depth at college are important gauges of faculty quality.

Course Catalogs

A course catalog describes each course at each grade level and gives you a better idea of the depth and difficulty of the curriculum. You can compare course catalogs from different schools to see which school you prefer. The booklets with school rules and regulations will give you an idea of the depth and breadth of the disciplinary system at each school.

Figure 3. A student profile from each school describes the academic strength of the most recent graduating class and, therefore, of the school itself.

Junior Year Statistics for the Class of 1992

Range	SAT Verbal	SAT Math
750–800	1	5
700–749	3	8
650–699	4	9
600–649	8	7
550–599	9	5
500–549	11	6
450–499	4	3
400–449	2	–
Below 400	1	–
	Verbal Mean: 572	Math Mean: 639

Junior Year CEEB Achievement Tests

Test	Students	Mean
American History	2	730
Biology	19	580
Chemistry	5	574
English Composition	37	587
French	3	657
Math (level 1)	30	604
Math (level 2)	8	761
Physics	6	657
Spanish	4	585

Advanced Placement Test Results

Examination	Students	Mean
American History	24	3.7
Biology	11	3.6
Computer Science A	5	3.8
English Comp. & Lang.	4	4.5
English Comp. & Lit..	2	4.0
French Language	1	3.0
French Literature	1	4.0
Calculus AB	7	2.4
Calculus BC	4	3.7
Spanish Language	11	3.1
Spanish Literature	1	3.0

Colleges Entered by the Class of 1991

Arizona, Univ. of	Franklin & Marshall (3)	Swarthmore
Boston College	Johns Hopkins (2)	Trinity (CT) (2)
Bucknell (2)	Johnson & Wales	Tufts
California/UCSD	Ohio Northern	Tulane
Clemson	Pennsylvania, Univ. of (2)	Vanderbilt (2)
Delaware, Univ. of (2)	Penn State	Virginia, Univ. of
Dickinson	Ricks	Virginia
Duke	Rollins	Commonwealth

Viewbooks and Videos

The general descriptive brochures and videocassettes, of course, will give you a broad picture of day-to-day life at each school—its personality, perhaps its teaching methods and certainly its educational philosophy. Moreover, these materials will provide magnificent pictures of the schools and the facilities of which they are proudest. So, you'll get a better idea of each school's physical plant.

But remember, once again, all these booklets and videos are promotional materials prepared by professionals hired by each school to put its best foot forward. So everything you see or read will be biased in favor of the school. Nevertheless, together with the other materials, brochures and videos should allow you to complete the second phase of your evaluation and reduce your list of schools to those that, on paper at least, seem perfect for your child. Don't include any schools you're not sure about—those that may only be OK. It's a safe bet that no school will seem better when you see it in real life than it does in the slick promotional materials it sends you. So forget about the "maybes" and limit your final list of schools to those that seem perfect on paper. Then begin your third and final phase of evaluation by visiting each one.

CHAPTER 6

EVALUATING SCHOOLS: THE FINAL PHASE

*T*he last step in the evaluation process is a personal visit to the school, where you'll meet with admissions representatives and the head of the school. Then you'll tour the school.

You'll probably have to make two visits to kindergartens and some elementary schools—a first one by yourself or with your spouse and a second with your child. Do *not* take a young child on your initial visit. No matter how mature your preschooler may be, you should not take him or her to visit any school during your preliminary decision-making process. The selection of a private school for a young child must be yours and yours alone—not your child's! Only after you've made, and are enthusiastic about, your decision should you expose a young child to the sometimes startling new environment of a new school with strange new adults and children.

For the late elementary- or middle- and upper-school grades, by all means take your son or daughter with you on your initial visit if the school permits it. The input of a mature, older child can be helpful in deciding which school to select.

One visit to each middle school or high school may be enough to determine which school is right for your child, although it's possible and even probable that you may find two, three or more schools that seem equally perfect. In that case, apply to them all, or, if you feel you need to, make a second visit to get to know each school and its administrators and teachers a little better.

PLANNING YOUR VISITS

In planning your visits, try to do so with an open mind, devoid of all preconceived ideas. Many parents mistakenly assume that a magnificent school exterior and physical plant go hand in hand with academic excellence and, conversely, that a slightly dowdy look translates into less-than-adequate academics. Neither is true. So, be patient about jumping to conclusions and making any decisions. There's no need to hurry. Be extremely wary of any love-at-first-sight responses that reflect your own personal wishes to return to your own youth and "do it all over again." Try as much as possible to be objective and concentrate on your child's needs.

And take as much time as you need at each visit. Ask as many questions as you want—as often as you want, of as many different people as you want. Your child's future is at stake, along with tens of thousands of dollars of your family's wealth.

To set up your initial visits, telephone or write for appointments the directors of admissions at all the schools on your list. Be certain to make sure in advance that your visit will include a complete tour of the school and interviews with the head of the school, the appropriate admissions representatives and one or two teachers. If the school permits it, try also to sit in on a class or two.

If your child has any special needs—special talents that need professional development, for example, or a learning disability—it's wise to discuss those over the telephone with the director of admissions or the head of the school before you actually visit the school. Don't waste time visiting a school, only to find out it cannot meet your child's needs.

Although a half-day visit may accomplish all you want at some schools, be prepared to spend a full day. Don't try to crowd visits to two schools in the same day. Visiting too many schools at a time is like visiting too many European cathedrals at a time. You'll soon forget the differences and get them all confused. So visit one school at a time; take copious notes at each; and give yourself some time after each visit—at least a day—to organize your notes and absorb and reflect on all you saw. The Private School Evaluation Form in Appendix A can help.

In selecting classes to visit in an elementary school, choose those that your child will enter the following year *and* the ones for the year after that, to get a broader picture of the school and the education your child will get over a reasonably extended period. Ask also to see the school's special facilities for any special needs your child may have—music rooms, for example, if your child has musical talents.

If your child will enter middle or secondary school, ask to visit the class where they are teaching his best subject and the class where they are teaching his worst subject so you can discuss your child's strengths *and* weaknesses with teachers who will have to deal directly with your child. In this way you will find out exactly how they might cope with your child's needs. The response of both teachers will be a concrete indication of just how much individual support the faculty gives each students.

Visiting Boarding Schools

Visits to boarding schools can be time-consuming and often costly, because they usually involve overnight hotel stays and quite a few meals away from home for you and your child and often other members of the family. So it's important that the preliminary evaluations discussed in the last chapter be as thorough as possible in order to reduce the number of schools you have to visit to as few as possible—certainly no more than eight. Do not try to visit more than four boarding schools in a single week, or more than one over a weekend. Crowding too many visits in too short a time puts unnecessary pressure on you and your child.

Plan your route on the boarding school "circuit" carefully and make hotel or motel reservations and school appointments long in advance. Some of the towns where boarding schools are located may only have small inns with few accommodations. Leave more than enough time to travel from one school to another and, if possible, include a few half-day or full-day breaks so that your child can relax at a hotel or motel swimming pool, away from the stress of interviews, admissions tests and constantly being on his or her best behavior.

Visiting a school does not commit you to making a formal application for your child's admission. Indeed, filling out applications is the final step in the process of selecting the perfect private school and is simply a confirmation of your decision. Each application usually requires a $30 to $50 nonrefundable filing fee. So the decision to apply should only come after you've picked one or more schools to which you're absolutely certain you are willing to entrust your child's educational life.

Your Day at School

Once again, do not take your child with you on your first visit to a kindergarten or elementary school, where the decision to apply or enroll must be yours alone. A small child has no way of knowing what educational approach will be best. Many elementary schools will actually insist on your coming alone for your first interview and refuse responsibility of caring for your child during that interview. If, after your initial visit, you and the school officials feel the school might be the right one, you can arrange a second visit and bring your child with you then.

On visits to middle schools and secondary schools, it's important to take your child along on the first visit because admissions officers will want to interview both of you—first together as a group, then individually.

The purpose of interviewing you together is to see how you and your preteen or teenager interact—to see whether you're comfortable together and present a picture of warmth, trust and friendship, or one of distance and even hostility. Is your youngster silent, uncommunicative or even hostile in your presence? Do you or your spouse dominate the conversation and answer all the questions, or do you let your child respond independently to questions—without any second-guessing or explanations on your part about what your child might mean?

Following the joint family interview, admissions officials will want to interview you (and your spouse, if present) apart from your child. They'll also interview your child privately. In some schools, a student host may then accompany your child to a few classes. Most schools will also require your child to take an admissions test—either the school's own test or a standardized admissions test—usually on another scheduled date, either at the school or some neutral site.

During your visit, you'll have an opportunity to meet privately with the head of the school, who may have the title of principal, headmaster or headmistress, depending on the school's custom. If the school permits it, you may also have a chance to sit in on a class or two and speak with any teachers you'd like to meet. And, together with your child, you'll also have a complete tour of the school, often conducted by a student guide.

The day may also include lunch in the student cafeteria with a faculty or administration host, and sometimes with students. This will give you a chance to sample the atmosphere of the school (as well as the food) in a relaxed setting outside the classroom. You and your child may also want to attend a sports practice in the afternoon or an intramural or interscholastic competition to get a sense of student spirit. Are such events well attended? Is the cheering genuine, halfhearted, mocking, abusive? Listen and look carefully throughout the day and get to know each school as well as possible *before* your child applies.

The order of events during your visits is relatively unimportant. It will vary from school to school. What is important, however, is to remember at all times that every interview, every personal contact and every chance to observe throughout the day will represent a two-way evaluation process. In other words, every time you and your child are being interviewed, both of you should also be interviewing the school's representatives.

So let's look at interviews first and see what kind of information you should try to elicit and what kind of information school representatives will be trying to elicit from you and your child. Remember also that your visit to and interviews at each school may represent the final, decisive stage in picking the perfect private school for your child. So it's important to approach this stage completely prepared—*with a knowledge of what you're seeking in a school and a list of questions to assure success in that search.* One common complaint among the heads of many private schools is that too many parents show up not knowing what they're looking for in a school. So do careful preliminary evaluations, and make lists of what you are looking for.

Interviews

Never forget that the word *interview* means to see one another—in other words, for two people to see *each other.* Don't approach the interview situation as if you and your child are on trial, and, above all, do not approach the application process concerned that if your child is not admitted to a particular school, he or she and your family will, in some way, be failures.

Your goal, and that of every good school you visit, should be to find the right "match" for your child. A school may well be reputed as "the best" for many children, and still be the worst for your child—and that is all you should consider as you begin your visits. With few exceptions, that is what admissions officers at good schools will have in mind as they interview you and your child. There is, of course, the possibility you may run into an incompetent, or even arrogant, admissions representative here and there. But the vast majority are skilled, caring people, and it's important to prepare your child for school visits and interviews by making it clear that you, as a parent, are at one with admissions officials in finding the school where your child will have the greatest chance for success in obtaining the best education.

Most of us tend to be nervous in interview situations. Our pasts are dotted with interviews that proved crucial to getting good jobs or being admitted to universities and professional schools. But the interviews at top private elementary and secondary schools are quite different, and it's important to approach them without feeling that you're being interviewed for a job or without trying to sell yourself, your child or your family.

Most admissions interviewers are well-trained educators eager to admit youngsters who will succeed and be happy in their schools. They are not gatekeepers trying to keep youngsters out; they are eagerly trying to let the right youngsters in, and if some of them feel their schools are not right for your child, they are almost certainly doing your child—and you and your family—a great kindness.

If your preliminary evaluations are done carefully and objectively, however, that probably won't happen too often. But if it does, you'll find that many admissions officials who say their schools are not right for your child will suggest, and perhaps even help you arrange, visits to one or more schools they feel would be more appropriate.

So, it's important to trust most admissions officials and the advice they offer. Most cannot afford to give bad advice. Their own reputations and that of their schools are always at stake when they speak to prospective parents—and most of them know that.

"We cannot accept children if we don't think they can do the work," says the admissions director of a prestigious New York day school. "It would be cruel to do so."

Questions They'll Ask You

"Tell me about your child" is something you'll hear over and over again in one form or another from virtually everyone you meet at every school you visit, whether it's an elementary, middle or upper school. It is meant as a friendly question. It is not meant to be intrusive, and is certainly not meant to put you on the defensive.

Chapter 2, you'll recall, stressed the importance of knowing your child and being able to recognize, understand and discuss your child's strengths and weaknesses. As you do so during the interview, remember that you'll be talking with experienced educators who have worked with, and know and understand, far more children in far greater depth than most parents can or ever will. So, to use a trite gangster-movie expression, don't try to con a con man. The school officials you meet will eventually talk to, test and evaluate your child themselves. Your ability and willingness to give them an accurate evaluation beforehand will not only reflect your honesty and, therefore, the ethical standards of your family, it will also reflect your family dynamics—and that is an important element every school tries to examine as closely as possible.

Family dynamics are based on how parents relate to each other and to their children, and vice versa. Interviewers want to know whether both parents are still together, whether one or both work, whether the child has been, or is being, raised by a parent or housekeeper. They'll want to know details of your child's life and role in the family unit. They'll ask about family structure, the number of siblings and their ages, genders, accomplishments and how they fit into the family structure.

They'll ask you to describe your relationships with your children; how much sleep you insist on your child's getting each night or whether you let your child decide; whether there's a special area set aside at home for your child to do homework; whether and how you control television watching and other leisure activities; whether you read to your children and help them create; whether you take them on excursions to, and adventures at, the zoo, museum, theater, opera and other interesting places and special events. How much exposure does your child get to music, art and culture? The school will want to know your philosophy of education and your expectations of your child and of the school.

"We cannot undo damage that parents may have inflicted on their children during their children's early years," explains one admissions specialist. "Nor can we undo in school, in six to seven hours a day over only 165 days, what happens to the child during the other 200 days of the year. Home and school have to be together. There has to be a mutual support system.

"Parents make indelible marks on their children's lives," she continued, "and our task is to find out what those marks are before we admit them. We need to know the social and emotional underpinnings that parents are giving their children—in addition to the child's academic skills and talents. Personal stability is essential for a child's growth in a school setting outside the parent's control. We can often determine the personal maturity of a child by talking to the parents—without ever even seeing the child."

The people you meet at school will also want to know why you've selected their school and why you're not considering public school or, if your child is older, why you're withdrawing your child from his or her present school. Be honest! Tell them of your preliminary evaluations that led you to their school. Tell them if you think your local public schools are deficient—and tell them why.

Another question school officials will explore is whether you, as a parent, will support the school and be at one with its educational goals for your child. And it's important that you feel strongly that you can indeed be at one with the school. Again, that's why your evaluation of a school's educational philosophy is so important—to see that it coincides with your own. Nothing can be more destructive than having parents pulling in one direction and the school in another. For a parent to pull a child out of an academically demanding school during the school year to go on a family ski holiday, for example, not only sends the child a terrible, contradictory message, it is educationally destructive. It undermines the child's education, ethics and belief in the value of education, and it undermines the authority of the school and, indeed, of all rules and regulations.

Questions They'll Ask Your Child

Directly or indirectly, almost all the questions the school asks you will be asked of your child—whether it's by a gentle kindergarten teacher asking your child to tell him or her a story or by the admissions director asking your child, "Tell me about yourself," or "what's your home like?"

In other words, for the school's own sake and for your child's, school officials are going to get to know all about your child and your family one way or another. So it's in your own, and your child's, best interests for all of you to be honest from the very beginning. *Above all, do not try to rehearse your child for interviews and school visits.* All you'll accomplish is to demonstrate your own anxieties and impart them to your child—and risk making your child too nervous to function effectively.

Remember: School officials want to get to know your child. They're going to do so eventually anyway. Let them do so now, for your child's sake. Let these professional educators help you determine whether their school is indeed best for your child. Let your child be himself or herself. Encourage your child to act as he or she always does—indeed, to have a good time getting to know some new people who want nothing more than to be friends and help your child succeed.

To imply anything else will certainly not be in your child's best interests. For no matter how well you rehearse, there is no way you will succeed in hiding a personality problem that may stand in the way of admission. You'd be far better off finding a school that can handle and solve such a problem instead of trying to foist it on a school that cannot, and will not, do so. If your child is unkempt, a mop of neatly combed hair and a new suit or dress won't disguise a thing. If your child is unruly, skilled educators will quickly discover that trait, no matter how well you may have rehearsed.

So be honest, and encourage your child to be honest. It's the only sure way of picking the perfect private school.

Remember that procedures will vary widely from school to school and according to your child's age. At elementary schools, admissions directors often try to put incoming applicants for kindergarten at ease by inviting them and their parents to have a glass of milk and a cookie. This will also give the school an idea of the applicant's emotional maturity. After a few minutes, applicants at some schools are asked to join a play group, where a skilled kindergarten teacher begins the process of testing, interviewing and evaluating each child, watching carefully to see whether each is intellectually, emotionally and socially ready for that particular school. In other schools, the teacher may test the child individually.

Testing Young Children

Whatever the process, most good private elementary schools make such testing and interviewing great fun for incoming kindergartners. Basically, "testing" consists of nothing more than puzzles, drawing, listening to stories and discussing them—and a host of other activities that are not only enjoyable for most children, but also allow the teacher/tester to study each child's math readiness, reading readiness, social readiness, attention span, eye-hand coordination, emotional stability, intellectual curiosity and all the other characteristics that show that a child is ready for the first year of school. Along the way, the teacher/tester also learns a lot about each child's interests and home life.

As mentioned earlier, private-school kindergartens differ dramatically from those in most public schools, where the goal is usually to help five-year-olds bridge the gap between preschool play groups and the 1st-grade learning environment. As such, they represent more of a social training ground for learning, sharing and group participation and how to outgrow the self-centered world of the home environment.

Private-school kindergartens, however, are not designed to help babies grow up. Preschool play groups serve that function, and kindergarten represents a pre-1st grade, where actual formal education begins with academically oriented reading and writing and math-oriented manipulative programs. Although kindergarten children may appear to be playing, skilled teachers—usually two in each class—turn what the children think is play into serious learning. In other words, good private schools turn serious learning and maturation into sheer fun—and vice versa—and that's what learning and growing up should be for all kids.

Private-school kindergarten children learn basic language skills. They learn to speak clearly and correctly, to narrate events in their lives, to listen attentively as others do the same, and they learn to read stories and short books and to *write* their own creative stories. They also learn to count, measure, tell time, add, subtract and understand the meaning of numbers in the sense of one number being the same as, smaller than, or larger, than another.

Private-school kindergartens teach basic, elementary elements of history, geography, civics, biology, geology, astronomy, physics, music, dance, drama, art and the concept of foreign languages. In every sense, a good kindergarten is the first year of school, and children emerge as students, ready and eager to learn on a more advanced level when they enter first grade. In dramatic contrast, public-school kindergarten children seem infantile in their intellectual, social and emotional behavior. Many enter 1st grade unable to read their own names or write their own initials.

99

Although some parents and many social critics scoff at the idea of putting four-year-olds through "testing" and interviews to qualify for admission to private kindergartens, the allegedly rigorous admissions process is not a result of class-conscious snobbery. Nor is it designed to lock children out. Rather, it is designed to admit mature children from families who place good education at the top of their list of priorities for their children. Moreover, for most bright, mature kids, the testing and interviews are, as stated earlier, a lot of fun. In the long run, they're good for the kids that take them, because they assure kids of being placed in the right grade at the right time.

A word of warning however: Don't be upset if your preschooler whines or cries or balks at your leaving her or him alone to face a strange teacher or a group of strange children at the kindergarten evaluation process. It happens all the time. Don't overreact—with either sympathy or anger or pleas to behave. Let the teacher/evaluator handle the situation as much as possible, to show you how able the school is to handle difficult situations and to give you greater insight into your child's readiness for kindergarten or whatever grade you're considering. Moreover, quiet support of the teacher/evaluator will show your child your trust in the school and in its teachers and the high value you place on schooling.

In some cases, it may be that your child is indeed too immature to begin rigorous private-school education, and would be better off postponing it for a year. Again, that is no reflection on your child or you or your family. It is simply the result of normal developmental differences in children, who all grow up at different rates.

Some schools will allow you to accompany your child into the testing situation and then withdraw after providing the necessary assurance that you'll be waiting right outside. Still other schools will give you the opportunity to return a second time if, for some reason, your child simply will not cooperate on that particular day. But do try to keep in mind the possibility that your child may not be ready for the rigors of a private-school kindergarten, and be prepared to postpone the experience for a year.

The admissions process for later elementary-school grades is only slightly different from that for kindergarten and the early grades, in that applicants often spend part of the day attending classes with a host student. That allows several teachers to observe and compare each applicant with the very children the applicant will be attending school with the following year. Depending on the school, an admissions test may be administered the same day at school, or at a test site on some other date.

As in the case of applicants to kindergarten, however, you should make a preliminary visit to the school on your own before bringing your child. And, as mentioned earlier, do not try to rehearse your child before his or her visit. Let your child be as natural as possible. Reassure your child that the visit will be a day of fun—an exciting adventure in which to see a beautiful new school and meet all sorts of interesting teachers and other students of the same age.

Interviews for Older Children

The process for older kids—those entering 7th through 12th grades—is far more formal, but again, don't try to rehearse. As with younger children, simply explain what lies ahead. When you arrive, the admissions representative will chat with you and your child for a few minutes in generalities, about the weather, current events, sports, people you know in common, etc. The aim is only to put you and your child at ease. After a while, the interviewer will direct questions toward your son or daughter—about school, hobbies and other interests—to see how your child responds in your presence and how you and your child interact in a social situation.

Essentially, your interviewer is hoping to engage you and your youngster in an easygoing, three- or four-way conversation between equals, with no one dominating the questions or answers or undermining the responses of other participants. Parents who continually interrupt their children and answer for them can destroy their children's chances of admission. It's the interaction and your child's emotional stability in your presence that count more than specific questions and answers in this joint interview.

At an appropriate moment, the interviewer will suggest that your son or daughter go off with a student guide or host on a tour of the school or to sit in on classes. Or another adult interviewer may enter and take your child off for a private one-on-one chat, while you continue a more in-depth, adult-to-adult interview with no children present. Each school has a different method and order for doing all these things. Some may send you and your child together on a school tour—again to see how you interact as a family and whether you allow each other to ask and answer questions independently.

Before the end of the visit, however, you and your child will have been through the entire admissions experience: group and individual interviews with admissions representatives, the head of the school and teachers; a complete tour of the school; a visit with other students, perhaps in class, in the gym or athletic fields or in the lunchroom. And perhaps your child will also have taken a test of some sort. Some schools may ask your child to bring some recent graded essays from his or her present school.

At some boarding schools, your child may want and be able to stay overnight with a student host and experience the complete routine of daily life at school for 24 hours, while you stay at a nearby hotel. Such overnights, however, are usually reserved for accepted candidates who are trying to decide between two or more schools.

So simply prepare your preteen or teenager for all these experiences without implying any timetable or giving too many details. Regardless of the order of the day's visit, your child will, of course, experience what may be his or her first private, formal interview ever—with an admissions staffer who has had loads of experience chatting with youngsters and putting them at their ease. As with younger children, it's important that your child act as naturally as possible and let the interviewer get to know her or him as well as possible—and you should emphasize this in explaining to your child what an interview is.

Tell your child, "It's a chance for the two of you to get to know each other," and that you'll be having a separate interview for the same purpose.

Throughout the preliminary evaluation process, you and your child should be reviewing the school's brochures and watching the videocassettes together. It's always a good idea while doing so to provoke questions from your child by wondering aloud, "I wonder if they have . . . ?" Then, when it's time for your visit, you can remind your child to ask all the questions that arose as you studied the brochures together. You might even say, while watching the videocassettes, "I've got so many questions, I'm going to write them down," and encourage your child to do the same. Encourage your teenager to keep a notebook and take it on the visit to write down all he or she sees.

But make the entire experience an adventure and great fun, and be certain to emphasize that it is you and your child as a family who are selecting a school—not the school that will be selecting you! Be certain that your youngster understands that failure to gain admission to a particular school will simply be due to the fact that the school is not the right one. And that, rest assured, will indeed be the reason.

As for specific questions the interviewer will ask your child, they will run the gamut of hobbies and interests and relationships in and out of school: "What do you like most about school?"; "What do you like least?"; "What do you do with your spare time . . . at school . . . at home?"; "What's your favorite subject . . . sport . . . book . . . television program?"; "What do you think about . . . (some current event)?"; And, of course, "Do you have any questions you want to ask?"

Overall, the interviewer's primary goal will simply be to get to know your child as well as possible and thus examine your child's compatibility with the school. So remind your child that there won't be any right or wrong answers—only honest ones, and that the interview is simply an opportunity for "the two of you to get to know each other and see if you like each other and if both of you feel the school is right for you."

Questions Your Child Should Ask

Children being children, yours will undoubtedly pepper *you* with questions about every school whose videos you watch and whose brochures you study—and then forget every one of those questions during the stress of an actual visit to each school. That's to be expected. So, don't be upset when, after a month of endless, annoyingly repetitive cross-examinations by your child at home, he or she responds with a vapid "no" when a kindly admissions representative asks, "Do you have any questions?"

If you're like many parents, you may well want to explode with an angry "WHAT?"—and then prod your child into remembering all the questions that monopolized the previous night's dinner conversation. Don't, however. Again, you and your child will usually be dealing with highly skilled interviewers, who are quite aware of the anxieties that children of all ages bring to the admissions offices and classrooms of a new school—regardless of their ages. Most are pretty good at evoking questions from even the smallest children, if parents simply give them the chance.

Aside from anxiety, there's another obvious reason your child may have no questions: You may well have answered them all at home! So, don't answer all your child's questions at home—or at least don't do so in a way that obviates your child's need to ask questions during the school visit.

By all means try to allay your child's deepest and often irrational fears—e.g., making new friends or confronting "mean" teachers. Envious children at your child's present school may well plant frightening thoughts in your child's mind: the sisters beat you in Catholic school; they lock you up when you're bad at boarding schools; and endless other bits of nastiness.

Never belittle or dismiss in an offhanded fashion such thoughts or any other fears your child may have about entering or changing schools, no matter how unimportant or childish they may seem to you. For your child, those fears *are* realistic and you should take them seriously and encourage your child to discuss them both at home and at the interview.

Questions such as How's the food? are perfectly normal and realistic for children of almost all ages. Discouraging such questions will only convince most children that all the questions they consider important are, in fact, unimportant to adults. To ensure your child's coming alive in the interview at school, respond to such questions with praise at home by saying, "That's a good question," or "That's an excellent question. I'm sure the food's good, but you be sure to ask at the interview so we can both find out."

Similarly, it is *not* unrealistic for some preschoolers to fear being away from home, or for many preteens and teenagers to fear the difficulties of making new friends in an entirely new school setting. No matter how socially gifted a child may be, meeting and making new friends can be terribly stressful, and your child—and you—have a right to know in advance how accepting students at the new school tend to be of new students.

Many children fear the work at a new school may be too hard for them, and it's important for your child and you to find out how much support the school gives new students to help them through academic adjustment problems.

So don't belittle such anxieties, and don't belittle or ignore any of the other realistic negatives your child may raise about private-school attendance: the loss of neighborhood friends and friends from one's old school; possible resentment of neighborhood kids; the far heavier work load and loss of free time and fun on weekday evenings and weekends because of homework; and if the school is far from home, the long, tiring daily travel to and from school.

These are realistic concerns, and it's essential that you discuss them with your child at home and encourage his or her discussing them during the interviews. Any interviewer will admire the maturity of a youngster who is able to deal openly and forthrightly with such normal anxieties.

Encourage your older child to ask questions about education, too. Most middle-school youngsters and teenagers are far more aware of the quality of their education than many parents suspect. Most know intuitively when they have a good or bad teacher—and their evaluations usually have nothing to do with whether the teacher is strict or not. Indeed, most teenagers quickly dismiss strictness as a relatively unimportant quality if the teacher is fair in dispensing discipline and, above all, if the teacher is "good" in the sense of working hard to dispense as much knowledge as the class can absorb. And many admissions representatives, in turn, know that when a bright 14-year-old applicant asks, "Are the teachers strict?" the youngster is often really asking in teen talk, "Are the teachers good?" or, "Will they help me if I find the work is too hard at first?"

So praise your child's enthusiasm and questions at home, but don't answer them in such depth that he or she has nothing left to ask during the interview at school.

If your child is only elementary-school age and forgets such questions, raise them yourself in his or her presence—including How's the food?—to show how seriously you take your child's concerns. But if your child is older and applying to middle or upper school, trust her or him to raise the questions independently. Don't do so yourself—even if your child produces a blank stare when asked for questions. There are times when children must succeed or fail on their own, and this is one of those times. For you to intervene may well mean your child's being rejected by some schools.

For, in addition to intellectual, social and emotional maturity, interviewers at each school will also be looking to see how enthusiastic your child is about coming to that particular school. Many deem an absence of questions as a lack of enthusiasm, and, regardless of how enthusiastic *you* may be, few academically demanding schools will accept a child who does not want to go there.

"Before we accept a youngster," says the headmistress of one prestigious private school, "that youngster must buy into the school. We insist that she express enthusiasm and eagerness to come here. We can't be bothered dragging kids in against their will."

Questions You Should Ask

Just as the admissions representative will ask you first and foremost to talk about your child, you, in turn, might well ask your interviewer, "Tell me about *your* child." Or, put in more appropriate terms, "Tell me about your typical student. What's he or she like? How would you describe the ideal candidate for this school? What kind of youngster do you think fits in best in this school?"

Any of those questions represents an appropriate way to begin to determine whether your child will fit in. You must, in other words, try to learn, before you fill in any applications, exactly what kind of youngster each school is seeking, and whether your own child matches, or comes close to matching, that description.

If your child has any special needs—no matter how insignificant they appear to you—*now*, in your initial interview, is the time to determine in no uncertain terms that the school can meet them. This applies equally to a special gift or interest in a particular area, a peculiarity that may be a borderline learning disability or simply a deep abiding interest in some hobby.

Don't save such questions until the end of your visit. You may find you've wasted your entire day and the school's valuable time—and that's not fair to anybody. Indeed, if you're dealing with something as obvious as a world-class talent or, at another extreme, a serious learning disability, you should, as suggested earlier, inquire over the telephone about the school's ability to deal with such needs before you make appointments to visit. Simply call the director of admissions or the head of the school and ask openly whether they deal with such talents or problems. You'll find that officials at all private schools are friendly, open and always enthusiastic about talking to parents about their children.

Remember at all times that most of the men and women you talk to at most private schools are dedicating their lives to helping parents raise and educate their children. Some may even be scholars who have taught or could teach at the college and university levels but have chosen to work with younger students. They adore working with kids and want nothing but the best for the kids they're teaching—and for your kids, whether or not they wind up teaching them also.

So be open and frank as you make arrangements to visit each school and as you meet the people who greet and talk to you there. Tell them the kind of school and the kind of education you're seeking for your child, and ask them to tell you the kind of youngster they are seeking and are best equipped to educate. Ask them the academic and social skills they expect a child to have mastered before entering the grade for which your child is applying. Ask what is expected of children in each grade in addition to what you've seen described in the course catalog.

Once you've described your own child and heard a description of the type of youngster the school seeks, ask frankly if the interviewer thinks, on the basis of what you've said, that your child might fit in well at the school.

If at that point there is agreement that your child could do well there, you're ready to begin asking a lot of probing questions as part of the final, in-depth phase of your evaluation.

In-depth Evaluations

Remember that it's highly likely that most of the schools you decided to visit will be similar, if not identical, because you were looking for one particular set of characteristics as you watched the videotapes and read all the school brochures. Therefore, your in-depth evaluation and the probing questions you ask will have to determine the subtle differences between each school—if indeed there are any.

Those differences will determine which schools you finally select to apply to. Be certain to prepare a carefully considered list of questions; repeat many of them to the various people you meet during your visit at each school; and write down the answers as carefully as possible. The differences in those answers from school to school will often be so subtle that you'll fail to remember them if you don't write them down. Ultimately, the care with which you take notes may determine your success in distinguishing which schools are better for your child.

Use the Private School Evaluation Form in Appendix A as a broad guide to help you organize your notes. Make copies of the form so you can take one to each school. After you've finished visiting all the schools, you should have a neat evaluation report of each school to compare with all the others.

The questions you ask should be designed to fill in whatever blanks remain after your preliminary evaluations and to answer questions left unanswered by the various school brochures, catalogs and selection aids. The questions to ask will vary widely, according to your child's particular needs and your own goals for your child. Not every parent will have to ask all of the questions suggested below. Pick out those that are appropriate for your child.

EVALUATION STANDARDS

There were, you'll recall, eight key standards for evaluating schools: accreditation; educational philosophy (or educational goals); educational results; faculty quality; financial condition; academic strength; physical plant; and personality, or school atmosphere. You should have determined accreditation earlier from Appendix B or from *Peterson's* and should be limiting your visits to accredited schools only.

Many of the questions regarding the other standards, however, may have been only partially answered during your preliminary evaluation. Let's reexamine those standards and look at questions to ask during your interviews and tours.

Educational Philosophy

As mentioned earlier, one of the most corrosive influences in public-school education has been the tendency of educators to lower academic standards to adjust to the least-motivated, unwilling students and their parents, rather than setting high standards and expecting (insisting) that students adjust upwards to meet those standards. At a private school, however, the admissions representative and the head of the school should be able to state the school's educational standards clearly and unequivocally, giving the relative emphasis placed on academics, individual creativity, ethical conduct, athletics, extracurricular activities and community service.

Clearly stated goals are important for three reasons. First, they give the faculty and staff a clear policy for working with students. Second, they tell students what is expected of them. Finally, they give you and other parents a chance to compare the school's goals with your own and, if the differences are too great, to take your child elsewhere.

The broad descriptions of educational philosophies in school brochures, however, often leave many questions unanswered. What you, as a parent, need to find out during your school visits is how each school's educational philosophy differs from that of other schools you're considering and how each school says it will apply its philosophy to your child's benefit.

Ask the head of the school for his or her own description of the school's educational philosophy. How does it differ from that of competitive schools you're considering and what does it mean in practical terms for your child— both short-term in the grade your child will enter and long-term over the entire elementary-, middle- or upper-school segment? What you must try to find out in concrete terms is what your child will learn—and how—in the years ahead.

Academic goals for each subject are usually stated in the course catalog. If you didn't get one by mail, ask for it at the beginning of your first interview and scan through those parts that will apply to your child in the coming year, so that you know what your child will have to master during the first year at school. Regardless of whether you think those goals are too high, too low or just right, it's important to be able to discuss them with your interviewer.

In addition to educational goals, it's also important to discuss social and emotional goals. Every child needs social and emotional support at school as well as at home. How will this school give the support that your child needs? A shy youngster, for example, may need a warm, nurturing, less structured approach, while an aggressive child might need a more structured, disciplined environment. A highly intellectual child might need continual intellectual stimulation to thrive at school and free rein to explore independently, to avoid the kind of boredom that often undermines academic motivation.

So, in discussing educational philosophy, see which approach the school uses and try to determine how it will serve your child's needs. How, for example, will the school challenge your youngster's mind? Does the school encourage risk taking and exploration by encouraging children to design their own experiments, for example, to learn about science—rather than simply giving children answers to memorize or urging them to look up answers in books? Are children allowed to make mistakes in the interests of independent discovery? Listen to the teacher's reactions to children's questions if you visit classes. Those reactions will often reflect the school's educational philosophy far more accurately than any brochure or video will.

Be open and frank about mentioning the other schools you're considering when asking what makes each school different. All private schools know they must compete for the best students, and none shies from that competition. So be direct. Ask the admissions representative and the head of the school what they think their school's advantages and disadvantages are in relation to comparable schools you're considering. What can each school do for your child that others cannot—and how do they plan to go about it?

Be certain also to ask the head of the school and anyone else you interview to describe what they consider some of the school's weaknesses. The school's brochures will certainly have outlined its strengths, but it's important for you to try to discover the school's weaknesses before your child enrolls and you've sent a nonrefundable payment for tuition and fees.

At healthy schools, don't expect whatever is wrong to be of a serious nature. Successful schools don't succeed by having serious problems. More than likely, the biggest problem will be shortage of funds to expand in a particular area or, perhaps, failure of some parents to prod their children to put forth more effort. Whatever the school's problems, however, they will eventually become yours, at least in part, and they may affect your child. So try to find out those problems while you're interviewing school officials. Then, later, as you tour the school, see if any of the school's weaknesses described by the head of the school are evident.

Rules and Regulations

Discipline and its application are important elements of any school's philosophy. You should already have received the school's rules and regulations, and, while you may agree with those rules one hundred percent, it's important to learn during your visit whether the faculty and administration actually enforce the rules or simply pay lip service to them while winking at infractions. Probe deeply into that question if rules, regulations and discipline are of concern to you—especially if you value a highly disciplined, structured approach to education more than you do a carefree, child-centered approach.

Today's kids of all ages and all cultural and economic backgrounds have easy access to alcohol, drugs and premature sexual experiences, and they're often pushed by peer pressure to rebel against authority by cheating, lying, stealing and engaging in other antisocial behavior. It's important to know in advance what kinds of peer pressures exist at each school and how school authorities handle violations of school rules and regulations. Many parents want to hear the head of their children's prospective school say unequivocally that anyone caught with alcohol or drugs of *any* kind are expelled on the spot, with no opportunity for appeal. Others prefer a more lenient, case-by-case approach. You must decide what you want. Ask whether the school has a comprehensive program of education on chemical and drug dependency. All good schools now have such programs.

Taking discipline a step further, ask whether school rules and regulations concerning student behavior extend beyond school grounds. Is a teenager who might be expelled for drinking on campus, for example, expelled if arrested on a drunk driving charge far from the campus over the weekend? Many schools consider their students representatives of the school at all times, wherever they happen to be, and they thus expect students to conduct themselves according to school rules and regulations everywhere, 365 days a year.

Parent-teacher Contacts

Be sure to ask, too, about communications between the school and the family. How does the school keep parents informed about their child's academic and social development? How often are school officials in touch with parents—formally and informally? Every school has at least one regular, formal Parents' Day each year. Some schools have two or three—one each semester or trimester. In addition to such formal contacts, however, are there frequent informal teacher-parent or school-parent contacts by telephone, if, for example, a student fails to hand in some homework or seems to be in academic or social difficulty? Does the school give parents early warning signs of such problems? How? (Many teachers send parents homework assignment sheets, for example, to combat the "I-don't-have-any-homework" syndrome.)

Educational Results

As mentioned earlier, almost any school can achieve impressive academic results with academically gifted youngsters, and those results will be amply evident in the school brochures and student profiles.

Success with academically gifted children, however, is only important to their parents. If your child is gifted, you'll need to ask different questions from parents of more average children. Be certain to ask both the admissions representative and the head of the school what provisions the school makes for assuring your child of reaching his or her full potential: private lessons, for example, in the case of a gifted musician; special studio time and facilities for an artist, etc.

Most children, however, are not geniuses, and it's these more average children that put schools to the test in terms of educational results. Unlike public schools, good private schools do not allow such children to languish in educational mediocrity—and certainly not to pull the school's educational standards down to their level. The educational results at any private school should reflect the school's academic standards and expectations—

and the degree to which it insists on students adjusting upward to meet those standards and expectations. Private schools have the right to dictate rules, regulations and academic standards and *force* students to conform— or get out!

To merit your consideration, any school should be able to explain in detail how it takes average children and motivates and teaches them and makes sure they learn *everything* they're supposed to learn in the curriculum.

So if your child is indeed about average, ask how the school spurs each child to reach beyond the limits the child may have set. Find out what steps the school takes to help a student who is having trouble in a particular area. Some schools provide peer tutoring, for example, for minor academic troubles. Others provide extra group or one-on-one tutoring by teachers during free periods or after school. How are special needs spotted early and dealt with by faculty at different grade levels? Are there special sections to ensure that older children transferring from public schools catch up to their private-school peers in such areas as the mechanics of writing, grammar, rhetoric, etc.? Are there special programs such as English as a Second Language for children who have grown up speaking a foreign language?

If your child is applying for kindergarten, ask what provisions are made for the child who is already reading, if that's the case with your child, or for the child who progressively falls behind as the year progresses. Find out whether lunch is part of the learning process and whether and how the youngest children are taught social skills, such as cleaning up after themselves and disposing of trash in the classroom, at lunch and elsewhere in the school.

Ask carefully about homework—how much there is at each grade level (even kindergarten kids have homework once in a while)—and how much parental involvement the school wants or expects. Obviously, this will change with student age and grade.

In middle schools and high schools, educational results are often easier to measure than in elementary schools. Your preliminary evaluations with school profiles should have given you a breakdown of the previous year's SAT scores for high-school juniors and seniors and the list of colleges last year's graduates are now attending.

For elementary and middle schools, however, you may have no such easy-to-find guides. So ask the admissions representative and the head of the school for some factual evidence to confirm the educational results of the school. Some elementary and middle schools, for example, compile average student scores on standardized achievement tests or on the Secondary School Admission Test. Other elementary schools simply point out the high caliber of secondary schools and colleges their students are now attending. It's immaterial how a school proves its educational results as long as it does so.

Educational results are inevitably a reflection of educational philosophy, and it's important for you to find out what results each private school obtains with its students and how they achieve those results.

Faculty Quality

You should have some feel for faculty quality by the time you visit each school. The faculty list the school should have sent you shows the number of advanced-degree holders on the faculty, the caliber of colleges and universities they attended, along with the subjects in which they majored and the subjects they now teach. The last two should usually coincide.

There are some additional measures of faculty quality, however, that may not be evident from your preliminary evaluations. One is average age and tenure. There should be a good mix of teachers of all ages, with about one-third with 10 years' or more tenure, one-third with five to 10 years', and one-third made up of younger teachers, who, because of their age, relate easily (and differently from older faculty) to their students. The young teachers, most of whom are recent college graduates, may not yet have decided to make teaching their career. Those who do may leave after three to five years to get their master's degree. Some will return, depending on how attractive the school makes it for them to do so. (You can determine approximate teacher age by the year they graduated from college.)

Teacher Salaries

In addition to average tenure, check on teacher salaries. As stated earlier, the average public-school teacher's salary in the United States is about $30,000, and ranges as high as $50,000 in states with the best public school systems. Average teacher salaries for independent schools are about 10% less, and 30% less at all other private schools. Independent-school salaries, however, range as high as $75,000 at the costliest, most prestigious schools, and many private schools offer teachers such perks as free on-campus housing and food, free medical care, free schooling for their children at the school, tuition reimbursement for professional advancement and a host of other benefits.

But the most important benefit for private-school teachers is the opportunity to work with small groups of bright, motivated, well-behaved kids who respect education and their teachers. So don't be misled by the sometimes dramatic differences in pay between private- and public-school teachers. The high salaries for some public-school teachers is often nothing more than combat pay to compensate them for the anarchy, physical violence and, often, threats of physical assault they face at work.

Nevertheless, private-school teachers do have bills to pay, and few will remain content if they have to struggle too hard financially—no matter how much they love their work. So compare teacher salaries against those at local public schools to see how great the differences are. If the differences are not more than 10%, and if the salaries are competitive with those at other, comparable private schools, you'll know the school is probably compensating its faculty enough to attract fine teachers.

Teaching Methods

Another measure of faculty quality is the way teachers teach—something you'll be able to discern only by sitting in on a class or two. Teacher quality can be seen in the interaction with students in the classroom setting. Look at the faces of the teachers and their students. Are they genuinely enjoying each other and the material they're discussing? Are the classes exciting? There's no way to measure excitement. It's like the electricity in the air at a hit show or great concert performance, and it's evident in classes whenever great teachers work with great kids. You'll know it and feel it when you experience it. Just look in the kids' faces! I remember walking into a 4th-grade music room at one school to find five children playing "Greensleeves" in perfect harmony on violins, xylophones and the piano. Without missing a beat or a note, they turned to me and broke into wide grins that reflected not only the beauty of their music but their joy from performing so well.

Financial Condition

As stated earlier, it's important to determine the financial condition of any school you consider so that you can avoid academic, social and emotional trauma for your child and considerable financial trauma for you if the school should close in mid-semester.

School brochures are often of little value in analyzing a school's financial condition. Despite high costs of attending independent schools, the tuition paid by parents—even those who pay "full fare"—covers only about 75% of the actual costs of educating each child. The gap must be filled each year with income from two other sources: the school's endowment fund and annual fund raising. The level of annual giving—i.e., the financial support of alumni and parents—and the size of, and income from, the endowment are thus key measures of any school's financial condition.

113

Again, be straightforward in asking about a school's financial condition. You have a right to know before making the kind of investment you're contemplating, and the best person to ask is the head of the school. It's usually pointless to ask anyone in admissions, whose job, after all, is to "sell" the school and who may truly not be familiar with school finances.

Ask about the school's long-term and short-term debts and whether the school has been operating at a deficit or not. If so, for how long? It's best not to apply to any school that has been accumulating consistent annual deficits. Academic brilliance, remember, does not insure financial acumen, and any school that consistently runs in the red is mismanaged and not a place to risk your money or your child's future.

Ask also whether the school has worked up a financial projection for the next three to five years. Such "look-ahead" plans are also a sign of good fiscal management.

Deficits are not the only signs of mismanagement. Falling enrollment can be another, although schools can compensate by allowing attrition to reduce the size of the faculty accordingly to keep the school in the black. So check whether the sizes of the student body and faculty have remained stable. Find out if the total number of courses offered has been declining, thereby reducing academic opportunities at the school. To compensate for declining income by cutting either faculty size or the academic program can damage, and even destroy, a private school's basic reason for existing.

Check also whether student-teacher ratios have increased or decreased dramatically over the past few years. Financially sound private schools try to maintain student–teacher ratios of about 12 students per teacher, although independent schools have an average student–teacher ratio of 9.3. Private elementary schools generally put more students in their classrooms than secondary schools do—an average of just under 13.9 students per teacher in elementary grades, versus an average of 10.7 students per teacher in secondary schools. Fewer than nine students per teacher is usually too costly, unless it is a special-needs school, and more than 15 can mean overcrowded classrooms. Remember, the average ratio for public schools is 17.6. In addition, check the average teacher's *total student load* (the number of students each teacher must teach each day) to see if there have been any significant changes in that number.

Another indication of deteriorating finances is a decline in student academic strength. A steady, dramatic decline in SAT scores, for example, can mean the school is admitting less-qualified students to fill the school—and its coffers—and that can mean a less-demanding academic program for your child. Some schools in financial trouble also try to "buy" extra students with partial scholarships to keep enrollment from dropping. In addition, many prep schools actively recruit overseas. By filling 15%, 20%

or even more of their classes with children of wealthy Asian families, such schools not only maintain a steady cash flow, they also fulfill their socio-legal requirements to open their doors to "children of color." But a large foreign-born population necessarily changes the character and atmosphere of a school, and you must decide whether you want to place your child in it.

Academic Strength

Although you may know each school's *absolute* academic strength in terms of average SAT scores, colleges attended, etc., what you need to determine on your visit is the school's *relative* academic strength, which will have far more effect on your child. In relative terms, the school working with kids whose SAT scores only range up to 600 may actually be stronger than the school with gifted kids whose scores range from 700 to a perfect 800—*if* the former is making its kids reach their full potential and the latter is not.

What's important to determine when you visit each school, then, is whether the school is helping children "reach." As you visit each class-room, watch the children's faces carefully as they interact with each other and with their teachers. Not much learning takes place if students don't seem attentive and are not actively taking part in classroom discussions. Joy, excitement and satisfaction usually spread across the faces of children who are learning and discovering.

And watch the teachers carefully. See if they lecture the students or encourage student participation. As mentioned before, the student, not the teacher, must be the most active participant in the learning process. The teacher is merely a leader, asking questions, provoking students to ask their own questions and guiding students to the right answers by getting them to look things up, to conduct experiments, to make observations and, finally, to reach conclusions. Regardless of age, students learn best by doing, and good teachers encourage even the youngest kindergartners to do things—to touch, handle, count and interrelate materials and use as many senses and faculties as possible.

Listen also to see if teachers interconnect knowledge from their own subject area to other subjects to make them part of a more meaningful and interesting whole. Literature is not written, nor music composed, nor art created, in a vacuum. All are tied to the history of their times, which in turn are influenced by advances in mathematics, science, technology and many other forces. So all the subjects taught in school are interrelated, and good teachers make a point of showing and explaining those interre-lationships to their students.

The degree to which a school encourages independent discovery, advanced study and research is also a good measure of academic strength. So ask about the number of class projects or, for older students, the number of independent research projects under way in each class you visit. Check, too, on the number and percentage of students enrolled in AP courses—those advanced courses mentioned earlier that are the equivalent of college freshman courses and designed by The College Board for students who have completed the high-school curriculum in each course.

Another mark of academic strength is the practice of grading a child for effort as well as academics. This lets parents know just how hard their children are trying in school. Grades for effort also serve as incentives to prod parents into motivating their children to work harder. Effort grades at private schools also represent a contrast to public schools, where parents and teachers often accept a child's failure to achieve as a simple reflection of poor aptitude in a particular subject. Effort grades show both parents and children that academic performance is most often a reflection of the amount of effort a child is willing to invest in his work.

In your interviews with admissions representatives and the head of the school, you cannot, of course, obtain a guarantee that your child will reach his or her potential at that school, but what you should try to get is a solid explanation of just how the school's teaching methods routinely help those children who are similar to yours grow to the fullest extent possible, intellectually, socially and emotionally.

Physical Plant

Although the brochures the school sent you will certainly list and picture most elements of the physical plant, only a personal tour can show you the current condition and importance of each element. A basketball court with dull, unvarnished, warped floorboards and a torn net beneath each basket is either an indication of deteriorating finances or total lack of interest in basketball. You should find out which.

If you're evaluating a city school, be certain to take a close look at the surrounding neighborhood. Slums have a way of spreading quickly through every city and creeping too close for comfort to even the most costly and prestigious private schools. So walk or drive a few blocks in every direction from the school. Your children may have to. If you have even the slightest doubt about neighborhood safety, talk to parents of children already attending the school. If necessary, call the local police station and speak to the community affairs officer.

As you're about to enter the school, whether it's in the city, suburbs or country, look carefully at the school yard or grounds and at the building exterior. Is the school yard safe, attractive and well maintained? Is the fencing in good shape? Does the building seem well cared for? Deteriorating building exteriors and landscaping may also be signs of deteriorating finances.

Are kids or adults loitering outside the school property? It's important to know that your child will be supervised at all times and never accosted by strangers when in the care of school authorities. Safety for your child must be as primary a concern as educational excellence.

Suburban and rural schools should present a picture of a perfect landscape of playing fields, tennis courts and other outdoor recreational facilities. City schools should be on quiet, clean streets.

As you enter the school, look at the physical condition of the floors, walls, ceilings. Are they well maintained and attractive? Are hallways well lit? Are floors clean or littered? Keep a sharp eye out for safety precautions—smoke detectors, fire extinguishers and well-marked fire exits. Does the school smell clean? Is it hot and stuffy or cold and damp? Again, these characteristics can reflect the financial condition of the school as well as its personality, in that careful attention to details of student safety and comfort represents deep caring by school administrators. Look for ramps and other facilities for handicapped children if the school says it accepts them.

If your child is enrolling in elementary or middle school, your tour guide will probably be the person on the admissions staff who interviewed you. Many secondary schools let students guide parents and their children. That allows student applicants and parents to relax from the stress of the formal interview situation and ask questions they might not ask an adult interviewer.

Above all, it allows them to ask a student how he or she likes the school. It also demonstrates to prospective parents that the school is so proud of itself that it dares entrust its students with the key public relations task of showing the school to prospective "buyers."

Regardless of who shows you the school, you'll want to look for the same things and ask the same questions. As you visit classrooms, for example, see if they're well lit and well furnished, with well-maintained chairs, tables or desks designed to fit the children who use that particular room. A kindergarten classroom is different from all others. It is usually larger, with a wide, open central space and a half-dozen or more "learning areas" spread nicely around the perimeter. Each learning area is usually devoted to a special subject—mathematics, for example, or science or geography. Tables and chairs must be movable and light enough for little children to carry and rearrange in clusters, according to the activity.

Kindergartens

A kindergarten should have an in-class library, plenty of blocks, educational toys, manipulative rods and cubes, art and writing supplies, plants and perhaps a few animals and a wide variety of other materials for learning reading and writing, mathematics, science, music and art, and for participating in dramatic play. Some schools integrate computers into daily learning activities in kindergarten.

Check bathrooms and coatrooms. Are they neat, clean and safe? Are younger children segregated from older ones to prevent bullying?

Check the playground to see that it's attractive and safe and that its equipment is in perfect condition, with no rust around the edges. The area should be big enough and have enough equipment for all the children to run, climb, swing, slide and play. Are any children waiting in lines or idle with nothing to do? A well-run school sees that all children are active in the playground and spend all their pent-up energies. Good teachers ensure that play is a learning experience as well as fun. Check the gym for adequacy as a bad-weather substitute.

Elementary School Grades

Look for many of the same things in 1st- and 2nd-grade classes. There should be considerable expansion of in-class libraries and fewer playthings. First and 2nd grades should have more formal seating arrangements, with a desk and chair for each child. The perimeter of the room should still be organized into neat learning areas. There should be more evidence of traditional schoolwork than in kindergarten—more wall charts, for example. Calculators, computers and word processors should be part of the standard equipment available to 1st and 2nd graders.

Third and 4th grade classrooms should present a picture of increased seriousness, scholarship and structure. At this age, too, instead of studying every subject with a single homeroom teacher in the same classroom all day, students normally begin switching to other specially equipped classrooms, where teacher-specialists teach art, music, science and foreign languages. Computers are now an integral part of daily learning.

As you look at classrooms in the upper grades, all will begin to look alike. The key element to look at is the physical condition of such classrooms—again, as an indication of both the financial condition of the school and of its concern for the children. Check the number of desks in each classroom to be certain the school is not crowding more and more students into each class to cut its costs. Check that science laboratories are well equipped and that each student's workbench has functioning equipment.

Supply cabinets should be filled with chemicals and other supplies for student experiments. Take the time to watch part of a lab in action, if you're looking at middle and upper schools.

Be certain to visit the library, regardless of your child's age. Does the library have a special area designed for the youngest children? A key indication of a superior school is the way it adapts its facilities for each age group. The library should have a separate card catalog that young children can manipulate and understand. Older children should have a standard card catalog section, along with data retrieval equipment (microfiche) and a computerized information index that prints out a bibliography for just about any topic a student may be studying. In addition to tens of thousands of books—about 50 books per student—every school library should have a wide variety of periodicals.

Visit the computer labs. There should be one lab for each broad age group, with 25 to 50 computers in the elementary school lab, a similar number of more advanced units for middle schoolers and an even more advanced lab for high schoolers. A good school sees to it that all its students are computer literate.

Ask, too, whether the school has a writing center. Because of the declining literacy of American school children, good schools are making extra efforts to ensure that their students develop good writing skills. Some have writing labs to supplement the normal work in English classes. Others have special weekly writing periods, during which students do nothing but write nonfiction narratives, fictional pieces, poetry or anything else they choose.

Visit the art, music and drama areas to check on the number of musical instruments, music stands and stage and backstage equipment. Are private practice rooms available? What works are in progress in art rooms, and in how many different media? Oils? Watercolors? Clay? Even if these areas are of little interest to you or your child, remember that you'll be paying for a broad liberal arts education unavailable in the vast majority of public schools. Be certain that your child will get your money's worth.

Athletic Facilities

Tour all sports facilities to see that they meet the needs of both girls and boys. At middle- and upper-school levels, there should be adequate facilities for intramural, as well as varsity and junior varsity, programs for interscholastic competition. The vast majority of students cannot make the varsity or junior varsity teams, but have just as much right to participate in sports as more gifted athletes. Most good private schools require regular participation in sports by all students, but it's important to check that the facilities for intramural sports are as good as those for interscholastic competition.

As you tour, see if the playing fields and track are well maintained and safe looking. Is the swimming pool clean and constantly supervised? Are gymnasium facilities well maintained and safe? Are locker rooms adequate for all participants? Does each youngster have an individual locker for sports and another elsewhere for coats, overshoes, books and personal items? Are lockers in good repair? Can students feel secure about storing valuables in lockers?

Are there adequate, clean showers and changing rooms, with boys and girls carefully segregated? Is there a separate locker room for visiting teams? Ask about first aid for participants in sports and whether a medically trained person is present at all athletic events—intramural as well as interscholastic.

Ask coaches whether girls have equal access to all facilities or whether boys have priority. Can girls field teams and participate in as many sports as boys?

If applicable, check whether there is an "adaptive gym center" for students with handicaps or health problems. A child with a handicap or chronic health problem could be extremely unhappy in a school with no appropriate recreational opportunities.

Extracurricular Activities

The brochures the school sent you undoubtedly list all available extracurricular activities, but when you visit the schools in person, you should ask to see some of the facilities to determine how serious the school is about them. A rich mix of extracurricular activities can be as important and rewarding to children as formal academics. Academic clubs in areas such as science or foreign languages, for example, allow students to extend their interests beyond the classroom, and to do so in a social setting free of the pressures of exams and homework.

Activities such as drama, singing, band, orchestra, photography, journalism and magazine and book publishing help develop talents and teach valuable skills seldom taught in classrooms. Hobbies such as chess, stamp or coin collecting or lepidopterology not only expand children's knowledge, they put them in contact with others outside the school with similar interests—often world-renowned experts eager to share knowledge with young enthusiasts in their fields.

So, depending on your child's interests, ask to see the newspaper and yearbook offices; the radio and television studios if they have them; the stage and theater facilities for dramatic and musical presentations; the music rooms and instruments; the darkroom and any other facilities that may interest your child and you. Ask about academic extracurricular facilities for groups such as the science club, and ask about student government to see if the school is teaching its youngsters how to govern themselves.

Obviously, elementary schools will have far fewer extracurricular activities, but good schools do incorporate into their daily curricula special projects that serve as substitutes for what will later become extracurricular activities in middle and upper school. Thus, many elementary-school grades produce their own class "newspapers," literary "magazines" and other publications. So ask elementary schools about special facilities or activities that develop skills normally not taught in the standard academic curriculum.

Other Facilities

Don't forget to visit the cafeteria—and taste some food—as part of your tour of every school. Visit the nurse's office to see whether it appears adequate. In both cafeteria and nurse's office, look for cleanliness. Does the aroma in the cafeteria whet your appetite? Do the health-care facilities inspire confidence?

Look at the main locker area in day schools. Your children will undoubtedly store valuables there. See that the lockers are in good condition and secure. In boarding schools, be sure to visit dormitories, a variety of children's rooms and several common rooms where youngsters gather to watch television, listen to music or simply enjoy each other's company. Peek into the bathrooms to see that they're clean and well maintained. Ask yourself always whether you'd be happy living at that school.

School "Personality"

Although you'll absorb a bit of the school's personality by reading its brochures and talking to the head of the school and the admissions staff, it's on your tour of the school that you'll get a better sense of that personality. Be certain to take careful notes. Ultimately, personality—the way you "feel" about a school—may be the deciding factor in selecting between otherwise identical schools, and only your notes will give you the data you need to make that decision. Unless you note in writing experiences such as mine, watching those 4th graders I described making magnificent music, you'll fail to distinguish and remember the subtle differences between the personalities of the schools you visit.

As you tour the school, see if the hallways have a happy look, with children's art work on the walls of elementary-school corridors. Or are the halls grim and forbidding? In addition to the physical look, pay close attention to the social atmosphere. What is the noise level in the corridors during and between classes? Look into the children's faces. Are they happy, pensive, scholarly, fearful, angry? Are they well dressed and well groomed?

When you first enter the school, at the beginning of the day, before your first interviews, stop and talk to students in the corridors. Ask for directions to the administration office when you arrive—even if you know the way—just for the opportunity of a brief encounter with randomly selected students. Do they escort you there or just grunt and point? Are they friendly and helpful? Ask questions of those you meet. Do they love the school? Why? What don't they like about it?

If you're touring a secondary school, ask your student guide similar questions. Watch his or her response. Is he or she cheerful and evidently proud of being at the school? If you're touring with an admissions staffer or the head of the school, do the children run up in delight to show their latest homework paper or work of art? Watch for joy and excitement as opposed to chaos; watch for signs of genuine affection between students and the adults who run the school. Watch, in other words, for the elements that make up the atmosphere of this school and its personality.

The kindergarten should have an especially happy look and be decorated with children's creative works. A room that's too neat may be a sign of an overstructured atmosphere, which can smother some children's imaginations. A messy room, on the other hand, may be an indication of chaos and an overly permissive atmosphere where children may fail to learn self-discipline and proper social behavior. Neither condition provides much fun or learning. A good kindergarten should fall somewhere in between. (It's good to remember that academic subjects are called *disciplines*—as in the discipline of writing or the discipline of mathematics. It's virtually impossible for children—or anyone else, for that matter—to learn a discipline in a state of chaos.)

Watch teachers interact with their students. Kindergarten teachers should be friendly, warm and understanding, but firm and able to control the situation at all times. Good kindergarten teachers seldom lose an opportunity to introduce some learning in every exchange with every child—even in the cafeteria.

Elementary-school classrooms for older children should maintain a happy look, with prominent displays of children's works mixed with more scholarly learning materials such as wall charts. Again, watch and listen to teachers interacting with their students. Is there genuine warmth? Do the kids and their teachers enjoy being together? Are teachers sensitive to the children—to the anxieties and problems children often bring to school each day or the dangers young adolescents face in today's world?

Although many of the teachers you see and meet will be busy teaching, some will be between classes. Use those brief opportunities to interview them. Just as you should, if you get a chance, ask a student, "What's it like going to school here?" you should ask the teachers you meet, "What's it like teaching here?" What do they like most about the school? What are their most serious problems—and how do they solve them? Is discipline or bad behavior a problem?

In every class, try to assess the atmosphere. Is the class orderly? Tense? Quiet? Are students and teachers interested and enthusiastic—or bored? What are students doing: drilling? taking tests? discussing and debating? listening to a lecture? Is real learning, as described earlier, taking place? Are the children eager and excited to be learning? Is the atmosphere exciting?

See if the school's stated educational philosophy is evident in the classroom. Is classroom atmosphere structured and formal, structured but informal, or carefree? Are the teachers demanding or nurturing? If you could, would you like to be a child again and sit in *that* classroom in *that* school with *that* teacher or with the other teachers you see and meet? Ultimately, *your* comfort at the school must be a deciding factor in evaluating the school's personality as right or wrong for your child.

As you explore the school, look carefully at all trophy cases and wall displays to determine the emphasis the school places on different activities. Do academic achievement awards predominate, or do athletic trophies, medals and ribbons dominate the displays, as they do in most public schools? The degree of emphasis a school places on academics, athletics and extracurricular activities determines the esteem in which achievers in each area are held, and that, in turn, affects the school atmosphere. Tragically, semi-literate athletes are heroes in most public schools and brilliant scholars are "nerds." Don't pick a private school with a similar atmosphere.

Safety

Part of any school's atmosphere is the degree of safety that it offers to the school community. If students have to run a gauntlet of neighborhood toughs each day, the atmosphere of a day school will be deeply affected. So be certain to get details about how each school—whether in the city, suburbs or country—ensures the physical safety of its students—at recess and when they arrive and leave school. How does the school keep intruders out? Is there school-bus service? Who supervises them on the bus?

Who is there to greet them in the morning as they arrive? Where do they get the school bus to return home? Who ensures that each child is on the correct bus?

Fire safety is another important question to discuss. Inspection by authorities is not reliable in many areas of the country. So it's up to you to make certain the school has taken adequate steps to protect its children against fire and smoke inhalation. Check that there are adequate fire alarms, smoke detectors and fire exits throughout the school and, if it's a boarding school, in the dormitories. Are all the fire exits easy to open from inside the building? Does the school hold regular fire and evacuation drills? How often?

You should also ask whether the school has an asbestos abatement program and lead-free water. Do not send your child to a school that exposes students to asbestos or lead!

If you're evaluating boarding schools, find out how the school ensures the safety of children off campus when the children go into the nearby town or village. Ask about on-campus security as well. There are usually no fences or gates to protect the grassy expanses of most boarding-school campuses, and protection from intruders is an important question to discuss at any boarding school you consider—especially coed and all-girls schools. What safeguards are there against drugs and alcohol on campus? Ask whether the school teaches its children about the effects and dangers of drugs and alcohol.

Although it's a touchy subject, it's absolutely essential also to discuss the question of sexual safety as well as physical safety. Does the school provide any sex education? At what age? Almost all good secondary schools usually offer a once-a-week course in human relations and sexuality—usually to 10th graders.

Get specifics on how the school protects its students against sexual molestation of all kinds, including date rape by schoolmates *and* faculty. And be certain to find out the school's policy on AIDS. Every school—particularly middle and secondary schools—should have a carefully worked out AIDS policy to protect its children against possible exposure to the HIV virus by other children and faculty members.

Do not compromise your child's safety. If a school cannot guarantee the on-campus and off-campus safety of children in its care, find a school that can.

CHAPTER 7

A FINAL WORD

*I*f you've taken careful notes while touring each school, you should now be ready to pick the perfect private school or schools for your child. The Private School Evaluation Form in Appendix A should help you organize your notes and make the decision easier and more clear cut.

If, after comparing the results of your study, you find several schools equally perfect—in other words, if you've got a "win-win" situation—apply to them all. And if your child is admitted to them all and they are indeed equal in every respect, let your child help decide which to attend if he or she is at least 10 or 12 and quite mature and experienced in making decisions. If your child is unenthusiastic about a school at that age, chances are the school already knows it from the interviews and may well not offer an invitation to enroll. Most schools want enthusiastic applicants.

If your child does indeed prefer one school over others, try to evoke as rational an explanation as possible for the preference. If, as is more likely, your child's preferences are based only on intangible "gut" feelings, respect those feelings and take them into consideration if you're picking a middle or upper school. For children entering kindergarten and elementary school, you'll have to do all the decision making.

Regardless of your child's age, it's a good idea to apply to more than one school, if possible—the "perfect" ones you most want your child to attend and one or two "safety" schools you're sure will accept your child.

Before leaving each school, don't hesitate to ask the admissions representative about your child's chances of admission and whether it will be worthwhile applying. If you're told the chances are poor, ask whether the admissions representative can suggest other schools more likely to admit your child.

If the school encourages your application and says your child's chances of admission are good, find out how much time after submitting your application the school takes to inform you of your child's status.

Beware, however, of overeager admissions representatives ready to admit your child on the spot. Unless the school is one of the strongest academically and financially and your child is clearly gifted or has measurably outstanding talents, the admissions representative may simply be trying to find paying bodies to fill and support a financially shaky school. An overeager admissions person who is obviously trying to sell you a school should be cause for a careful check of the school's finances. If you are a prep school or college graduate, ask people you know at your old schools if they can get you additional information about the current condition and reputation of the school you're considering.

Educational Consultants

If, after you've completed your evaluation, you find you're unable to develop a list of schools you consider appropriate for your child, you may want to ask an educational consultant to do the job for you. There may be many of them listed in the telephone book, because anyone can set up as an educational consultant. There are no licensing or certification procedures or professional qualifications. So, *only use a consultant who is a member of The Independent Educational Consultants Association* (IECA). IECA membersip is the only assurance you have of a consultant's professional qualifications. To get the names of consultants in your area or to check whether someone you're considering is a member in good standing, contact IECA in Forestdale, Massachusetts. Tel: (508) 477–2127.

Consultants often charge $1,000 or more. Most have an intimate knowledge of almost all the private schools listed in Appendix B. Most conduct preliminary interviews with parents by telephone, then invite you and your child to their offices, where they'll ask almost all the questions this book has asked. Some may also test your child before matching him or her up with schools they believe will be most appropriate for you to visit. They'll set up the visits for you, and then you and your child will still have to go through the entire admissions process—interviews, tours, etc.—described in the last chapter.

The advantage of good educational consultants is that they'll save you the work of preliminary evaluation and send you to schools where your child will have the best chances of admission. Admission won't be guaranteed, however, and no honest consultant will ever give you such a guarantee. Indeed, one or two of the schools your consultant recommends might reject your child. But there is always a possibility that all the schools your consultant recommends will accept your child—which will leave you and your child with some happy choices to make.

A Final Word

Applying

Filling out and filing an application is the simplest step in picking a school for your child. Figure 4 is a typical application. As you can see, the application represents a mere formality. It's your visit to each school and the interviews and tests that represent the heart of the admissions process.

Don't forget to enclose the required application fee, which can run as high as $50. Then, all you can do is wait for a reply. If your child is accepted, you'll be expected to send a deposit before a specific date. It's always best to send it by registered mail to assure its getting there and holding your child's seat in the coming school year. The rest of the tuition for the first semester will be due in August, and payment for the second semester will be due in December.

During the summer, your child will have to have a complete physical examination, and you'll have to send the school a doctor's certification that your child is in good health and has had all the required shots.

Responsibilities of Private School Parents

If your child is accepted by, and enrolls in, private school, both your child and you—and the rest of the family, for that matter—will enter a new educational and social world unknown to (indeed unimagined by) the vast majority of Americans, whose children routinely attend public schools. Most have never seen or even heard of America's most prestigious private schools. Most respond with blank stares at the mention of such names as Exeter, Hotchkiss or even Collegiate, which is said to be the oldest school in America—older even than Harvard! And that's because the world of private schools is so far removed from the lives of most Americans.

Attending public school is every American child's right. Attending private school, however, is a privilege. It is important never to forget this key difference, or to permit your child to forget it. It is tragic, but true, that private school now represents one of the few ways of assuring your child a good education, which most Americans once assumed was not only their right but was available in all public schools.

In addition to an unexcelled educational opportunity, enrollment in a private school will mean your child will join a private club. Some of these "clubs" can often ease entry into the most selective colleges and universities and into the halls of power and leadership in business, industry, government and the professions. Membership in such clubs often lasts a lifetime, and can produce deep friendships and associations that last equally long.

Figure 4. A typical private school application form. Unlike those used in the college application process, application forms for elementary and secondary schools are relatively simple formalities at the end of a mutual evaluation process for families and schools.

APPLICATION FOR
ADMISSION

APPLICATION FOR ADMISSION FOR THE YEAR BEGINNING SEPTEMBER 19

NAME

| FOR GRADE | BOARDING | DAY | M or F |

A Final Word

CANDIDATE

NAME OF STUDENT (FIRST)   (MIDDLE)   (LAST)   (NICKNAME)

NAME OF PARENTS OR GUARDIANS (INCLUDE FIRST NAME OF MOTHER)

HOME ADDRESS

TOWN OR CITY   ZIP CODE   TELEPHONE (AREA CODE)

NUMBER OF YEARS AT THIS ADDRESS

FULL NAME OF SCHOOL DISTRICT IN WHICH YOU CURRENTLY RESIDE

CANDIDATE'S FATHER	CANDIDATE'S MOTHER
NAME (FIRST) (MIDDLE) (LAST)	NAME (FIRST) (MAIDEN NAME) (LAST)
HOME ADDRESS	HOME ADDRESS
HOME TELEPHONE (AREA CODE)	HOME TELEPHONE (AREA CODE)
EMPLOYER	EMPLOYER
NATURE OF BUSINESS	NATURE OF BUSINESS
ADDRESS	ADDRESS
(ZIP CODE)	(ZIP CODE)
BUSINESS TELEPHONE	BUSINESS TELEPHONE
POSITION IN FIRM	POSITION IN FIRM
PROFESSIONAL SCHOOL(S) (DEGREE AND DATE)	PROFESSIONAL SCHOOL(S) (DEGREE AND DATE)
COLLEGE(S) (NAME AND DATE)	COLLEGE(S) (NAME AND DATE)

CANDIDATE'S NATURAL PARENTS ARE: ☐ MARRIED   ☐ SEPARATED   ☐ DIVORCED   ☐ FATHER DECEASED   ☐ MOTHER DECEASED

CANDIDATE LIVES WITH: ☐ PARENTS   ☐ FATHER   ☐ MOTHER   ☐ GUARDIAN   ☐ OTHER

ADDRESS TO WHOM ALL CORRESPONDENCE, BILLS AND NOTICES SHOULD BE SENT

ADDRESS (IF DIFFERENT FROM ABOVE)

NAME AND RELATIONSHIP OF ANY FRIENDS/RELATIVES WHO HAVE ATTENDED HACKLEY SCHOOL

STUDENT'S DATE OF BIRTH   HEIGHT   WEIGHT   PHYSICAL CONDITION

STUDENT'S CURRENT SCHOOL   TOWN

ADDRESS OF SCHOOL   ZIP CODE

FULL NAME OF SCHOOL DISTRICT IN WHICH YOU PRESENTLY RESIDE

Please list all other schools attended, starting with kindergarten, and give dates:

SCHOOL   CITY   DATES OF ATTENDANCE

(CONTINUE ON LAST PAGE IF NECESSARY.)

NAMES, AGES AND CURRENT SCHOOLS OF BROTHERS AND SISTERS:

Has the applicant ever been subject to major disciplinary action (suspension, dismissal, probation) in any school? ☐ Yes ☐ No
If yes, please explain on last page.

Has the applicant been under continuing care for any physical or emotional difficulty? ☐ Yes ☐ No
If yes, please give dates and details on last page.

Please list all extracurricular activities, other than sports, in which the applicant has been involved in the past year. Underline those in which he has been officer.

Please list sports in which the applicant has participated in order of preference, and underline those in which he has played on organized teams.

Please list hobbies which the applicant pursues, in order of preference.

What are the reasons for your application to Hackley?

PLEASE TURN PAGE.

A Final Word

Have you had an interview at the Hackley School this year?   ☐ Parents   ☐ Candidate
(if not, please arrange one when submitting this application.)

Have arrangements been made for a School visit?   ☐ Yes   ☐ No

Have arrangements been made to take the admissions test?   ☐ Yes   ☐ No

Is applicant applying for financial aid?   ☐ Yes   ☐ No
*(If yes, a statement of school policy and procedure will be sent to you.
Aid is based on "need plus merit" and applications are processed through The School Scholarship Service.)*

DATE OF APPLICATION   PARENT'S SIGNATURE

Please return this form, with a nonrefundable $30.00 application fee (fee includes testing at Hackley) payable to Hackley School, to:

Director of Admissions
Hackley School
293 Benedict Avenue
Tarrytown, New York 10591

131

Flagrant violation of private-school rules, however, can mean swift expulsion from that club and ostracism by one's mates. Don't even think or let your child think in terms of rights at private school, for there is only one right: to obey the school's rules and do the work demanded.

As a private club, a private school adopts rules set by a majority of members, who have the right to set any rules they choose—regardless of whether nonmembers agree or not. A boys' school does not have to admit girls if it doesn't want to, and girls' schools do not have to admit boys. They are private!

Always remember, then, that it was you and your child who knocked at the school's doors asking for membership—not vice versa. It is important to understand this concept before enrolling your child and that you agree with and support it. And it's important always to make the concept clear to your child throughout his or her school career.

If there are rules, regulations or basic elements of a school's educational philosophy with which you disagree, don't waste time or energy trying to change them. You will only succeed in producing turmoil in your child's educational life at a time when a calm environment is required for success.

Many private schools have survived a century or more and are the way they are because those who *own* them—the alumni, their *elected* representatives on the boards of trustees and their appointed administrators and faculty—want their schools to be that way. And they have that right. Again, they are private! So, if you disagree with the way a school is run, *don't enroll your child!* If you do, be prepared to "buy into the school" and make its values, its educational philosophy and its rules and regulations your own.

In every sense, parents must be as one with the private schools in which they enroll their children. And if, after a year or two, you find yourself disillusioned by, and in strong disagreement with, the school, transfer your child to another school.

Ensuring Your Child's Success

To help your child succeed academically at every level of any demanding private school, it's important to monitor your child's schoolwork—to know what your child is doing at school and, therefore, what he or she should be doing at home. Depending on the grade, homework in private school can take up a child's entire evening, every weekday night, and usually a half day over the weekend. Making certain your child has done the required work is a primary obligation of parents of all private-school students other than those at boarding schools. For younger children, that means not just accepting their word, but actually checking that the homework has been done carefully, completely and correctly. In other words, parents should, if possible, supplement the teaching at school with some teaching of their own at home to help their children learn.

And when your child comes home and insists, as all children do from time to time, that there is no homework, call the teacher to find out. To avoid such confrontations, the best practice is to ask the teacher at the beginning of the term what his or her homework practices are. Many teachers provide parents, as well as students, with regular homework assignment schedules to avoid such confrontations. The schedules also let parents know in advance when their children should be studying for forthcoming quizzes and examinations.

Another major factor in a child's academic success at school is the cultural level of the child's home. Children whose homes are filled with books and whose parents read to them each night when they're young invariably do better at school. Try also to enrich your child's life and supplement and reinforce education at school with trips to museums, theaters, concert halls and other cultural attractions.

Above all, do not diminish or belittle the importance of academics in any way. To pull a child out of school for something as frivolous as a sports event or a family vacation is to send an educationally destructive message to that child—i.e., that playing is more important than learning, hard work and fulfilling one's responsibilities.

Another way to spur your child on to academic success is to teach the concept that hard work is the most important factor in academic achievement. Few demanding private schools will excuse poor school performance on the basis of a child's having no aptitude in a particular area. Nor will they tolerate such student assertions as "the work is too hard" or "the teacher is too strict" or "I don't understand the work." The rule for private-school students is to work harder when they do poorly and to keep studying until they do understand or to ask the teacher for extra help.

Another key to a child's success at school is consistent expectations. That means that, in addition to continual supervision of, and involvement with, their children's academic work, private-school parents are expected to monitor their children's behavior and social conduct at home and everywhere else out of school to support the school's rules, regulations and behavioral expectations.

Still another element in any child's success is good health. It's important that your child get enough sleep and has a proper diet. Private school is far more demanding physically as well as intellectually than public school, where children may spend many idle hours during the day doing absolutely nothing but "hanging out." Not so in private schools, where they're kept active almost every minute of the day, with classes in the morning and required sports participation in the afternoon.

So check on the school's and your pediatrician's recommendations—especially for younger children. Then set and enforce the rules for sleeping and eating, and don't simply "let nature take its course." The degree of concentration and the amount of work required in private school is too great to allow children to decide what's best for them. Indeed, the entire theory of private-school education is based on the notion that children do *not* know what's best for them and that the role of wise parents and educators is to teach them what is best.

That's why it's important, too, to limit TV viewing—your own as well as your child's. You cannot expect your child's top priority to be academics if the top priority of the rest of the family is television.

If sending your child to private school sounds like hard work for you as well as your child, it is! The private-school parent has far more responsibilities than the parent of a public-school child. In simplest terms, private-school parents cannot allow their children to "drift" through school. Drifting in demanding private schools inevitably results in failure and dismissal. The only way to ensure success at any demanding private school is to provide each child with constant supervision and guidance by a team of caring adults that includes parents, teachers, faculty advisors, coaches and school officials—all acting as *one!*

Financial Responsibilities

As mentioned earlier, private school represents an enormous financial investment—probably $150,000 over the 13 years from kindergarten through 12th grade. Kindergarten tuition at many schools ranges up to $7,500. Annual costs of succeeding grades at day schools are now approaching $15,000, while tuition, room and board at some boarding schools is more than $20,000 a year. Books and school supplies can add several hundred dollars more; athletic equipment still more hundreds of dollars; lunches at day schools, another $500 to $750 a year; and other fees such accident insurance, fees for special class or school trips, another $250. In addition, costs of clothes for children at schools with dress codes can easily add $1,000 or more to annual costs, depending on how quickly your child grows.

And even these enormous outlays will not cover the entire, actual costs of educating your child. Indeed, the fees you'll pay will only cover about 60% to 90%, at most, of the costs of your child's education. The school your child attends, in other words, will spend more, often far more, than you actually pay it to educate your child—even if your child gets no scholarship and you pay the full price demanded of you.

A Final Word

There are several reasons for this deficit: The first is the cost of building, improving and expanding the physical plant—i.e., the capital costs, which are necessarily spread over many decades, but nevertheless shared by every parent of every generation of school child. Secondly, there are the costs of new programs—for example, a costly but essential salary increase or health insurance scheme for faculty and staff. And finally, all schools have worthy scholarship students who add to the school in so many other ways that the school feels it worthwhile for others to pay all or part of the costs of their education.

As we saw earlier, the financial gap between what you pay to educate your child and the actual costs is covered with funds from two sources—income from the school's endowment and voluntary gifts from loyal alumni, past parents who are grateful for what the school did for their children, and current parents who support the school and what it stands for.

So, the school will ask you to make voluntary financial (and tax-deductible) contributions each year, over and above the tuition and other fees you'll be required to pay. The annual fund-raising campaigns often come as a shock to parents new to private-school education and unaware that their huge tuition payments are not enough to cover school operating costs.

If you can afford to contribute to your child's school's annual fund-raising campaign, by all means do so. Supporting that effort by contributing and helping to raise funds is every private-school parent's responsibility. Most parents know this. Most realize that such funds are the only way to preserve what is the last bastion of decent education in the United States.

Besides annual fund-raising, most schools also solicit capital gifts from the school "family" to replace or improve the physical plant, to build new facilities, to improve existing programs or add new ones and to build the endowment fund.

In addition to financial contributions, most private schools will also ask you to contribute your time to the school. Unlike public schools, private schools are unburdened by layers of administrators and bureaucrats who siphon off moneys better spent on good teachers and teaching materials. So private schools usually ask parents to help organize special cultural and fund-raising events at school. Parents may be asked to help supervise or drive students on class or team trips; to buy advertising in the school newspaper or yearbook; to provide or appear as unpaid speakers or performers at school; to help youngsters get summer jobs; and to help the school and its students, graduates and faculty in any way possible, including serving on parents' organizations and even, possibly, on the board of trustees.

In every respect, enrolling in a good private school means joining an extended family and assuming many of the responsibilities that go with any

135

family membership. And if you find the perfect private school for your child, you'll also find that, as in any family, the more you contribute, the more rewards your child will reap.

The private school tradition in America goes back more than three centuries, to the earliest era of the colonies, more than 200 years before Americans even envisioned the concept of "free," or public, schools. The private schools of America have produced generation after generation of American leaders, from Nathan Hale to George Bush. Generations of the same families have attended and supported individual schools because of the consistently high standards of education and ethical values these schools and their faculties have maintained.

The gratitude and loyalty felt by alumni and their parents for that education and for the entire private-school experience is evident in their strong, lifelong support—both emotional and financial.

I hope you'll find as perfect a private school to help you raise and educate your child as I did for my son. And good luck!

APPENDIX A

PRIVATE SCHOOL EVALUATION FORM

*U*se the form below as a broad guide for evaluating each private school you consider for your child. Make as many copies as you need so that you have one form for each school, and can compare them side by side. In the left-hand margin in each section, write the questions you feel will most evoke the information you need to see if a school will meet the needs of your child. Copy any questions from the pages of this book that you think are appropriate and jot down your own questions.

Practical Considerations

1. Location

2. Grades taught

3. Type of school (mark appropriate categories)

   A. College prep

     i. Day

     ii. Boarding

   B. Religious

     i. Day

     ii. Boarding

   C. Military

     i. Day

     ii. Boarding

   D. Special needs (specify: _____
_____)

     i. Day

     ii. Boarding

4. Gender

   A. Coed

   B. All girls

   C. All boys

5. Financial aid

Evaluation Standards

1. Accreditation

    A. Regional accreditation association

    B. NAIS (see Appendix B)

2. Educational philosophy

    A. Educational goals

    B. Teaching methods

    C. Student support

    D. Depth of education

    E. Type of student

        i. Gifted

        ii. Gifted + average

        iii. Average

        iv. Underachievers

        v. Special needs

            a. Special gifts

            b. Learning disabilities

            c. Postgraduates

    F. Behavioral controls

        i. Dress code

        ii. Rules and regulations (strict, average, relaxed, etc.)

        iii. Ethical and moral training

    G. Leadership training

    H. Relative emphasis

        i. Academics

        ii. Athletics

        iii. Extracurricular activities

        iv. Special needs

        v. Community service

3. Educational results

    A. Range of scores on standardized achievement tests

    B. Range of SAT scores

    C. AP courses

        i. Percent of students enrolled

        ii. Range of scores

    D. Colleges attending

4. Faculty quality

    A. M.A.'s

    B. Doctorates

    C. Majors vs. subjects taught

    D. Average tenure

    E. Salaries

    F. Perks

Appendix A

5. Financial strength and stability

  A. Operating results (deficits, etc.)

  B. Endowment

  C. Income

    i. Tuition and fees

    ii. Endowment

    iii. Annual giving

  D. Significant structural changes

    i. Enrollment

    ii. Academic results

    iii. Composition of student body

    iv. Faculty size

    v. Student/teacher ratios and loads

    vi. Size, scope of curricular & extracurricular offerings

6. Academic strength

  A. Is learning taking place, and how?

    i. Independent student work

    ii. Interconnection of subjects

  B. Motivational tools (effort grades, etc.)

  C. How will school help your child reach potential?

7. Physical plant

  A. Neighborhood

  B. School grounds

  C. Buildings

    i. Exteriors

    ii. Interiors

      a. Hallways

      b. Classrooms

      c. Dormitory bedrooms

      d. Washrooms

      e. Locker/cloakroom facilities

      f. Cafeteria

      g. Health care (nurse's office/infirmary)

  D. Academic facilities

    i. Classrooms

    ii. Science laboratories

    iii. Computer labs

    iv. Library

  E. Athletic facilities

    i. Sports offered (list)

      a. Boys

      b. Girls

    ii. Playing areas

139

iii. Changing rooms/shower areas

iv. Equipment

F. Extracurricular activities (list; describe facilities)

G. Safety

  i. Building

    a. Fire prevention and evacuation provisions

    b. Asbestos abatement and lead-free water

  ii. Equipment

  iii. Precautions against intruders

    a. On school grounds

    b. School perimeter, neighborhood, in transit

  iv. Sexual safety

    a. Against molestation and "date rape"

    b. Against AIDS

  v. Drug and alcohol prevention

8. School personality

  A. Hallway atmosphere (art on walls, etc.)

  B. Children's attitudes

  C. Teacher attitudes

  D. Teacher-student interaction

  E. Classroom atmosphere

Conclusion

What makes this school different from other, similar schools?

1. _____

_____

2. _____

_____

3. _____

_____

4. _____

_____

APPENDIX B

MEMBER SCHOOLS OF THE NATIONAL ASSOCIATION OF INDEPENDENT SCHOOLS

CONTENTS

EXPLANATION OF TERMS

Boarding schools: Schools in which at least 95% are full-time boarders, and the rest are day students.

Boarding/day schools: Schools in which 50% to 94% are full-time boarders, and the rest are day students.

Day/boarding schools: Schools in which fewer than half are boarders, and day students make up between 51% and 94% of the student body.

PG students: Postgraduate students who have graduated from high school but are, for whatever reason, repeating their senior year.

(For further information about NAIS or its member schools, call or write The National Association of Independent Schools, 1800 M Street N.W., Suite 460 South, Washington, DC 20036. Tel: [202] 833-4757.)

Member Schools of the National Association of Independent Schools
(Alphabetically by state, and by city within each state)

.

Alabama

Advent Episcopal Day School
Birmingham   (205) 252-2535
Preschool–8th grade
Coed day school—332 students

The Altamont School
Birmingham   (205) 879-2006
5th–12th grade
Coed day school—295 students

Highlands Day School
Birmingham   (205) 256-9731
Preschool–7th grade
Coed day school—294 students

Lyman Ward Military Academy
Camp Hill   (205) 896-4127
6th–12th grade
Boys' boarding—172 students

Bayside Academy
Daphne   (205) 626-2840
Preschool–12th grade
Coed day school—325 students

Houston Academy
Dothan   (205) 794-4106
Preschool–12th grade
Coed day school—464 students

Indian Springs School
Helena   (205) 988-3350
8th–12th grade (PG)
Coed day/boarding—244 students

Randolph School
Huntsville   (205) 881-1701
K–12th grade
Coed day school—476 students

Springwood School
Lanett   (205) 644-2191
K–12th grade
Coed day school—290 students

St. Luke's Episcopal School
Mobile   (205) 666-2991
Preschool–8th grade
Coed day school—482 students

St. Paul's Episcopal School
Mobile   (205) 342-6700
Preschool–12th grade
Coed day school—1,342 students

UMS-Wright Preparatory School
Mobile   (205) 479-6551
Preschool–12th grade
Coed day school—1,040 students

The Montgomery Academy
Montgomery   (205) 272-8210
K–12th grade
Coed day school—728 students

Arizona

The Orme School
Mayer   (602) 632-7601
8th–12th grade
Coed boarding—132 students

All Saints' Episcopal Day School
Phoenix   (602) 274-4866
K–8th grade
Coed day school—387 students

Phoenix Country Day School
Phoenix   (602) 955-8200
Preschool–12th grade
Coed day school—540 students

The Judson School
Scottsdale   (602) 948-7731
K–12th grade (PG)
Coed boarding/day—305 students

Arkansas

Pulaski Academy
Little Rock   (501) 225-9320

California

Redwood Day School
Alameda   (510) 865-8464
K–8th grade
Coed day school—178 students

Cornelia Connelly School
Anaheim   (714) 776-1717
9th–12th grade
Girls' day—147 students

Tuscaloosa Academy
Tuscaloosa   (205) 758-4462
Preschool–12th grade
Coed day school—456 students

Verde Valley School
Sedona   (602) 284-2272
9th–12th grade(PG)
Coed boarding/day—69 students

The Fenster School of Southern
   Arizona
Tucson   (602) 749-3340
9th–12th grade
Coed boarding/day—50 students

Green Fields Country Day School
Tucson   (602) 297-2288
4th–12th grade
Coed day school—173 students

St. Gregory College Prep. School
Tucson   (602) 327-6395
7th–12th grade
Coed day school—260 students

Preschool–12th grade
Coed day school—925 students

Menlo School
Atherton   (415) 688-3863
7th–12th grade
Coed day school—448 students

Sacred Heart Schools
Atherton   (415) 322-1866
Preschool–12th grade
Coed day school—693 students

East Bay French-American School
Berkeley   (510) 549-3867
Preschool–8th grade
Coed day school—404 students

Viewpoint School
Calabasas   (818) 340-2901
Preschool–12th grade
Coed day school—506 students

Army and Navy Academy
Carlsbad   (619) 729-2385
7th–12th grade
Boys' boarding/day—274 students

Cate School
Carpinteria   (805) 684-4127
9th–12th grade
Coed boarding/day—245 students

Foothill Country Day School
Claremont   (714) 626-5681
K–8th grade
Coed day school—180 students

The Webb Schools
Claremont   (714) 626-3587
9th–12th grade
Coed boarding/day—371 students

Harbor Day School
Corona del Mar   (714) 640-1410
K–8th grade
Coed day school—396 students

Marin Country Day School
Corte Madera   (415) 924-3743
K–8th grade
Coed day school—495 students

The Athenian School
Danville   (510) 837-5375

6th–12th grade
Coed day/boarding—244 students

East Bay Sierra School
El Cerrito   (415) 527-4714
K–6th grade
Coed day school—272 students

Crystal Springs Uplands School
Hillsborough   (415) 342-4175
6th–12th grade
Coed day school—344 students

Nueva Center for Learning
Hillsborough   (415) 348-2272
Preschool–8th grade
Coed day school—289 students

Idyllwild School of Music/Art
Idyllwild   (714) 659-2171
7th–12th grade (PG)
Coed boarding/day—114 students

Flintridge Preparatory School
La Canada   (818) 790-1178
7th–12th grade
Coed day school—511 students

The Bishop's School
La Jolla   (619) 459-4021
7th–12th grade
Coed day school—609 students

La Jolla Country Day School
La Jolla   (619) 453-3440
Preschool–12th grade
Coed day school—768 students

Brentwood School
Los Angeles   (213) 476-9633
7th–12th grade
Coed day school—480 students

Curtis School Foundation
Los Angeles   (310) 476-1251
K–8th grade
Coed day school—516 students

The John Thomas Dye School
Los Angeles   (310) 476-2811
Preschool–6th grade
Coed day school—3,313 students

Marlborough School
Los Angeles   (213) 935-1147
7th–12th grade
Girls' day—498 students

Marymount High School
Los Angeles   (310) 472-1205
9th–12th grade
Girls' day—304 students

Pilgrim School
Los Angeles   (213) 385-7351
K–12th grade
Coed day school—606 students

St. James' School, Wilshire
Los Angeles   (213) 382-2315
K–6th grade
Coed day school—310 students

Turningpoint
Los Angeles   (310) 476-8585
Preschool–7th grade
Coed day school—149 students

Windward School
Los Angeles   (310) 391-7127
7th–12th grade
Coed day school—288 students

Hillbrook School
Los Gatos   (408) 356-6116

Preschool–8th grade
Coed day school—278 students

Dunn School
Los Olivos   (805) 688-6471
6th–12th grade
Coed day/boarding—169 students

Midland School
Los Olivos   (805) 688-5114
9th–12th grade
Coed boarding—75 students

Phillips Brooks School
Menlo Park   (415) 854-4545
Preschool–6th grade
Coed day school—212 students

Mount Tamalpais School
Mill Valley   (415) 383-9434
K–8th grade
Coed day school—240 students

Santa Catalina School
Monterey   (408) 655-9372
Preschool–12th grade
Girls' day/boarding—489 students

The York School
Monterey   (408) 372-7338
8th–12th grade
Coed day school—202 students

John Woolman School
Nevada City   (916) 273-3183
9th–12th grade (PG)
Coed day/boarding—35 students

Campbell Hall
North Hollywood   (818) 980-7280
K–12th grade
Coed day school—734 students

Harvard-Westlake School
North Hollywood   (310) 980-6692
7th–12th grade
Coed day school—1,534 students

Oakwood School
North Hollywood   (818) 766-5177
K–12th grade
Coed day school—574 students

The College Preparatory School
Oakland   (510) 652-0111
9th–12th grade
Coed day school—298 students

The Head-Royce School
Oakland   (510) 531-1300
K–12th grade
Coed day school—578 students

St. Paul's School
Oakland   (510) 451-4356
K–8th grade
Coed day school—168 students

Happy Valley School
Ojai   (805) 646-4343
9th–12th grade
Coed boarding/day—70 students

The Oak Grove School
Ojai   (805) 646-8236
Preschool–12th grade
Coed day/boarding—141 students

Ojai Valley School
Ojai   (805) 646-1423
K–12th grade
Coed boarding/day—239 students

The Thacher School
Ojai   (805) 646-4377

9th–12th grade
Coed boarding/day—225 students

St. Matthew's Parish School
Pacific Palisades   (310) 454-1358
Preschool–8th grade
Coed day school—312 students

The Palm Valley School
Palm Springs   (619) 328-0861
K–12th grade
Coed day school—200 students

Castilleja School
Palo Alto   (415) 328-3160
7th–12th grade
Girls' day/boarding—308 students

Keys School
Palo Alto   (415) 328-1711
K–6th grade
Coed day school—147 students

Chadwick School
Palos Verdes Peninsula
(310) 377-1543
K–12th grade
Coed day school—719 students

Polytechnic School
Pasadena   (818) 792-2147
Preschool–12th grade
Coed day school—822 students

The Chandler School
Pasadena   (818) 795-9314
K–8th grade
Coed day school—428 students

Mayfield Junior School
Pasadena   (818) 796-2774
K–8th grade
Coed day school—415 students

Appendix B

Mayfield Senior School
Pasadena (818) 799-9121
9th–12th grade
Girls' day school—237 students

Westridge School
Pasadena (818) 799-1153
4th–12th grade
Girls' day school—387 students

Robert Louis Stevenson School
Pebble Beach (408) 624-1257
9th–12th grade
Coed day/boarding—499 students

Woodside Priory School
Portola Valley (415) 851-8221
7th–12th grade
Boys' day/boarding—107 students

Valley Preparatory School
Redlands (714) 793-3063
Preschool–6th grade
Coed day school—251 students

The Branson School
Ross (415) 454-3612
9th–12th grade
Coed day school—320 students

Sacramento Country Day School
Sacramento (916) 481-8811
Preschool–12th grade
Coed day school—442 students

San Domenico School
San Anselmo (415) 454-0200
Preschool–12th grade
Girls' day/boarding—442 students

All Saints' Episcopal School
San Diego (619) 298-1671
Preschool–8th grade
Coed day school—107 students

Francis W. Parker School
San Diego (619) 569-7900
Preschool–12th grade
Coed day school—946 students

Cathedral School for Boys
San Francisco (415) 771-6600
K–8th grade
Boys' day school—184 students

French American International
  School
San Francisco (415) 626-8564
K–12th grade
Coed day school—447 students

The Hamlin School
San Francisco (415) 922-0300
K–8th grade
Girls' day school—351 students

Katherine Delmar Burke School
San Francisco (425) 751-0177
K–8th grade
Girls' day school—359 students

Lick-Wilmerding High School
San Francisco (415) 333-4021
9th–12th grade
Coed day school—330 students

San Francisco Day School
San Francisco (415) 931-2422
K–8th Grade
Coed day school—391 students

San Francisco University High
  School
San Francisco   (415) 346-8400
9th–12th grade
Coed day school—385 students

Schools of the Sacred Heart
San Francisco   (415) 563-2900
Preschool–12th grade
Girls' day school—803 students

Town School for Boys
San Francisco   (415) 921-3747
K–8th grade
Boys' day school—393 students

The Urban School/San Francisco
San Francisco   (415) 626-2919
9th–12th grade
Coed day school—175 students

Clairbourn School
San Gabriel   (818) 286-3108
Preschool–8th grade
Coed day school—404 students

Marin Academy
San Rafael   (415) 453-4550
9th–12th grade
Coed day school—278 students

Saint Mark's School
San Rafael   (415) 472-7911

K–8th grade
Coed day school—303 students

Crane School
Santa Barbara   (805) 969-7732
K–8th grade
Coed day school—215 students

Laguna Blanca School
Santa Barbara   (805) 687-2461
K–12th grade
Coed day school—258 students

Crossroads School for Arts &
  Sciences
Santa Monica   (310) 829-7391
K–12th grade
Coed day school—847 students

Wildwood School
Santa Monica   (213) 828-4431
K–6th grade
Coed day school—255 students

Sonoma Country Day School
Santa Rosa   (707) 575-7115
K–8th grade
Coed day school—167 students

Center for Early Education
West Hollywood   (213) 651-0707
Preschool–6th grade
Coed day school—464 students

Colorado

The Aspen Country Day School
Aspen   (303) 925-1909
Preschool–12th grade
Coed day school—141 students

St. Scholastica Academy
Canon City   (719) 275-7461
7th–12th grade
Girls' boarding/day—104 students

Appendix B

The Colorado Rocky Mountain
School
Carbondale   (303) 963-2562
Preschool–12th grade
Coed boarding/day—172 students

The Colorado Springs School
Colorado Springs   (719) 475-9747
K–12th grade
Coed day/boarding—182 students

Fountain Valley School
Colorado Springs   (719) 390-7035
9th–12th grade
Coed boarding/day—213 students

Colorado Academy
Denver   (303) 986-1501
Preschool–12th grade
Coed day school—589 students

Garland Country Day School
Denver   (303) 399-0390
K–9th grade
Coed day school—589 students

St. Anne's Episcopal School
Denver   (303) 756-9481

Preschool–8th grade
Coed day school—403 students

Theodor Herzl Jewish Day School
Denver   (303) 755-1846
K–6th grade
Coed day school—277 students

Kent Denver School
Englewood   (303) 770-7660
6th–12th grade
Coed day school—496 students

St. Mary's Academy
Englewood   (303) 762-8300
Preschool–12th grade
Girls' day school—696 students

The Whiteman School
Steamboat Springs
(303) 879-1350
9th–12th grade
Coed boarding/day—63 students

Vail Mountain School
Vail   (303) 476-3850
K–12th grade
Coed day school—179 students

Connecticut

Avon Old Farms School
Avon   (203) 673-3201
9th–12th grade (PG)
Boys' boarding/day—387 students

The Woodhall School
Bethlehem   (203) 266-7788
9th–12th grade (PG)
Boys' boarding—31 students

Wightwood School
Branford   (203) 481-0363
Preschool–8th grade
Coed day school—95 students

Cheshire Academy
Cheshire   (203) 272-5396
6th–12th grade (PG)
Coed boarding/day—225 students

The Marvelwood School
Cornwall   (203) 672-6612
9th–12th grade
Coed boarding day—100 students

Wooster School
Danbury   (203) 743-6311
6th–12th grade
Coed day school—150 students

Fairfield Country Day School
Fairfield   (203) 259-2723
K–9th grade
Boys' day school—196 students

The Unquowa School
Fairfield   (203) 336-3801
Preschool–8th grade
Coed day school—165 students

Miss Porter's School
Farmington   (203) 677-1321
9th–12th grade
Girls' boarding/day—263 students

Greens Farms Academy
Greens Farms   (203) 255-1556
K–12th grade
Coed day school—479 students

Brunswick School
Greenwich   (203) 869-0601
Preschool–12th grade
Boys' day school—558 students

Convent of the Sacred Heart
Greenwich   (203) 531-6500
Preschool–12th grade
Girls' day school—310 students

Greenwich Academy
Greenwich   (203) 869-4020

Preschool–12th grade
Girls' day school—561 students

Greenwich Country Day School
Greenwich   (203) 622-8500
Preschool–9th grade
Coed day school—727 students

The Mead School
Greenwich   (203) 637-3800
Preschool–8th grade
Coed day school—219 students

Whitby School—American
Montessori
Greenwich   (203) 869-8464
Preschool–9th grade
Coed day school—235 students

Hamden Hall Country Day School
Hamden   (203) 865-6158
Preschool–12th grade
Coed day school—584 students

The Institute of Living School
Hartford   (203) 241-6923
1st–12th grade
Coed day/boarding—86 students

Watkinson School
Hartford   (203) 236-5618
6th–12th grade
Coed day school—214 students

Mooreland Hill School
Kensington   (203) 223-6428
6th–9th grade
Coed day school—81 students

Kent School
Kent   (203) 927-3501
9th–12th grade (PG)
Coed boarding—524 students

Appendix B

The Hotchkiss School
Lakeville (203) 435-2591
9th–12th grade (PG)
Coed boarding/day—535 students

Indian Mountain School
Lakeville (203) 435-0871
5th–9th grade
Coed day/boarding—145 students

The Forman School
Litchfield (203) 567-8712
9th–12th grade
Coed boarding/day—221 students

The Country School
Madison (203) 421-3113
Preschool–8th grade
Coed day school—159 students

Westover School
Middlebury (203) 758-2423
9th–12th grade
Girls' boarding/day—164 students

The Independent Day School
Middlefield (203) 347-7235
Preschool–8th grade
Coed day school—216 students

Academy of Our Lady of Mercy
Milford (203) 877-2786
9th–12th grade
Girls' day school—432 students

New Canaan Country School
New Canaan (203) 972-0771
K–9th grade
Coed day school—492 students

St. Luke's School
New Canaan (203) 966-5612

6th–12th grade
Coed day school—250 students

The Foote School
New Haven (203) 777-3463
K–9th grade
Coed day school—420 students

Hopkins School
New Haven (203) 397-1001
7th–12th grade
Coed day school—545 students

The Williams School
New London (203) 443-5333
7th–12th grade
Coed day school—255 students

Canterbury School
New Milford (203) 355-3103
9th–12th grade (PG)
Coed boarding/day—301 students

Washington Montessori School
New Preston (203) 868-0551
Preschool–8th grade
Coed day school—205 students

Pomfret School
Pomfret (203) 928-7731
9th–12th grade
Coed boarding/day—301 students

The Rectory School
Pomfret (203) 928-7759
6th–9th grade
Boys' boarding/day—136 students

Salisbury School
Salisbury (203) 435-2531
9th–12th grade (PG)
Boys' boarding/day—233 students

The Ethel Walker School
Simsbury   (203) 658-4467
7th–12th grade (PG)
Girls' boarding/day—150 students

Westminster School
Simsbury   (203) 658-4444
9th–12th grade (PG)
Coed boarding/day—342 students

South Kent School
South Kent   (203) 927-3539
9th–12th grade (PG)
Boys' boarding—150 students

King & Low-Heywood Thomas
   School
Stamford   (203) 322-3413
Preschool–12th grade
Coed day school—463 students

The Long Ridge School
Stamford   (203) 322-7693
Preschool–5th grade
Coed day school—88 students

Pine Point School
Stonington   (203) 535-0606
K–9th grade
Coed day school—222 students

Suffield Academy
Suffield   (203) 688-7315
9th–12th grade (PG)
Coed boarding/day—293 students

Choate Rosemary Hall
Wallingford   (203) 269-7722
9th–12th grade (PG)
Coed boarding/day—1,020 students

The Gunnery
Washington   (203) 868-7334
9th–12th grade (PG)
Coed boarding/day—204 students

Rumsey Hall School
Washington Depot
(203) 868-0535
3rd–9th grade
Coed boarding/day—185 students

Saint Margaret's-McTernan School
Waterbury   (203) 757-9891
K–12th grade
Coed day school—396 students

The Taft School
Watertown   (203) 274-2516
9th–12th grade (PG)
Coed boarding/day—541 students

Kingswood-Oxford School
West Hartford   (203) 233-9631
6th–12th grade
Coed day school—724 students

Renbrook School
West Hartford   (203) 236-1661
Preschool–9th grade
Coed day school—492 students

The Oxford Academy
Westbrook   (203) 399-6247
9th–12th grade (PG)
Boys' boarding—23 students

The Loomis Chaffee School
Windsor   (203) 688-4934
9th–12th grade (PG)
Coed day/boarding—723 students

Appendix B

Delaware

Archmere Academy
Claymont   (302) 798-6632
9th–12th grade
Coed day school—439 students

Sanford School
Hockessin   (302) 239-5263
Preschool–12th grade
Coed day school—540 students

St. Andrew's School
Middletown   (302) 378-9511
9th–12th grade
Coed boarding—253 students

The Independence School Inc.
Newark   (302) 239-0330
Preschool–8th grade
Coed day school—599 students

The Pilot School
Wilmington   (302) 478-1740
K–8th grade
Coed day school—155 students

The Tatnall School
Wilmington   (302) 998-2292
Preschool–12th grade
Coed day school—685 students

Tower Hill School
Wilmington   (302) 575-0550
Preschool–12th grade
Coed day school—657 students

Wilmington Friends School
Wilmington   (302) 576-3900
Preschool–12th grade
Coed day school—695 students

District of Columbia

Beauvoir
(202) 537-6485
Preschool–3rd grade
Coed day school—258 students

Capitol Hill Day School
(202) 547-2244
Preschool–8th grade
Coed—225 students

Edmund Burke School
(202) 362-8882
7th–12th grade
Coed day school—219 students

Georgetown Day School
(202) 333-7727
Preschool–12th grade
Coed—992 students

Georgetown Visitation Preparatory
   School
(202) 337-3350
9th–12th grade
Girls' day school—392 students

Maret School
(202) 939-8800
K–12th grade
Coed day school—494 students

National Cathedral School
(202) 537-6300
4th–12th grade
Girls' day school—548 students

National Presbyterian School
(202) 537-7500
Preschool–6th grade
Coed day school—196 students

St. Albans School
(202) 537-6435
4th–12th grade
Boys' day/boarding—546 students

St. Anselm's Abbey School
(202) 269-2350
6th–12th grade
Boys' day school—183 students

St. Patrick's Episcopal Day
(202) 342-2805
Preschool–6th grade
Coed day school—389 students

Sheridan School
(202) 362-7900

K–8th grade
Coed day school—205 students

The Sidwell Friends School
(202) 537-8100
Preschool–12th grade
Coed day school—1,023 students

Washington Episcopal School
(301) 652-7878
Preschool–6th grade
Coed day school—200 students

Washington International School
(202) 364-1800
Preschool–12th grade
Coed day school—613 students

Florida

Saint Andrew's School
Boca Raton   (407) 483-8900
6th–12th grade (PG)
Coed day/boarding—585 students

Saint Stephen's Episcopal School
Bradenton   (813) 746-2121
Preschool–12th grade
Coed day school—321 students

Saint Paul's School
Clearwater   (813) 536-2756
Preschool–8th grade
Coed day school—384 students

Pine Crest School
Fort Lauderdale   (305) 492-4120
Preschool–8th grade (PG)
Coed day school—702 students

The University School of Nova
    University

Fort Lauderdale   (305) 476-1902
Preschool–12th grade
Coed day school—1,364 students

Canterbury School
Fort Myers   (813) 481-4323
Preschool–12th grade
Coed day school—409 students

Oak Hall School
Gainesville   (904) 332-3609
6th–12th grade
Coed day school—244 students

Gulf Stream School
Gulf Stream   (407) 276-5225
Preschool–8th grade
Coed day school—205 students

The Bolles School
Jacksonville   (904) 733-9292
Preschool–12th grade (PG)
Coed day/boarding—1,200 students

154

Episcopal High School
of Jacksonville
Jacksonville   (904) 396-5751
7th–12th grade
Coed day school—533 students

Jacksonville Country Day School
Jacksonville   (904) 641-6644
Preschool–6th grade
Coed—428 students

Riverside Presbyterian Day School
Jacksonville   (904) 353-5511
Preschool–6th grade
Coed day school—395 students

The Cushman School
Miami   (305) 757-1966
Preschool–6th grade
Coed day school—307 students

Miami Country Day School
Miami   (305) 759-2843
Preschool–12th grade
Coed—795 students

Palmer Trinity School
Miami   (305) 251-2230
6th–12th grade
Coed day school—233 students

Ransom Everglades School, Inc.
Miami   (305) 460-8800
7th–12th grade
Coed day school—693 students

Community School of Naples
Naples   (813) 597-7575
Preschool–9th grade
Coed day school—192 students

The Benjamin School
North Palm Beach
(305) 626-3747
Preschool–12th grade
Coed day school—737 students

St. Johns Country Day School
Orange Park   (904) 264-9572
Preschool–12th grade
Coed day school—561 students

Palm Beach Day School
Palm Beach   (407) 655-1188
K–9th grade
Coed day school—309 students

The Out-of-Door Academy
Sarasota   (813) 349-3223
Preschool–8th grade
Coed day school—354 students

Admiral Farragut Academy South
St. Petersburg   (813) 384-5500
5th–12th grade (PG)
Coed boarding/day—215 students

Shorecrest Preparatory School
St. Petersburg   (813) 522-2111
Preschool–12th grade
Coed day school—837 students

Saint Michael's School
Stuart   (407) 283-1222
Preschool–8th grade
Coed day school—242 students

Maclay School
Tallahassee   (904) 893-2138
Preschool–12th grade
Coed day school—889 students

Berkeley Preparatory School
Tampa   (813) 885-1673
Preschool–12th grade
Coed day school—852 students

Independent Day School
Tampa   (813) 961-3087
Preschool–8th grade
Coed day school—197 students

St. Mary's Episcopal Day School
Tampa   (813) 289-8966
K–8th grade
Coed day school—383 students

Tampa Preparatory School
Tampa   (813) 251-8481

9th–12th grade
Coed day school—293 students

Saint Edward's School
Vero Beach   (407) 231-4136
Preschool–12th grade
Coed day school—746 students

Rosarian Academy
West Palm Beach   (407) 832-5131
Preschool–12th grade
Girls' day/boarding—382 students

Trinity Preparatory School of
   Florida
Winter Park   (407) 671-4140
6th–12th grade
Coed day school—441 students

Georgia

Athens Academy
Athens   (404) 549-9225
Preschool–12th grade
Coed day school—651 students

Holy Innocents' Episcopal School
Atlanta   (404) 255-4026
Preschool–8th grade
Coed day school—914 students

The Lovett School
Atlanta   (404) 262-3032
Preschool–12th grade
Coed day school—1,465 students

Marist School
Atlanta   (404) 457-7201
7th–12th grade
Coed day school—943 students

Mills Springs Academy
Atlanta   (404) 255-5951
K–12th grade
Coed day school—130 students

Pace Academy
Atlanta   (404) 262-1345
K–12th grade
Coed day school—810 students

Trinity School, Inc.
Atlanta   (404) 237-9286
Preschool–6th grade
Coed day school—445 students

The Westminster Schools
Atlanta   (404) 355-8673
K–12th grade
Coed day school—1,725 students

The Augusta Preparatory Day
School
Augusta   (404) 863-1906
Preschool–12th grade
Coed day school—347 students

Woodward Academy
College Park   (404) 765-8200
Preschool–12th grade
Coed day school—2,199 students

Brookstone School
Columbus   (404) 324-1392
Preschool–12th grade
Coed day school—737 students

Brenau Academy
Gainesville   (404) 534-6148
9th–12th grade (PG)
Girls' boarding/day—65 students

The Walker School
Marietta   (404) 427-2689
Preschool–12th grade
Coed day school—612 students

The Heritage School
Newnan   (404) 253-9898
Preschool–12th grade
Coed day school—197 students

Rabun Gap-Nacoochee School
Rabun Gap   (404) 746-5736
7th–12th grade
Coed boarding/day—195 students

Darlington School
Rome   (404) 235-6051
Preschool–12th grade (PG)
Coed day/boarding—840 students

Saint Andrew's School
Savannah   (912) 897-4941
Preschool–12th grade
Coed day school—270 students

Savannah Country Day School
Savannah   (912) 925-8800
Preschool–12th grade
Coed day school—849 students

Frederica Academy
St. Simons Island   (912) 638-9981
K–12th grade
Coed day school—303 students

Brookwood School
Thomasville   (912) 226-8070
K–12th grade
Coed day school—319 students

Guam

St. John's School
Tumon Bay   (671) 646-8080

Preschool–12th grade
Coed day school—627 students

Hawaii

Academy of the Pacific
Honolulu   (808) 595-6359
7th–12th grade
Coed day school—156 students

Hanahauoli School
Honolulu   (808) 949-6461
Preschool–6th grade
Coed day school—295 students

Iolani School
Honolulu   (808) 949-5355
K–12th grade
Coed day school—1,744 students

The Kamehameha Schools
Honolulu   (808) 842-8211
Preschool–12th grade
Coed day/boarding—3,072 students

La Pietra
Honolulu   (808) 922-2744
6th–12th grade
Girls' day school—197 students

Mid-Pacific Institute
Honolulu   (808) 973-5000
7th–12th grade
Coed day/boarding—1,132 students

Punahou School
Honolulu   (808) 944-5711
K–12th grade
Coed day school—3,705 students

St. Andrew's Priory School
Honolulu   (808) 536-6102

Idaho

The Community School
Ketchum   (208) 622-3955

Illinois

Ancona School
Chicago   (312) 924-2356
Preschool–8th grade
Coed day school—212 students

Bernard Zell Anshe Emet
Day School
Chicago   (312) 281-1858

K–12th grade
Girls' day school—629 students

Le Jardin Academy
Kailua   (808) 261-0707
Preschool–8th grade
Coed day school—414 students

Hawaii Preparatory Academy
Kamuela   (808) 885-7321
K–12th grade
Coed day/boarding—713 students

The Parker School
Kamuela   (808) 885-7933
8th–12th grade
Coed day school—127 students

Seabury Hall
Maui   (808) 572-7235
6th–12th grade
Coed day/boarding—302 students

Assets School
Pearl Harbor   (808) 423-1356
K–8th grade
Coed day school—279 students

K–12th grade
Coed day school—244 students

Preschool–12th grade
Coed day school—332 students

Francis W. Parker School
Chicago   (312) 549-0172
Preschool–12th grade
Coed day school—780 students

Appendix B

The Harvard School
Chicago   (312) 624-0394
Preschool–12th grade
Coed day school—168 students

Latin School of Chicago
Chicago   (312) 787-0820
Preschool–12th grade
Coed day school—877 students

Morgan Park Academy
Chicago   (312) 881-6700
K–12th grade
Coed day school—474 students

Sacred Heart Schools at
Sheridan Road
Chicago   (312) 262-4446
K–12th grade
Coed day school—389 students

University of Chicago Laboratory
   Schools
Chicago   (312) 702-9450
Preschool–12th grade
Coed day school—1,499 students

Avery Coonley School
Downers Grove   (708) 969-0800
Preschool–8th grade
Coed day school—337 students

Chicago Junior School
Elgin   (708) 888-7910
Preschool–8th grade
Coed day/boarding—206 students

The Elgin Academy
Elgin   (708) 695-0300
K–12th grade
Coed day school—305 students

Roycemore School
Evanston   (708) 866-6055
Preschool–12th grade
Coed day school—217 students

Lake Forest Academy
Lake Forest   (708) 234-3210
9th–12th grade
Coed boarding/day—283 students

Lake Forest Country Day School
Lake Forest   (708) 234-2350
Preschool–9th grade
Coed day school—450 students

Woodlands Academy/Sacred Heart
Lake Forest   (708) 234-4300
9th–12th grade
Girls' day/boarding—208 students

Creative Children's Academy
Mount Prospect   (708) 577-5864
Preschool–9th grade
Coed day school—174 students

Saint Mary's Academy
Nauvoo   (217) 453-6619
9th–12th grade
Girls' boarding—85 students

Keith Country Day School
Rockford   (815) 399-8823
Preschool–12th grade
Coed day school—308 students

The North Shore Country Day
   School
Winnetka   (708) 446-0674
Preschool–12th grade
Coed day school—384 students

Indiana

The Culver Academies
Culver   (219) 842-3311
9th–12th grade (PG)
Coed boarding/day—668 students

Evansville Day School
Evansville   (812) 476-3039
Preschool–12th grade
Coed day school—316 students

Marian Heights Academy
Ferdinand   (812) 367-1431
9th–12th grade
Girls' boarding—175 students

Canterbury School
Fort Wayne   (219) 436-0746
Preschool–12th grade
Coed day school—470 students

Howe Military School
Howe   (219) 562-2131

6th–12th grade
Coed boarding—180 students

The Orchard Country Day School
Indianapolis   (317) 251-9253
Preschool–8th grade
Coed day school—571 students

Park Tudor School
Indianapolis   (317) 254-2700
Preschool–12th grade
Coed day school—745 students

La Lumiere School
La Porte   (219) 326-7450
9th–12th grade (PG)
Coed boarding/day—86 students

The Stanley Clark School
South Bend   (219) 291-4200
K–8th grade
Coed day school—807 students

Iowa

St. Katharine's-St. Mark's School
Bettendorf   (319) 359-1366
Preschool–12th grade
Coed day school—195 students

Maharishi School of the Age
Fairfield   (515) 472-1157
Preschool–12th grade
Coed day school—744 students

Kansas

Wichita Collegiate School
Wichita   (316) 634-0433

Preschool–12th grade
Coed day school—807 students

Kentucky

Capital Day School
Frankfurt   (502) 227-7172
Preschool–8th grade
Coed day school—167 students

St. Francis School
Goshen   (502) 228-1197
K–8th grade
Coed day school—240 students

Appendix B

The Lexington School
Lexington   (606) 278-0501
Preschool–9th grade
Coed day school—479 students

Sayre School
Lexington   (606) 254-1361
Preschool–12th grade
Coed day school—423 students

Kentucky Country Day School
Louisville   (502) 423-0440

K–12th grade
Coed day school—635 students

The Louisville Collegiate School
Louisville   (502) 451-5330
K–12th grade
Coed day school—535 students

St. Francis High School
Louisville   (502) 585-2057
9th–12th grade
Coed day school—120 students

Louisiana

Episcopal High School of Baton
  Rouge
Baton Rouge   (504) 753-3180
4th–12th grade
Coed day school—757 students

Episcopal School of Acadiana
Cade   (318) 365-1416
6th–12th grade
Coed day school—261 students

Metairie Park Country Day School
Metairie   (504) 837-5204
K–12th grade
Coed day school—685 students

St. Martin's Episcopal School
Metairie   (504) 733-0353
Preschool–12th grade
Coed day school—867 students

Isidore Newman School
New Orleans   (504) 899-5641
K–12th grade
Coed day school—1,075 students

The Louise S. McGehee School
New Orleans   (504) 561-1224
Preschool–12th grade
Girls' day school—280 students

St. Andrew's Episcopal School
New Orleans   (504) 861-3743
Preschool–6th grade
Coed day school—160 students

St. George's Episcopal School
New Orleans   (504) 891-5509
Preschool–8th grade
Coed day school—207 students

St. Paul's Episcopal School
New Orleans   (504) 488-1319
K–8th grade
Coed day school—192 students

Trinity Episcopal School
New Orleans   (504) 525-8661
Preschool–8th grade
Coed day school—419 students

Southfield School
Shreveport   (318) 868-5375
Preschool–12th grade
Coed day school—270 students

Maine

Hyde School
Bath   (207) 443-5584
8th–12th grade (PG)
Coed boarding—167 students

Gould Academy
Bethel   (207) 824-2161
9th–12th grade (PG)
Coed boarding/day—182 students

Fryeburg Academy
Fryeburg   (207) 935-2001
9th–12th grade (PG)
Coed day/boarding—442 students

Hebron Academy
Hebron   (207) 966-2100
9th–12th grade (PG)
Coed boarding/day—192 students

Kents Hill School
Kents Hill   (207) 685-4914
9th–12th grade (PG)
Coed boarding/day—122 students

Lee Academy
Lee   (207) 738-2252

9th–12th grade
Coed day/boarding—257 students

Bridgton Academy
North Bridgton   (207) 647-3322
12th grade   (for PG students)
Boys' boarding—158 students

Maine Central Institute
Pittsfield   (207) 487-3355
9th–12th grade (PG)
Coed day/boarding—470 students

Waynflete School
Portland   (207) 774-5721
Preschool–12th grade
Coed day school—494 students

Berwick Academy
South Berwick   (207) 384-2164
1st–12th grade
Coed day school—348 students

North Yarmouth Academy
Yarmouth   (207) 846-9051
6th–12th grade
Coed day school—184 students

Maryland

The Key School
Annapolis   (301) 263-9231
Preschool–12th grade
Coed day school—445 students

The Boys' Latin School of
   Maryland
Baltimore   (301) 377-5192
K–12th grade
Boys' day school—475 students

The Bryn Mawr School
Baltimore   (301) 323-8800
Preschool–12th grade
Girls' day school—868 students

Calvert School
Baltimore   (301) 243-6054
Preschool–6th grade
Coed day school—386 students

Friends School/Baltimore Inc.
Baltimore   (301) 435-2800
Preschool–12th grade
Coed day school—951 students

Gilman School
Baltimore   (301) 323-3800
K–12th grade
Boys' day school—951 students

Roland Park Country School
Baltimore   (301) 323-5500
K–12th grade
Girls' day school—586 students

Ruxton Country School
Baltimore   (301) 823-2271
K–8th grade
Coed day school—124 students

Harford Day School
Bel Air   (301) 838-4848
Preschool–8th grade
Coed day school—245 students

Worcester Country School
Berlin   (301) 641-3575
Preschool–12th grade
Coed day school—338 students

Country Day School of Sacred
   Heart-Stone Ridge
Bethesda   (301) 657-4322
Preschool–12th grade
Girls' day school—583 students

The Holton-Arms School
Bethesda   (301) 365-5300
3rd–12th grade
Girls' day school—623 students

Landon School
Bethesda   (301) 320-3200
3rd–12th grade
Boys' day school—585 students

Mater Dei School
Bethesda   (301) 365-2700
1st–8th grade
Boys' day school—191 students

The Norwood School
Bethesda   (301) 365-2595
K–6th grade
Coed day school—275 students

St. Andrew's Episcopal School
Bethesda   (301) 530-4900
6th–12th grade
Coed day school—352 students

The Park School
Brooklandville   (301) 825-2351
Preschool–12th grade
Coed day school—680 students

St. Paul's School
Brooklandville   (301) 825-4400
K–12th grade
Boys' day school—770 students

The Gunston School
Centreville   (301) 758-0620
9th–12th grade
Girls' boarding/day—68 students

Kent School, Inc.
Chestertown   (301) 778-4100
Preschool–8th grade
Coed day school—145 students

West Nottingham Academy
Colora   (301) 658-5556
9th–12th grade (PG)
Coed boarding/day—100 students

The Country School
Easton   (301) 822-1935
K–8th grade
Coed day school—222 students

Garrison Forest School
Garrison   (301) 363-1500
Preschool–12th grade
Girls' day/boarding—484 students

Gibson Island Country School
Gibson Island   (301) 255-5370
Preschool–5th grade
Coed day school—69 students

Oldfields School
Glencoe   (301) 472-4800
8th–12th grade
Girls' boarding/day—178 students

Glenelg Country School
Glenelg   (301) 531-2229
K–12th grade
Coed day school—334 students

The Calverton School
Huntington   (301) 535-0216
Preschool–12th grade
Coed day school—225 students

The Newport Schools
Kensington   (301) 942-4550
Preschool–12th grade
Coed day school—237 students

McDonogh School
McDonogh   (301) 363-0600

K–12th grade
Coed day/boarding—1,172 students

St. James' Academy
Monkton   (301) 771-4816
K–6th grade
Coed day school—201 students

St. John's Episcopal School
Olney   (301) 774-6804
K–8th grade
Coed day school—133 students

The Bullis School
Potomac   (301) 299-8500
4th–12th grade
Coed day school—474 students

The McLean School/Maryland Inc.
Potomac   (301) 299-8277
K–9th grade
Coed day school—234 students

Georgetown Preparatory School
Rockville   (301) 493-5000
9th–12th grade
Boys' day/boarding—411 students

Green Acres School
Rockville   (301) 881-4100
Preschool–8th grade
Coed day school—295 students

Salisbury School
Salisbury   (301) 742-4464
Preschool–8th grade
Coed day school—185 students

Sandy Spring Friends School
Sandy Spring   (301) 774-7455
6th–12th grade (PG)
Coed day/boarding—222 students

Appendix B

Severn School
Severna Park   (301) 617 7700
6th–12th grade
Coed day school—450 students

The Chelsea School
Silver Spring   (301) 585-1430
1st–12th grade
Coed day school—82 students

Saint James School
St. James   (301) 733-9330
8th–12th grade
Coed boarding/day—137 students

St. Timothy's School
Stevenson   (301) 486-7400
9th–12th grade
Girls' boarding/day—107 students

Notre Dame Preparatory School
Towson   (301) 825-6202
6th–12th grade
Girls' day school—549 students

Queen Anne School
Upper Marlboro   (301) 249-5000
7th–12th grade
Coed day school—153 students

Massachusetts

The Common School
Amherst   (413) 256-8989
Preschool–6th grade
Coed day school—118 students

Phillips Academy
Andover   (508) 749-4000
9th–12th grade (PG)
Coed boarding/day—1202 students

The Pike School
Andover   (508) 475-1197
Preschool–9th grade
Coed day school—395 students

Cushing Academy
Ashburnham   (508) 827-5911
9th–12th grade (PG)
Coed boarding/day—401 students

The Arlington School
Belmont   (617) 855-2124
9th–12th grade
Coed day school—31 students

Belmont Day School
Belmont   (617) 484-3078
Preschool–6th grade
Coed day school—173 students

Belmont Hill School
Belmont   (617) 484-4410
7th–12th grade
Boys' day school—406 students

Shore Country Day School
Beverly   (508) 927-1700
Preschool–9th grade
Coed day school—418 students

Glen Urquhart School
Beverly Farms   (508) 927–1064
K–8th grade
Coed day school—152 students

The Advent School
Boston   (617) 742-0520
K–6th grade
Coed day school—118 students

Commonwealth School
Boston   (617) 266-7525
9th–12th grade
Coed day school—112 students

Newman Preparatory School
Boston   (617) 267-4530
9th–12th grade
Coed day school—220 students

The Winsor School
Boston   (617) 735-9500
5th–12th grade
Girls' day school—376 students

Thayer Academy
Braintree   (617) 843-3580
6th–12th grade
Coed day school—564 students

The Park School
Brookline   (617) 277-2456
Preschool–9th grade
Coed day school—501 students

Governor Dummer Academy
Byfield   (508) 465-1763
9th–12th grade
Coed boarding/day—348 students

Buckingham Browne & Nichols
   School
Cambridge   (617) 547-6100
Preschool–12th grade
Coed day school—940 students

Cambridge Friends School
Cambridge   (617) 354-3880
K–8th grade
Coed day school—208 students

Fayerweather Street School
Cambridge   (617) 876-4746
K–8th grade
Coed day school—160 students

Manter Hall School
Cambridge   (617) 876-7532
10th–12th grade
Coed day school—16 students

Shady Hill School
Cambridge   (617) 868-1260
Preschool–9th grade
Coed day school—478 students

Beaver Country Day School
Chestnut Hill   (617) 734-6950
6th–12th grade
Coed day school—282 students

Brimmer and May School
Chestnut Hill   (617) 566-7462
Preschool–12th grade
Girls' day school—280 students

The Chestnut Hill School
Chestnut Hill   (617) 566-4394
Preschool–6th grade
Coed day school—157 students

Concord Academy
Concord   (508) 369-6080
9th–12th grade
Coed day/boarding—322 students

The Fenn School
Concord   (508) 369-5800
4th–9th grade
Boys' day school—257 students

Appendix B

Middlesex School
Concord   (508) 369-2550
9th–12th grade
Coed boarding/day—313 students

Nashoba Brooks School of
   Concord
Concord   (508) 369-4591
Preschool–8th grade
Girls' day school—278 students

Dedham Country Day School
Dedham   (617) 329-0850
Preschool–8th grade
Coed day school—213 students

Noble and Greenough School
Dedham   (617) 326-3700
7th–12th grade
Coed day/boarding—452 students

Ursuline Academy
Dedham   (617) 326-6161
7th–12th grade
Girls' day school—342 students

The Bement School
Deerfield   (413) 774-7061
K–9th grade
Coed day/boarding—185 students

Deerfield Academy
Deerfield   (413) 772-0241
9th–12th grade (PG)
Coed boarding/day—245 students

Eaglebrook School
Deerfield   (413) 774-7411
6th–9th grade
Boys' boarding/day—245 students

Charles River School
Dover   (508) 785-0068
Preschool–8th grade
Coed day school—168 students

Riverview School
East Sandwich   (508) 888-0489
9th–12th grade
Coed boarding—99 students

The Williston Northampton School
Easthampton   (413) 527-1520
7th–12th grade (PG)
Coed day/boarding—471 students

Falmouth Academy
Falmouth   (508) 563-9386
7th–12th grade
Coed day school—134 students

Applewild School
Fitchburg   (508) 342-6053
Preschool–9th grade
Coed day school—247 students

Touchstone Community School
Grafton   (508) 839-0038
K–6th grade
Coed day school—109 students

Stoneleigh-Burnham School
Greenfield   (413) 774-2711
9th–12th grade (PG)
Girls' boarding/day—161 students

Groton School
Groton   (508) 448-3363
8th–12th grade
Coed boarding/day—322 students

Lawrence Academy
Groton   (508) 448-6535
9th–12th grade
Coed day/boarding—331 students

Derby Academy
Hingham   (617) 749-0746
Preschool–9th grade
Coed day school—241 students

Berkshire Country Day School
Lenox   (413) 637-0755
Preschool–9th grade (PG)
Coed day school—224 students

Lexington Christian Academy
Lexington   (617) 862-7850
6th–12th grade
Coed day school—191 students

The Carroll School
Lincoln   (617) 259-8342
1st–12th grade
Coed day school—218 students

Brookwood School
Manchester   (508) 526-7596
K–8th grade
Coed day school—290 students

Tower School
Marblehead   (508) 631-5800
Preschool–9th grade
Coed day school—244 students

Tabor Academy
Marion   (508) 748-2000
9th–12th grade
Coed boarding/day—462 students

Hillside School
Marlborough   (508) 485-2824

5th–8th grade
Boys' boarding—42 students

Milton Academy
Milton   (617) 698-7800
K–12th grade
Coed day/boarding—949 students

Walnut Hill School
Natick   (508) 653-4312
8th–12th grade (PG)
Coed boarding/day—192 students

St. Sebastian's Country Day School
Needham   (617) 449-5200
7th–12th grade
Boys' day school—277 students

Newton Country Day School of the
    Sacred Heart
Newton   (617) 244-4246
5th–12th grade
Girls' day school—170 students

Brooks School
North Andover   (508) 686-6101
9th–12th grade
Coed boarding/day—316 students

Friends Academy
North Dartmouth   (508) 999-1356
K–9th grade
Coed day school—307 students

Smith College Campus School
Northampton   (413) 584-2700
Preschool–6th grade
Coed day school—325 students

Linden Hill School
Northfield   (413) 498-2906
5th–9th grade
Boys' boarding—26 students

Northfield Mount Hermon School
Northfield   (413) 498-5311
9th–12th grade (PG)
Coed boarding/day—1,142 students

Cape Cod Academy
Osterville   (508) 428-5400
K–12th grade
Coed day school—196 students

Miss Hall's School
Pittsfield   (413) 443-6401
9th–12th grade
Girls' boarding—179 students

Landmark School
Prides Crossing   (508) 927-4440
3rd–12th grade (PG)
Coed boarding/day—310 students

Austin Preparatory School
Reading   (617) 944-4900
6th–12th grade
Boys' day school—447 students

Berkshire School
Sheffield   (413) 229-8511
9th–12th grade
Coed boarding/day—414 students

Saint John's High School
Shrewsbury   (617) 842-8934
9th–12th grade
Boys' day school—1,094 students

The Pingree School
South Hamilton   (508) 468-4415
9th–12th grade
Coed day school—237 students

Fay School
Southborough   (508) 485-0100

1st–9th grade
Coed day/boarding—353 students

Saint Mark's School
Southborough   (508) 485-0050
9th–12th grade
Coed boarding/day—321 students

The MacDuffie School
Springfield   (413) 734-4971
6th–12th grade (PG)
Coed day/boarding—140 students

Willow Hill School
Sudbury   (508) 443-2581
7th–12th grade
Coed day school—35 students

Chapel Hill-Chauncy Hall School
Waltham   (617) 894-2644
9th–12th grade (PG)
Coed boarding/day—162 students

Perkins School for the Blind
Watertown   (617) 924-3434
Preschool–12th grade
Coed boarding/day—181 students

Dana Hall School
Wellesley   (617) 235-3010
7th–12th grade
Girls' day/boarding—303 students

Tenacre Country Day School
Wellesley   (617) 235-2282
Preschool–6th grade
Coed day school—174 students

The Fessenden School
West Newton   (617) 964-5350
K–9th grade
Boys' day/boarding—389 students

The Roxbury Latin School
West Roxbury   (617) 325-4920
7th–12th grade
Boys' day school—274 students

The Cambridge School
Weston   (617) 642-8600
9th–12th grade (PG)
Coed day/boarding—177 students

The Meadowbrook School
Weston   (617) 894-1193
Preschool–6th grade
Coed day school—181 students

The Rivers School
Weston   (617) 235-9300
7th–12th grade
Coed day school—280 students

Wilbraham & Monson Academy
Wilbraham   (413) 596-6811
7th–12th grade (PG)
Coed boarding/day—203 students

The Pine Cobble School, Inc.
Williamstown   (413) 458-4680
Preschool–9th grade
Coed day school—151 students

The Winchendon School
Winchendon   (508) 297-1223
8th–12th grade (PG)
Coed boarding—138 students

Bancroft School
Worcester   (508) 853-2640
K–12th grade
Coed day school—513 students

Notre Dame Academy
Worcester   (508) 757-6200
9th–12th grade
Girls' day school—274 students

Worcester Academy
Worcester   (508) 754-5302
7th–12th grade (PG)
Coed day/boarding—343 students

Michigan

Greenhills School
Ann Arbor   (313) 769-4010
6th–12th grade
Coed day school—427 students

Detroit Country Day School
Birmingham   (313) 646-7717
Preschool–12th grade
Coed day school—1,228 students

Academy of the Sacred Heart
Bloomfield Hills   (313) 646-8900
Preschool–12th grade
Girls' day school—328 students

The Cranbrook Schools
Bloomfield Hills   (313) 645-3000
Preschool–12th grade
Coed day/boarding—1,234 students

Kensington Academy
Bloomfield Hills   (313) 647-8060
Preschool–8th grade
Coed day school—126 students

Roeper City and Country School
Bloomfield Hills   (313) 642-1500
Preschool–12th grade
Coed day school—471 students

Friends School in Detroit
Detroit   (313) 259-6722
Preschool–8th grade
Coed day school—107 students

The Valley School
Flint   (313) 767-4004
Preschool–12th grade
Coed day school—152 students

The Leelanau School
Glen Arbor   (616) 334-3072
8th–12th grade
Coed boarding/day—93 students

The Grosse Pointe Academy
Grosse Pointe Farms
(313) 886-1221
Preschool–8th grade
Coed day school—438 students

University Liggett School
Grosse Pointe Woods
(313) 884-4444
Preschool–12th grade
Coed day school—752 students

Interlochen Arts Academy
Interlochen   (616) 276-9221
9th–12th grade (PG)
Coed boarding—418 students

Minnesota

Saint John's Preparatory School
Collegeville   (612) 363-3315
9th–12th grade
Coed day/boarding—216 students

The Marshall School
Duluth   (218) 727-7266
7th–12th grade
Coed day school—294 students

Shattuck-St. Mary's School
Faribault   (507) 334-6466
7th–12th grade (PG)
Coed boarding/day—185 students

Convent of the Visitation School
Mendota Heights   (612) 454-6474
Preschool–12th grade
Girls' day school—481 students

The Blake School
Minneapolis   (612) 338-2586
K–12th grade
Coed day school—1,067 students

Breck School
Minneapolis   (612) 377-5000
Preschool–12th grade
Coed day school—1,107 students

Mounds Park Academy
St. Paul   (612) 777-2555
K–12th grade
Coed day school—513 students

St. Paul Academy and Summit
   School
St. Paul   (612) 698-2451
K–12th grade
Coed day school—829 students

Mississippi

St. Andrew's Episcopal School
Jackson   (601) 982-5065
Preschool–12th grade
Coed day school—943 students

The Piney Woods Country Life
   School
Piney Woods   (601) 845-2214

Preschool–12th grade
Coed boarding/day—366 students

All Saints' Episcopal School
Vicksburg   (601) 636-5266
8th–12th grade (PG)
Coed boarding/day—179 students

Missouri

Chesterfield Day School
Chesterfield   (314) 469-6622
Preschool–6th grade
Coed day school—232 students

The Barstow School
Kansas City   (816) 942-3255
Preschool–12th grade
Coed day school—345 students

The Pembroke Hill School
Kansas City   (816) 753-1300
Preschool–12th grade
Coed day school—1,029 students

Missouri Military Academy
Mexico   (314) 581-1776
4th–12th grade (PG)
Boys' boarding—305 students

The Churchill School
St. Louis   (314) 997-4343
3rd–11th grade
Coed day school—100 students

Community School
St. Louis   (314) 991-0005
Preschool–6th grade
Coed day school—248 students

The Forsyth School
St. Louis   (314) 726-4542
Preschool–6th grade
Coed day school—237 students

John Burroughs School
St. Louis   (314) 993-4040
7th–12th grade
Coed day school—566 students

Logos High School
St. Louis   (314) 997-7002
9th–12th grade
Coed day school—87 students

Mary Institute & St. Louis Country
   Day
St. Louis   (314) 993-5100
Preschool–12th grade
Coed day/boarding—611 students

The Principia
St. Louis   (314) 434-2100
Preschool–12th grade
Coed day school—1,121 students

Rohan Woods School
St. Louis   (314) 821-6270
Preschool–6th grade
Coed day school—113 students

Rossman School
St. Louis   (314) 434-5877
Preschool–6th grade
Coed day school—204 students

Saint Louis Priory School
St. Louis   (314) 434-3690
7th–12th grade
Boys' day school—332 students

Nebraska
Brownell-Talbot School
Omaha   (402) 556-3772

Nevada
The Meadows School
Las Vegas   (702) 254-1610
K–12th grade
Coed day school—454 students

New Hampshire
Proctor Academy
Andover   (603) 735-5126
9th–12th grade
Coed boarding/day—298 students

Cardigan Mountain School
Canaan   (603) 523-4321
6th–9th grade
Boys' boarding—164 students

St. Paul's School
Concord   (603) 225-3341
9th–12th grade
Coed boarding—494 students

Dublin School
Dublin   (603) 563-8584
9th–12th grade
Coed boarding/day—87 students

Thomas Jefferson School
St. Louis   (314) 843-4151
7th–12th grade (PG)
Coed boarding/day—60 students

Whitfield School
St. Louis   (314) 434-5141
7th–12th grade
Coed day school—223 students

Preschool–12th grade
Coed day school—291 students

Milton I. Schwartz Hebrew
   Academy
Las Vegas   (702) 255-4500
Preschool–8th grade
Coed day school—259 students

Phillips Exeter Academy
Exeter   (603) 772-4311
9th–12th grade (PG)
Coed boarding/day—993 students

The White Mountain School
Littleton   (603) 444-2928
9th–12th grade (PG)
Coed boarding/day—109 students

The Derryfield School
Manchester   (603) 669-4524
7th–12th grade
Coed day school—300 students

Kimball Union Academy
Meriden   (603) 469-3211
9th–12th grade (PG)
Coed boarding/day—265 students

New Hampton School
New Hampton   (603) 744-5401
9th–12th grade (PG)
Coed boarding/day—246 students

The Holderness School
Plymouth   (603) 536-1257
9th–12th grade (PG)
Coed boarding/day—262 students

Tilton School
Tilton   (603) 286-4342

9th–12th grade (PG)
Coed boarding/day—232 students

High Mowing School
Wilton   (603) 654-2391
9th–12th grade
Coed boarding/day—92 students

Brewster Academy
Wolfeboro   (603) 569-1600
9th–12th grade (PG)
Coed boarding/day—309 students

New Jersey

Blair Academy
Blairstown   (908) 362-6121
9th–12th grade (PG)
Coed boarding/day—359 students

Woodland Country Day School
Bridgeton   (609) 935-7270
Preschool–8th grade
Coed day school—222 students

St. Mary's Hall
Burlington   (609) 386-3500
Preschool–12th grade
Coed day school—201 students

The Wardlaw-Hartridge School
Edison   (908) 754-1882
K–12th grade
Coed day school—425 students

Dwight-Englewood School
Englewood   (201) 569-9500
7th–12th grade
Coed day school—653 students

Elizabeth Morrow School
Englewood   (201) 568-5566

Preschool–6th grade
Coed day school—498 students

Far Hills Country Day School
Far Hills   (201) 766-0622
Preschool–9th grade
Coed day school—310 students

Gill/St. Bernard's School
Gladstone   (908) 234-1611
Preschool–12th grade
Coed day school—380 students

The Peddie School
Hightstown   (609) 490-7555
8th–12th grade (PG)
Coed boarding/day—498 students

The Lawrenceville School
Lawrenceville   (609) 896-0400
8th–12th grade (PG)
Coed boarding/day—764 students

Newark Academy
Livingston   (201) 992-7000
6th–12th grade
Coed day school—473 students

The Pingry School
Martinsville   (201) 647-5555
K–12th grade
Coed day school—971 students

The Montclair Kimberley Academy
Montclair   (201) 746-9800
Preschool–12th grade
Coed day school—1,019 students

Moorestown Friends School
Moorestown   (609) 235-2900
Preschool–12th grade
Coed day school—513 students

Delbarton School
Morristown   (201) 538-3231
7th–12th grade
Boys' day school—495 students

The Morristown-Beard School
Morristown   (201) 539-3032
7th–12th grade
Coed day school—408 students

The Peck School
Morristown   (201) 539-8660
K–8th grade
Coed day school—304 students

The Wilson School
Mountain Lakes   (201) 539-0181
K–12th grade
Coed day school—186 students

The Pennington School
Pennington   (609) 737-1838
7th–12th grade
Coed day/boarding—317 students

Admiral Farragut
  Academy   (North)

Pine Beach   (201) 349-1253
5th–12th grade (PG)
Boys' boarding/day—174 students

Mount Saint Mary Academy
Plainfield-Watchung
(201) 757-0108
9th–12th grade
Girls' day/boarding—331 students

Purnell School
Pottersville   (908) 439-2154
10th–12th grade
Girls' boarding—95 students

Chapin School
Princeton   (609) 924-2449
K–8th grade
Coed day school—229 students

The Hun School of Princeton
Princeton   (609) 921-7600
6th–12th grade (PG)
Coed day/boarding—498 students

Princeton Day School
Princeton   (609) 924-6700
Preschool–12th grade
Coed day school—832 students

Princeton Montessori School
Princeton   (609) 924-4594
K–8th grade
Coed day school—106 students

Stuart Country Day School of the
  Sacred Heart
Princeton   (609) 921-2330
Preschool–12th grade
Girls' day school—438 students

The Rumson Country Day School
Rumson   (201) 842-0527
K–9th grade
Coed day school—297 students

Saddle River Day School
Saddle River   (201) 327-4050
4th–12th grade
Coed day school—285 students

Far Brook School
Short Hills   (201) 379-3442
Preschool–8th grade
Coed day school—204 students

The Winston School
Short Hills   (201) 379-4114
1st–8th grade
Coed day school—28 students

New Mexico

Albuquerque Academy
Albuquerque   (505) 828-3200
6th–12th grade
Coed day school—875 students

Manzano Day School
Albuquerque   (505) 243-6659
Preschool–5th grade
Coed day school—393 students

Menaul School
Albuquerque   (505) 345-7727
8th–12th grade
Coed day/boarding—244 students

New York

Albany Academy for Girls
Albany   (518) 463-2201
Preschool–12th grade
Girls' day school—273 students

Rutgers Preparatory School
Somerset   (201) 545-5600
Preschool–12th grade
Coed day school—528 students

Kent Place School
Summit   (908) 273-0900
Preschool–12th grade
Girls' day school—429 students

Oak Knoll School/Holy Child
Summit   (908) 273-3018
K–12th grade
Girls' day school—468 students

Ranney School
Tinton Falls   (201) 542-4777
Preschool–12th grade
Coed day school—570 students

Sandia Preparatory School
Albuquerque   (505) 344-1671
6th–12th grade
Coed day school—414 students

Rio Grande School
Santa Fe   (505) 983-1621
K–6th grade
Coed day school—121 students

Santa Fe Preparatory School
Santa Fe   (505) 982-1829
7th–12th grade
Coed day school—205 students

The Doane Stuart School
Albany   (518) 465-5222
Preschool–12th grade
Coed day/boarding—277 students

Kildonan School
Amenia   (914) 373-8111
3rd–12th grade (PG)
Boys' boarding/day—70 students

Rippowam-Cisqua School
Bedford   (914) 234-3674
Preschool–9th grade
Coed day school—503 students

The Academy of St. oseph
Brentwood   (526) 273-2406
K–12th grade
Girls' day school—613 students

The Buffalo Seminary
Buffalo   (716) 885-6780
9th–12th grade
Girls' day school—136 students

The Elmwood Franklin School
Buffalo   (716) 877-5035
Preschool–8th grade
Coed day school—321 students

The Nichols School
Buffalo   (716) 875-5035
5th–12th grade
Coed day school—621 students

The Rockland Country Day School
Congers   (914) 268-6802
Preschool–12th grade
Coed day school—172 students

New York Military Academy
Cornwall-on-Hudson
(914) 534-3710
5th–12th grade (PG)
Coed boarding/day—272 students

Storm King School
Cornwall-on-Hudson
(914) 534-7892
9th–12th grade (PG)
Coed boarding/day—124 students

Manlius Pebble Hill School
DeWitt   (315) 446-2452
Preschool–12th grade
Coed day school—290 students

The Masters School
Dobbs Ferry   (914) 693-1400
6th–12th grade (PG)
Girls' boarding/day—237 students

The Waldorf School/Garden City
Garden City   (516) 742-3434
Preschool–12th grade
Coed day school—249 students

The Green Vale School
Glen Head   (516) 621-2420
Preschool–9th grade
Coed day school—446 students

Hoosac School
Hoosick   (518) 686-7331
8th–12th grade (PG)
Coed boarding—97 students

The Harvey School
Katonah   (914) 232-3161
6th–12th grade
Coed day/boarding—189 students

Nat'l Sports Academy Lake Placid
Lake Placid   (518) 523-3460
8th–12th grade
Coed boarding/day—40 students

North Country School
Lake Placid   (518) 523-9329
4th–8th grade
Coed boarding/day—71 students

Northwood School
Lake Placid   (518) 523-3357
9th–12th grade (PG)
Coed boarding/day—113 students

Friends Academy
Locust Valley   (516) 676-0393
Preschool–12th grade
Coed day school—690 students

Portledge School
Locust Valley   (516) 672-1475
Preschool–12th grade
Coed day school—235 students

Saint Gregory's School
Loudonville   (518) 785-6621
Preschool–8th grade
Boys' day school—182 students

The Dutchess Day School
Millbrook   (914) 677-5014
K–8th grade
Coed day school—132 students

Millbrook School
Millbrook   (914) 677-8261
9th–12th grade
Coed boarding/day—171 students

Darrow School
New Lebanon   (518) 794-7700
9th–12th grade (PG)
Coed boarding/day—95 students

New York City

Bronx
The Horace Mann Barnard School
Bronx   (718) 548-5000
Preschool–12th grade
Coed day school—1,649 students

The Fieldston School
Riverdale   (718) 543-5000
7th–12th grade
Coed day school—712 students

Riverdale Country School
Riverdale   (718) 549-8810
Preschool–12th grade
Coed day school—860 students

Brooklyn
Adelphi Academy
(718) 238-3308
Preschool–12th grade
Coed day school—232 students

Berkeley Carroll School
(718) 789-6060
Preschool–12th grade
Coed day school—614 students

Brooklyn Friends School
(718) 852-1029
Preschool–12th grade
Coed day school—328 students

Polytechnic Preparatory Country
   Day School
(718) 836-9800
5th–12th grade
Coed day school—633 students

Saint Ann's School
Brooklyn Heights   (718) 522-1660
Preschool–12th grade
Coed day school—897 students

The Packer Collegiate Institute
(718) 875-6644
Preschool–12th grade
Coed day school—722 students

Manhattan
Allen-Stevenson School
(212) 288-6710
K–9th grade
Boys' day school—309 students

The Anglo-American School
(212) 724-6360
K–12th grade
Coed day school—280 students

The Barnard School
(212) 795-1050
K–12th grade
Coed day school—93 students

The Birch Wathen Lenox School
(212) 861-0404
Preschool
Coed day school—260 students

The Brearley School
(212) 744-8582
K–12th grade
Girls' day school—612 students

The Browning School
(212) 838-6280
K–12th grade
Boys' day school—307 students

The Buckley School
(212) 535-8787
K–9th grade
Boys' day school—347 students

The Caedmon School
(212) 879-2296
Preschool–6th grade
Coed day school—163 students

The Calhoun School
(212) 877-1700
Preschool–12th grade
Coed day school—434 students

The Cathedral School of St. John
the Divine
(212) 316-7500
K–8th grade
Coed day school—237 students

The Chapin School
(212) 744-2335
K–12th grade
Girls' day school—580 students

The Churchill School & Center
(212) 722-0610
K–8th grade
Coed day school—132 students

Collegiate School
(212) 769-6500
1st–12th grade
Boys' day school—549 students

Columbia Grammar and Prep
School
(212) 749-6200
K–12th grade
Coed day school—618 students

Convent of the Sacred Heart
(212) 722-4745
Preschool–12th grade
Girls' day school—481 students

Corlears School
(212) 741-2800
Preschool–4th grade
Coed day school—142 students

The Dalton School
(212) 722-5160
Preschool–12th grade
Coed day school—1,277 students

The Day School
(212) 369-8040
Preschool–12th grade
Coed day school—351 students

The Episcopal School/City of NY
(212) 879-9764
Preschool-Kindergarten
Coed day school—217 students

The Ethical Culture Schools
(212) 874-5200
Preschool–12th grade
Coed day school—1,522 students

Friends Seminary
(212) 979-5030
Preschool–12th grade
Coed day school—577 students

Grace Church School
(212) 475-5609
Preschool–8th grade
Coed day school—350 students

The Hewitt School
(212) 288-1919
K–12th grade
Girls' day school—323 students

Little Red School House and
     Elisabeth Irwin High School

(212) 477-5316
Preschool–12th grade
Coed day school—366 students

Loyola School
(212) 288-3522
9th–12th grade
Coed day school—197 students

Marymount School of New York
(212) 744-4486
Preschool–12th grade
Girls' day school—258 students

The Nightingale-Bamford School
(212) 289-5020
K–12th grade
Girls' day school—471 students

Professional Children's School
(212) 582-3116
4th–12th grade
Coed day school—177 students

Regis High School
(212) 288-1100
9th–12th grade
Boys' day school—507 students

Robert Louis Stevenson School
(212) 787-6400
7th–12th grade
Coed day school—45 students

Rudolf Steiner School
(212) 535-2130
Preschool–12th grade
Coed day school—218 students

Saint David's School
(212) 369-0058
Preschool–8th grade
Boys' day school—325 students

Appendix B

St. Bernard's School
(212) 289-2878
1st–9th grade
Boys' day school—322 students

St. Hilda's and St. Hugh's School
(212) 932-1980
Preschool–12th grade
Coed day school—238 students

St. Luke's School
(212) 924-5960
Preschool–8th grade
Coed day school—190 students

St. Thomas Choir School
(212) 247-3311
5th–8th grade
Boys' boarding—41 students

The Spence School
(212) 289-5940
K–12th grade
Girls' day school—555 students

The Town School
(212) 288-4383
Preschool–8th grade
Coed day school—350 students

Trinity School
(212) 873-1650
K–12th grade
Coed day school—899 students

Winston Preparatory School
(212) 496-8400
7th–12th grade
Coed day school—65 students

United Nations International
    School

(212) 684-7400
K–12th grade
Coed day school—1,398 students

Queens
Garden School, Inc.
Jackson Heights   (718) 335-6363
Preschool–12th grade
Coed day school—341 students

The Kew-Forest School
Forest Hills   (718) 268-4667
1st–12th grade
Coed day school—386 students

Staten Island
Staten Island Academy
Staten Island   (718) 987-8100
Preschool–12th grade
Coed day school—342 students

Old Westbury School/Holy Child
Old Westbury   (516) 626-9129
Preschool–12th grade
Coed day school—330 students

East Woods School
Oyster Bay   (516) 922-4400
Preschool–9th grade
Coed day school—273 students

Trinity-Pawling School
Pawling   (914) 855-3100
9th–12th grade (PG)
Boys' boarding/day—253 students

Oakwood School
Poughkeepsie   (914) 462-4200
9th–12th grade (PG)
Coed boarding/day—102 students

Poughkeepsie Day School
Poughkeepsie   (914) 452-7600
Preschool–12th grade
Coed day school—158 students

Allendale Columbia School
Rochester   (716) 381-4560
Preschool–12th grade
Coed day school—438 students

The Harley School
Rochester   (716) 442-1770
Preschool–12th grade
Coed day school—428 students

The Norman Howard School
Rochester   (716) 461-1600
6th–12th grade
Coed day school—51 students

Buckley Country Day School
Roslyn   (516) 627-1910
Preschool–8th grade
Coed day school—306 students

Rye Country Day School
Rye   (914) 967-1417
Preschool–12th grade
Coed day school—763 students

School of the Holy Child
Rye   (914) 967-5622
9th–12th grade
Girls' day school—191 students

The Park School (Buffalo)
Snyder   (716) 839-1242
Preschool–12th grade
Coed day school—258 students

The Gow School
South Wales   (716) 652-3450
7th–12th grade (PG)
Boys' boarding—148 students

The Knox School
St. James   (516) 584-5500
7th–12th grade (PG)
Coed boarding/day—165 students

The Stony Brook School
Stony Brook   (516) 751-1800
7th–12th grade
Coed boarding/day—342 students

Hackley School
Tarrytown   (914) 631-0128
K–12th grade
Coed day/boarding—765 students

Emma Willard School
Troy   (518) 274-4440
Preschool–12th grade (PG)
Girls' day/boarding—474 students

Tuxedo Park School
Tuxedo Park   (914) 351-4737
Preschool–9th grade
Coed day school—136 students

Windward School
White Plains   (914) 949-6968
K–12th grade
Coed day school—180 students

Lawrence Country Day School-
Woodmere Academy
Woodmere   (516) 374-9000
Preschool–12th grade
Coed day school—475 students

Appendix B

North Carolina

Christ School
Arden (704) 684-6232
8th–12th grade
Boys' boarding—127 students

The Asheville School
Asheville (704) 254-6345
9th–12th grade (PG)
Coed boarding/day—188 students

Carolina Day School
Asheville (704) 274-0757
Preschool–12th grade
Coed day school—353 students

The Charlotte Country Day
  Schools
Charlotte (704) 366-1241
Preschool–12th grade
Coed day school—1,438 students

Charlotte Latin School
Charlotte (704) 846-1100
Preschool–12th grade
Coed day school—1,027 students

Providence Day School
Charlotte (704) 364-6848
Preschool–12th grade
Coed day school—973 students

Durham Academy
Durham (919) 489-6569
Preschool–12th grade
Coed day school—916 students

Greensboro Day School
Greensboro (919) 288-8590
K–12th grade
Coed day school—755 students

Morgan School Patterson Preserve
Lenoir (704) 758-2374
7th–12th grade (PG)
Coed boarding/day—77 students

Forsyth Country Day School
Lewisville (919) 945-3151
Preschool–12th grade
Coed day school—572 students

Oak Ridge Military Academy
Oak Ridge (919) 643-4131
7th–12th grade (PG)
Coed boarding/day—147 students

Ravenscroft School
Raleigh (919) 847-0900
Preschool–12th grade
Coed day school—802 students

Saint Mary's College
Raleigh (919) 828-2521
10th–12th grade
Girls' boarding/day—216 students

The O'Neal School
Southern Pines (919) 692-6920
Preschool–12th grade
Coed day school—296 students

Cape Fear Academy
Wilmington (919) 791-0287
Preschool–12th grade
Coed day school—338 students

Greenfield School
Wilson (919) 237-8046
Preschool–12th grade
Coed day school—311 students

Salem Academy
Winston-Salem   (919) 721-2646
9th–12th grade
Girls' boarding/day—147 students

The Summit School
Winston-Salem   (919) 722-2777
Preschool–9th grade
Coed day school—671 students

Ohio

The Grand River Academy
Austinburg   (216) 275-2811
9th–12th grade (PG)
Boys' boarding/day—111 students

Columbus School for Girls
Columbus   (614) 252-0781
Preschool–12th grade
Girls' day school—609 students

Olney Friends School
Barnesville   (614) 425-3655
9th–12th grade
Coed boarding—38 students

Marburn Academy
Columbus   (614) 433-0822
1st–12th grade
Coed day school—73 students

Old Trail School
Bath   (216) 666-1118
Preschool–8th grade
Coed day school—460 students

The Wellington School
Columbus   (614) 457-7883
K–12th grade
Coed day school—453 students

Canton Country Day School
Canton   (216) 453-8279
K–8th grade
Coed day school—153 students

The Miami Valley School
Dayton   (513) 434-4444
Preschool–12th grade
Coed day school—349 students

Cincinnati Country Day School
Cincinnati   (513) 561-7298
Preschool–12th grade
Coed day school—796 students

The Columbus Academy
Gahanna   (614) 475-2311
K–12th grade
Boys' day school—596 students

The Seven Hills Schools
Cincinnati   (513) 271-9027
Preschool–12th grade
Coed day school—936 students

Gilmour Academy
Gates Mills   (216) 442-1104
Preschool–12th grade
Coed day/boarding—545 students

Hathaway Brown School
Cleveland   (216) 932-4214
Preschool–12th grade
Girls' day school—571 students

Hawken School
Gates Mills   (216) 423-4446
K–12th grade
Coed day school—810 students

Western Reserve Academy
Hudson   (216) 650-4400
9th–12th grade (PG)
Coed boarding/day—377 students

University School
Hunting Valley   (216) 831-2200
K–12th grade
Boys' day school—821 students

Lake Ridge Academy
North Ridgeville   (216) 777-9434
K–12th grade
Coed day school—409 students

Laurel School
Shaker Heights   (216) 464-1441
Preschool–12th grade
Girls' day school—551 students

Maumee Valley Country Day
   School
Toledo   (419) 381-1313
Preschool–12th grade
Coed day school—510 students

The Andrews School
Willoughby   (216) 942-3600
7th–12th grade
Girls' day/boarding—146 students

Oklahoma

Casady School
Oklahoma City   (405) 755-0550
Preschool–12th grade
Coed day school—917 students

Heritage Hall
Oklahoma City   (405) 751-6797
Preschool–12th grade
Coed day school—748 students

Westminster Day School
Oklahoma City   (405) 524-0631
Preschool–8th grade
Coed day school—575 students

Holland Hall School
Tulsa   (918) 481-1111
Preschool–12th grade
Coed day school—992 students

Oregon

St. Mary's School
Medford   (503) 773-7877
7th–11th grade
Coed day school—247 students

The Catlin Gabel School
Portland   (503) 297-1894
Preschool–12th grade
Coed day school—639 students

Oregon Episcopal School
Portland   (503) 246-7771
Preschool–12th grade
Coed day/boarding—648 students

Sunriver Preparatory School
Sunriver   (503) 593-1244
Preschool–12th grade
Coed day school—129 students

Pennsylvania

The Swain School
Allentown   (215) 433-4542
Preschool–8th grade
Coed day school—270 students

Moravian Academy
Bethlehem   (215) 691-1600
Preschool–12th grade (PG)
Coed day/boarding—613 students

The Baldwin School
Bryn Mawr   (215) 525-2700
K–12th grade
Girls' day school—476 students

Country Day School of the Sacred
    Heart
Bryn Mawr   (215) 527-3915
Preschool–12th grade
Girls' day school—216 students

Delaware Valley Friends School
Bryn Mawr   (215) 526-9595
7th–12th grade
Coed day school—68 students

The Shipley School
Bryn Mawr   (215) 525-4300
K–12th grade
Coed day school—586 students

Montgomery School
Chester Springs   (215) 827-7222
Preschool–8th grade
Coed day school—187 students

The Erie Day School
Erie   (814) 452-4273
Preschool–8th grade
Coed day school—118 students

Germantown Academy
Fort Washington   (215) 646-3300
Preschool–12th grade
Coed day school—996 students

MMI Preparatory School
Freeland   (717) 636-1108
7th–12th grade
Coed day school—151 students

Friends School
Haverford   (215) 642-2334
Preschool–6th grade
Coed day school—161 students

The Haverford School
Haverford   (215) 642-3020
Preschool–12th grade
Boys' day school—661 students

Milton Hershey School
Hershey   (717) 534-3500
K–12th grade
Coed boarding—1,106 students

Abington Friends School
Jenkintown   (215) 886-4350
Preschool–12th grade
Coed day school—661 students

Upland Country Day School
Kennett Square   (215) 444-3035
Preschool–9th grade
Coed day school—218 students

Kimberton Waldorf School
Kimberton   (215) 933-3635
Preschool–12th grade
Coed day school—318 students

Wyoming Seminary College
  Preparatory School
Kingston   (717) 283-6000
Preschool–12th grade (PG)
Coed day/boarding—690 students

The Buckingham Friends School
Lahaska   (215) 794-7491
K–8th grade
Coed day school—178 students

Lancaster Country Day School
Lancaster   (717) 392-2916
K–12th grade
Coed day school—474 students

Valley School of Ligonier
Ligonier   (412) 238-6652
K–9th grade
Coed day school—197 students

Linden Hall
Lititz   (717) 626-8512
9th–12th grade (PG)
Girls' boarding/day—71 students

The Hillside School
Macungie   (215) 967-5449
1st–7th grade
Coed day school—103 students

Malvern Preparatory School
Malvern   (215) 644-5454
6th–12th grade
Boys' day school—443 students

The Phelps School
Malvern   (215) 644-1754
7th–12th grade (PG)
Boys' boarding—128 students

The Meadowbrook School
Meadowbrook   (215) 884-3238

Preschool–6th grade
Coed day school—191 students

Media-Providence Friends School
Media   (215) 565-1960
Preschool–8th grade
Coed day school—182 students

The Mercersburg Academy
Mercersburg   (717) 328-2151
9th–12th grade (PG)
Coed boarding/day—376 students

The Episcopal Academy
Merion   (215) 667-9612
Preschool–12th grade
Coed day school—976 students

Akiba Hebrew Academy
Merion Station   (215) 839-3540
6th–12th grade
Coed day school—358 students

The Miquon School
Miquon   (215) 828-1231
Preschool–6th grade
Coed day school—149 students

Carson Long Military Institute
New Bloomfield   (717) 582-2121
6th–12th grade (PG)
Boys' boarding—201 students

Solebury School
New Hope   (215) 862-5261
7th–12th grade (PG)
Coed day/boarding—117 students

George School
Newtown   (215) 968-3811
9th–12th grade
Coed boarding day—541 students

Newtown Friends School
Newtown   (215) 968-2225
K–8th grade
Coed day school—274 students

The Church Farm School
Paoli   (215) 363-7500
7th–12th grade
Boys' boarding—155 students

Perkiomen School
Pennsburg   (215) 679-9511
7th–12th grade (PG)
Coed boarding/day—206 students

Chestnut Hill Academy
Philadelphia   (215) 247-4700
K–12th grade
Boys' day school—489 students

Friends Select School
Philadelphia   (215) 561-5900
Preschool–12th grade
Coed day school—521 students

Germantown Friends School
Philadelphia   (215) 951-2300
K–12th grade
Coed day school—883 students

The Philadelphia School
Philadelphia   (215) 545-5323
K–8th grade
Coed day school—199 students

St. Barnabas Episcopal School
Philadelphia   (215) 438-9670
K–6th grade
Coed day school—74 students

St. Peter's School
Philadelphia   (215) 925-3963

Preschool–8th grade
Coed day school—206 students

St. Joseph Preparatory School
Philadelphia   (215) 978-1950
9th–12th grade
Boys' day school—730 students

Springside School
Philadelphia   (215) 247-7200
Preschool–12th grade
Girls' day school—393 students

William Penn Charter School
Philadelphia   (215) 844-3460
K–12th grade
Coed day school—810 students

The Ellis School
Pittsburgh   (412) 661-5992
K–12th grade
Girls' day school—429 students

Fox Chapel Country Day School
Pittsburgh   (412) 963-8644
Preschool–5th grade
Coed day school—132 students

St. Edmund's Academy
Pittsburgh   (412) 521-1907
Preschool–8th grade
Coed day school—286 students

Shady Side Academy
Pittsburgh   (412) 963-8800
K–12th grade
Coed day/boarding—874 students

The Winchester Thurston School
Pittsburgh   (412) 578-7500
K–12th grade
Girls' day school—340 students

The Hill School
Pottstown   (215) 326-1000
8th–12th grade (PG)
Boys' boarding/day—475 students

The Wyndcroft School
Pottstown   (215) 326-0544
Preschool–8th grade
Coed day school—187 students

Agnes Irwin School
Rosemont   (215) 525-8400
K–12th grade
Girls' day school—497 students

The Hill Top Preparatory School
Rosemont   (215) 527-3230
7th–12th grade
Coed day school—84 students

Rosemont School of the Holy
   Child
Rosemont   (215) 525-1876
Preschool–8th grade
Coed day school—275 students

The Kiski School
Saltsburg   (412) 639-3586
9th–12th grade (PG)
Boys' boarding/day—211 students

Scranton Preparatory School
Scranton   (717) 941-7737
9th–12th grade
Coed day school—784 students

Sewickley Academy
Sewickley   (412) 741-2230
Preschool–12th grade
Coed day school—670 students

The Woodlynde School
Strafford   (215) 687-9660
K–12th grade
Coed day school—227 students

The Grier School
Tyrone   (814) 684-3000
7th–12th grade (PG)
Girls' boarding—130 students

Academy of Notre Dame de
   Namur
Villanova   (215) 687-0650
6th–12th grade
Girls' day school—439 students

Valley Forge Military Academy
Wayne   (215) 688-1800
7th–12th grade (PG)
Boys' boarding—386 students

Westtown School
Westtown   (215) 399-0123
Preschool–12th grade
Coed day/boarding—589 students

The Harrisburg Academy
Wormleysburg   (717) 763-7811
Preschool–12th grade
Coed day school—328 students

Friends' Central School
Wynnewood   (215) 649-7440
Preschool–12th grade
Coed day school—705 students

York Country Day School
York   (717) 843-9805
Preschool–12th grade
Coed day school—216 students

Puerto Rico

Baldwin School
Bayamon   (809) 720-2421
Preschool–12th grade
Coed day school—609 students

Caribbean Consolidated Schools
San Juan   (809) 765-4411
Preschool–12th grade
Coed day school—792 students

The Caribbean School
Ponce   (809) 843-2048
Preschool–12th grade
Coed day school—633 students

St. John's School
Santurce   (809) 728-5343
Preschool–12th grade
Coed day school—735 students

Rhode Island

St. Andrew's School
Barrington   (401) 246-1230
6th–12th grade
Coed day/boarding—113 students

Rocky Hill School
East Greenwich   (401) 884-9070
Preschool–12th grade
Coed day school—257 students

The Providence Country Day
    School
East Providence   (401) 438-5170
5th–12th grade
Coed day school—204 students

St. George's School
Newport   (401) 847-7565
9th–12th grade
Coed boarding/day—325 students

St. Michael's Country Day School
Newport   (401) 849-5970
Preschool–8th grade
Coed—182 students

The New School
Portsmouth   (401) 849-4646

Preschool–8th grade
Coed day school—157 students

Portsmouth Abbey School
Portsmouth   (401) 683-2000
9th–12th grade
Coed boarding/day—206 students

Gordon School
Providence   (401) 434-3833
Preschool–8th grade
Coed day school—396 students

Lincoln School
Providence   (401) 331-9696
Preschool–12th grade
Girls' day school—396 students

Moses Brown School
Providence   (401) 831-7350
Preschool–12th grade
Coed day school—757 students

The Wheeler School
Providence   (401) 421-8100
Preschool–12th grade
Coed day school—666 students

South Carolina

Aiken Preparatory School
Aiken   (803) 648-3223
Preschool–9th grade
Coed day/boarding—157 students

Camden Military Academy
Camden   (803) 432-6001
7th–12th grade (PG)
Boys' boarding—203 students

Ashley Hall
Charleston   (803) 722-4088
Preschool–12th grade
Girls' day school—424 students

Charleston Day School
Charleston   (803) 722-7791
1st–8th grade
Coed day school—171 students

Porter-Gaud School
Charleston   (803) 556-3620
1st–12th grade
Coed day school—789 students

Ben Lippen School
Columbia   (803) 786-7200
6th–12th grade
Coed day/boarding—303 students

Hammond School
Columbia   (803) 776-0295
K–12th grade
Coed day school—520 students

Heathwood Hall Episcopal School
Columbia   (803) 765-2309
Preschool–12th grade
Coed day school—732 students

Christ Church Episcopal School
Greenville   (803) 299-1522
K–12th grade
Coed day school—599 students

Cambridge Academy
Greenwood   (803) 229-2875
Preschool–12th grade
Coed day school—285 students

Hilton Head Preparatory School
Hilton Head Island
(803) 671-2286
9th–12th grade (PG)
Coed Boarding—355 students

The Spartanburg Day School
Spartanburg   (803) 582-7539
Preschool–12th grade
Coed day school—527 students

Tennessee

The Webb School
Bell Buckle   (615) 389-9322
7th–12th grade (PG)
Coed day/boarding—166 students

Brentwood Academy
Brentwood   (615) 373-0611

7th–12th grade
Coed day school—424 students

The Baylor School
Chattanooga   (615) 267-8505
7th–12th grade
Coed day/boarding—727 students

Girls' Preparatory School
Chattanooga   (615) 634-7600
7th–12th grade
Girls' day school—585 students

The McCallie School
Chattanooga   (615) 622-2163
7th–12th grade
Boys' day/boarding—695 students

Saint Nicholas School
Chattanooga   (615) 624-0965
Preschool–6th grade
Coed day school—194 students

Battle Ground Academy
Franklin   (615) 794-3501
7th–12th grade
Coed day school—346 students

Harpeth Academy
Franklin   (615) 794-8436
K–6th grade
Coed day school—192 students

University School of Jackson
Jackson   (901) 664-0812
Preschool–12th grade
Coed day school—645 students

Webb School of Knoxville
Knoxville   (615) 693-0011
5th–12th grade
Coed day school—751 students

Grace-St. Luke's Episcopal School
Memphis   (901) 278-0200
Preschool–9th grade
Coed day school—492 students

Hutchison School
Memphis   (901) 761-2220

Preschool–12th grade
Girls' day school—787 students

Lausanne Collegiate School
Memphis   (901) 683-5233
Preschool–12th grade
Coed day school—380 students

Memphis University School
Memphis   (901) 761-5271
7th–12th grade
Boys' day school—582 students

St. Mary's Episcopal School
Memphis   (901) 682-4626
Preschool–12th grade
Girls' day school—728 students

Ensworth School
Nashville   (615) 383-0661
K–8th grade
Coed day school—487 students

Harding Academy
Nashville   (615) 356-5510
K–8th grade
Coed day school—372 students

The Harpeth Hall School
Nashville   (615) 297-9543
6th–12th grade
Girls' day school—388 students

Montgomery Bell Academy
Nashville   (615) 298-5514
7th–12th grade
Boys' day school—473 students

The Oak Hill School
Nashville   (615) 297-6544
Preschool–6th grade
Coed day school—428 students

Appendix B

University School of Nashville
Nashville   (615) 327-8158
K–12th grade
Coed day school—843 students

St. Andrew's-Sewanee School
St. Andrews   (615) 598-5651
7th–12th grade
Coed day/boarding—232 students

Texas

The Oakridge School
Arlington   (817) 451-4994
Preschool–12th grade
Coed day school—543 students

The Lamplighter School
Dallas   (214) 369-9201
Preschool–4th grade
Coed day school—475 students

St. Stephen's Episcopal School
Austin   (512) 327-1213
7th–12th grade
Coed day/boarding—292 students

St. John's Episcopal School
Dallas   (214) 328-9131
Preschool–8th grade
Coed day school—415 students

Episcopal High School
Bellaire   (713) 660-7840
9th–12th grade
Coed day school—458 students

St. Mark's School of Texas
Dallas   (214) 363-6491
1st–12th grade
Boys' day school—766 students

The Episcopal School of Dallas
Dallas   (214) 358-4368
5th–12th grade
Coed day school—399 students

The Winston School
Dallas   (214) 691-6950
1st–12th grade
Coed day school—124 students

Good Shepherd Episcopal School
Dallas   (214) 357-1610
Preschool–8th grade
Coed day school—360 students

The Selwyn School
Denton   (817) 382-6771
Preschool–12th grade
Coed day/boarding—179 students

Greenhill School
Dallas   (214) 661-1211
Preschool–12th grade
Coed day school—1,175 students

Fort Worth Academy
Fort Worth   (817) 370-1191
K–8th grade
Coed day school—186 students

The Hockaday School
Dallas   (214) 363-6311
Preschool–12th grade
Girls' day/boarding—894 students

Fort Worth Country Day School
Fort Worth   (817) 732-7718
K–12th grade
Coed day school—858 students

193

Trinity Valley School
Fort Worth   (817) 292-6060
K–12th grade
Coed day school—689 students

Marine Military Academy
Harlingen   (512) 423-6006
8th–12th grade (PG)
Boys' boarding—411 students

The Awty International School
Houston   (713) 686-4850
Preschool–12th grade
Coed day school—473 students

Grace School
Houston   (713) 782-4421
Preschool–8th grade
Coed day school—355 students

The Kinkaid School
Houston   (713) 782-1640
Preschool–12th grade
Coed day school—1,242 students

River Oaks Baptist School
Houston   (713) 623-6938
Preschool–8th grade
Coed day school—573 students

St. John's School
Houston   (713) 850-0222
K–12th grade
Coed day school—1134 students

Cistercian Preparatory School
Irving   (214) 438-4956

Utah

Long Trail School
Dorset   (802) 867-5717

5th–12th grade
Boys' day school—306 students

Trinity School of Midland
Midland   (915) 697-3281
Preschool–12th grade
Coed day school—457 students

Saint Mary's Hall
San Antonio   (512) 655-7721
Preschool–12th grade (PG)
Coed day/boarding—749 students

San Antonio Academy
San Antonio   (512) 733-7331
Preschool–8th grade
Boys' day/boarding—279 students

TMI-Texas Military Institute
San Antonio   (512) 698-7171
6th–12th grade (PG)
Coed day/boarding—260 students

San Marcos Baptist Academy
San Marcos   (512) 353-2400
6th–12th grade
Coed boarding/day—269 students

The John Cooper School
The Woodlands   (713) 367-0900
Preschool–9th grade
Coed day school—277 students

Vanguard School
Waco   (817) 772-8111
7th–12th grade
Coed day school—164 students

7th–12th grade
Coed day school—48 students

Burr and Burton Seminary
Manchester   (802) 362-1775
9th–12th grade
Coed day school—308 students

Wasatch Academy
Mount Pleasant   (801) 462-2411
9th–12th grade
Coed boarding/day—122 students

The Grammar School, Inc.
Putney   (802) 387-5364
K–8th grade
Coed day school—93 students

Vermont

The Waterford School
Sandy   (801) 572-1780
Preschool–12th grade
Coed day school—468 students

Vermont Academy
Saxtons River   (802) 869-2121
9th–12th grade (PG)
Coed boarding/day—236 students

St. Johnsbury Academy
St. Johnsbury   (802) 748-8171

The Greenwood School
Putney   (802) 387-4545
3rd–9th grade
Boys' boarding—39 students

The Putney School
Putney   (802) 387-5566
9th–12th grade (PG)
Coed boarding/day—146 students

Rowland Hall-St. Mark's School
Salt Lake City   (801) 355-7485
Preschool–12th grade
Coed day school—871 students

9th–12th grade (PG)
Coed day/boarding—799 students

Stratton Mountain School
Stratton Mountain
(802) 297-1886
8th–12th grade
Coed boarding/day—64 students

Pine Ridge School
Williston   (802) 434-2161
7th–12th grade
Coed boarding—103 students

Virginia

Browne Academy
Alexandria   (703) 960-3000
Preschool–8th grade
Coed day school—264 students

Episcopal High School
Alexandria   (703) 379-6530
9th–12th grade
Coed boarding—287 students

St. Stephen's & St. Agnes School
Alexandria   (703) 751-2700
K–12th grade
Coed day school—458 students

Powhatan School
Boyce   (703) 837-1009
K–8th grade
Coed day school—170 students

The Miller School of Albemarle
Charlottesville   (804) 823-4805
5th–12th grade
Boys' boarding—100 students

St. Anne's-Belfield School
Charlottesville   (804) 296-5106
Preschool–12th grade
Coed day/boarding—725 students

Tandem School
Charlottesville   (804) 296-1303
5th–12th grade
Coed day school—119 students

Chatham Hall
Chatham   (804) 432-2941
9th–12th grade
Girls' boarding/day—115 students

Christchurch School
Christchurch   (804) 758-2306
9th–12th grade
Boys' boarding/day—219 students

Blue Ridge School
Dyke   (804) 985-2811
9th–12th grade
Boys' boarding—200 students

Broadwater Academy
Exmore   (804) 442-9041
Preschool–12th grade
Coed day school—382 students

Fork Union Military Academy
Fork Union   (804) 842-3212
6th–12th grade (PG)
Boys' boarding—594 students

Randolph-Macon Academy
Front Royal   (703) 636-5200

7th–12th grade (PG)
Coed boarding/day—381 students

Loudoun Country Day School
Leesburg   (703) 777-3841
Preschool–8th grade
Coed day school—176 students

Seven Hills School
Lynchburg   (804) 847-1013
6th–12th grade
Coed day school—102 students

Virginia Episcopal School
Lynchburg   (804) 384-6221
9th–12th grade
Coed boarding/day—218 students

Carlisle School
Martinsville   (703) 632-7288
Preschool–12th grade
Coed day school—344 students

The Langley School
McLean   (703) 356-1920
Preschool–8th grade
Coed day school—446 students

The Madeira School
McLean   (703) 556-8200
9th–12th grade
Girls' boarding/day—326 students

The Potomac School
McLean   (703) 356-4100
Preschool–12th grade
Coed day school—802 students

Foxcroft School
Middleburg   (703) 687-5555
9th–12th grade (PG)
Girls' boarding/day—131 students

The Hill School
Middleburg   (703) 687-5897
K–8th grade
Coed day school—178 students

Hampton Roads Academy
Newport News   (804) 249-1489
6th–12th grade
Coed day school—389 students

Norfolk Academy
Norfolk   (804) 461-6236
1st–12th grade
Coed day school—1,167 students

Norfolk Collegiate School
Norfolk   (804) 480-2885
K–12th grade
Coed day school—537 students

The Williams School
Norfolk   (804) 627-1383
K–8th grade
Coed day school—122 students

Flint Hill School
Oakton   (703) 242-0705
K–12th grade
Coed day school—446 students

Grymes Memorial School
Orange   (703) 672-1010
Preschool–8th grade
Coed day school—159 students

Benedictine High School
Richmond   (804) 342-1300
9th–12th grade
Boys' day school—217 students

The Collegiate Schools
Richmond   (804) 740-7077

K–12th grade
Coed day schools—1,338 students

Saint Catherine's School
Richmond   (804) 288-2804
Preschool–12th grade
Girls' day/boarding—710 students

St. Christopher's School
Richmond   (804) 282-3185
Preschool–12th grade
Boys' day school—778 students

St. Gertrude High School
Richmond   (804) 358-9114
9th–12th grade
Girls' day school—173 students

The Steward School
Richmond   (804) 740-3394
K–12th grade
Coed day school—242 students

Trinity Episcopal School
Richmond   (804) 272-5864
8th–12th grade
Coed day school—236 students

North Cross School
Roanoke   (703) 989-6641
Preschool–12th grade
Coed day school—493 students

Stuart Hall
Staunton   (703) 885-0356
8th–12th grade
Girls' boarding/day—72 students

Nansemond-Suffolk Academy
Suffolk   (804) 539-8789
Preschool–12th grade
Coed day school—907 students

St. Margaret's School
Tappahannock   (804) 443-3357
8th–12th grade (PG)
Girls' boarding/day—104 students

Cape Henry Collegiate School
Virginia Beach   (804) 481-2446
Preschool–12th grade
Coed day school—471 students

Virgin Islands

Forest Ridge
Bellevue   (206) 641-0700
5th–12th grade
Girls' day school—230 students

The Little School
Bellevue   (206) 827-8708
Preschool–4th grade
Coed day school—209 students

The Good Hope School
Frederiksted,
St. Croix   (809) 772-0022
Preschool–12th grade
Coed day school—422 students

Washington

The Overlake School
Redmond   (206) 868-1000
5th–12th grade
Coed day school—199 students

The Bush School
Seattle   (206) 322-7978
K–12th grade
Coed day school—530 students

Epiphany School
Seattle   (206) 323-9011
Preschool–6th grade
Coed day school—135 students

Highland School
Warrenton   (703) 347-1221
K–8th grade
Coed day school—148 students

Woodberry Forest School
Woodberry Forest
(703) 672-3900
9th–12th grade
Boys' boarding—361 students

St. Thomas School
Medina   (206) 454-5880
Preschool–6th grade
Coed day school—180 students

All Saints Cathedral School
St. Thomas   (809) 774-0231
Preschool–12th grade
Coed day school—431 students

The Antilles School
St. Thomas   (809) 774-1966
Preschool–12th grade
Coed day school—410 students

The Evergreen School
Seattle   (206) 364-2650
Preschool–8th grade
Coed day school—241 students

Lakeside School
Seattle   (206) 368-3600
5th–12th grade
Coed day school—674 students

University Preparatory Academy
Seattle   (206) 525-2714
6th–12th grade
Coed day school—261 students

Saint George's School
Spokane   (509) 466-1636
K–12th grade
Coed day school—255 students

The Annie Wright School
Tacoma   (206) 272-2216

West Virginia

The Linsly School
Wheeling   (304) 233-3260
5th–12th grade
Coed day/boarding—419 students

Wisconsin

Wayland Academy
Beaver Dam   (414) 885-3373
9th–12th grade
Coed boarding/day—258 students

St. John's Military Academy
Delafield   (414) 646-3311
7th–12th grade
Boys' boarding—266 students

University Lake School
Hartland   (414) 367-6011
K–12th grade
Coed day school—252 students

Preschool–12th grade (PG)
Girls' day/boarding—401 students

Charles Wright Academy
Tacoma   (206) 564-2171
Preschool–12th grade
Coed day school—556 students

Wheeling Country Day School
Wheeling   (304) 232-2430
Preschool–6th grade
Coed day school—144 students

Northwestern Military
   and Naval Academy
Lake Geneva   (414) 248-4465
7th–12th grade
Boys' boarding—65 students

University School of Milwaukee
Milwaukee   (414) 352-6000
Preschool–12th grade
Coed day school—1,030 students

The Prairie School
Racine   (414) 631-3845
Preschool–12th grade
Coed day school—470 students

Foreign Members *

Australia

Camberwell Grammar School
Camberwell, Victoria 3103
Tel: 61-03-836-6266

K–12th grade
Boys' day school—1,162 students

---

* For more information on foreign NAIS schools, contact NAIS in Washington, DC
Tel: (202) 833-4757. For information on education in countries with no NAIS
schools, contact the Director, Pupil Personnel Services, Department of State,
Washington, DC 20520-8100

Canberra Grammar School
Canberra, 2603
Tel: 61-06-295-1833
Preschool–12th grade
Boys' day/boarding—1,373 students

Geelong Grammar School
Geelong, Victoria
Tel: 61-05-273-9200
Preschool–12th grade
Coed boarding/day—1,765 students

Ivanhoe Grammar School
Ivanhoe, Victoria 3079
Tel: 61-03-497-1877

K–12th grade
Boys' day school—1,818 students

Methodist Ladies' College
Kew, Victoria 3101
Tel: 61-03-810-1333
Preschool–12th grade
Girls' day/boarding—2,280 students

Wesley College
Prahran, Victoria 3181
Tel: 61-03-51-8694
K–12th grade
Coed day school—2,734 students

Austria

The American International School
Salmannsdorferstrasse 47
A-1190 Vienna

Preschool–12th grade
Coed day school—3,592 students

Bahamas

St. Andrew's School
P.O. Box N-7546, Nassau
Tel: (809) 324-2621

Preschool–12th grade
Coed day school—292 students

Belgium

International School of Brussels
1170 Brussels

Preschool–12th grade
Coed day school—1,072 students

Bermuda

Saltus Grammar School
Hamilton HMJX
Tel: (809) 292-6177
K–12th grade
Boys' day school—629 students

The Bermuda High School
Tel: (809) 295-6153
K–12th grade
Girls' day school—531 students

Appendix B

Brazil

Associacao Escola Graduada de
  Sao Paulo
01051 Sao Paulo

Preschool–12th grade
Coed day school—1,091 students

Canada

St. Andrew's College
Aurora, Ontario L4G3H7
Tel: (416) 727-3178
7th–12th grade
Boys' boarding/day—433 students

Lower Canada College
Montreal, Quebec H4A 2M5
Tel: (514) 482-9916
3rd–12th grade
Boys' day school—592 students

Albert College
Belleville, Ontario K8P 1A6
Tel: (613) 968-5726
7th–12th grade
Coed boarding/day—205 students

Miss Edgar's/Miss Cramp's School
Montreal, Quebec H3Y 3H6
Tel: (514) 935-6357
1st–11th grade
Girls' day school—331 students

Grenville Christian College
Brockville, Ontario K6V 5V8
Tel: (613) 345-5521
Preschool–12th grade
Coed boarding/day—241 students

St. George's School of Montreal
Montreal, Quebec H3Y 1R9
Tel: (514) 937-9289
Preschool–11th grade
Coed day school—468 students

Hillfield Strathallan College
Hamilton, Ontario L9C 1G3
Tel: (416) 389-1367
Preschool–12th grade
Coed day school—977 students

Selwyn House School
Montreal, Quebec H3Y 2H8
Tel: (514) 931-9481
1st–11th grade
Boys' day school—532 students

Lakefield College School
Lakefield, Ontario K0L 2H0
Tel: (705) 652-3324
7th–12th grade
Coed boarding/day—268 students

The Study
Montreal, Quebec H3Y 1S4
Tel: (514) 482-9352
K–11th grade
Girls' day school—265 students

Bishop's College School
Lennoxville, Quebec J1M 1Z8
Tel: (819) 566-0227
7th–12th grade
Coed boarding/day—276 students

Trafalgar School for Girls
Montreal, Quebec H3G 2J7
Tel: (514) 935-2644
7th–11th grade
Girls' day school—277 students

Pickering College
Newmarket, Ontario L3Y 4X2
Tel: (416) 895-1700
7th–12th grade
Boys' boarding/day—164 students

Appleby College
Oakville, Ontario L6K 3P1
Tel: (416) 845-4681
4th–12th grade
Boys' day/boarding—486 students

Strathcona-Tweedsmuir School
Okotoks, Alberta T0L 1T0
Tel: (403) 938-4431
1st–12th grade
Coed day school—541 students

Ashbury College
Ottawa. Ontario K1M 0T3
Tel: (613) 749-5954
7th–12th grade
Coed day/boarding—470 students

Trinity College School
Port Hope, Ontario L1A 3W2
Tel: (416) 885-4565
8th–12th grade
Boys' boarding/day—390 students

Ridley College
St. Catherines, Ontario L2R 7C3
Tel: (416) 684-8193
5th–12th grade (PG)
Coed boarding/day—605 students

Stanstead College
Stanstead, Quebec J0B 3E0
Tel: (819) 876-2223
7th–12th grade (PG)
Coed boarding/day—162 students

The Bishop Strachan School
Toronto, Ontario M4V 1X2
Tel: (416) 483-4325
Preschool–12th grade
Girls' day/boarding—761 students

Branksome Hall
Toronto, Ontario M4W 1N4
Tel: (416) 920-9741
K–12th grade
Girls' day/boarding—784 students

Havergal College
Toronto, Ontario M5N 2H9
Tel: (416) 483-3519
Preschool–12th grade
Girls' day/boarding—717 students

St. Clement's School
Toronto, Ontario M4R 1G8
Tel: (416) 483-4835
1st grade–12th grade
Girls' day school—402 students

The Toronto French School
Toronto, Ontario M4N 1T7
Tel: (416) 484-6533
Preschool–12th grade
Coed day school—1,290 students

Upper Canada College
Toronto, Ontario M4V 1W6
Tel: (416) 488-1225
3rd–12th grade
Boys' day/boarding—1,003 students

Crofton House School
Vancouver, B.C. V6N 3E1
Tel: (604) 263-3255
1st–12th grade
Girls' day school—492 students

Appendix B

Fraser Academy
Vancouver, B.C. V6K 2H8
Tel: (604) 736-5575
6th–12th grade
Coed day school—81 students

St. George's School
Vancouver, B.C. V6S 1V6
Tel: (604) 224-1304
2nd–12th grade
Boys' day/boarding—695 students

York House School
Vancouver, B.C. V6J 2V6
Tel: (604) 736-6551
K–12th grade
Coed day school—605 students

Collinwood School
Victoria, B.C.
Tel: (604) 925-3331
K–12th grade
Coed day school—630 students

Egypt
Cairo American College
P.O. Box 39, Maadi
Cairo

France
American School of Paris
92210 Saint-Cloud

Germany
The Franfurt International School
An der Valdlust 15

Great Britain
TASIS England American School
Contact New York Office:

Glenlyon-Norfolk School
Victoria, B.C.
Tel: (604) 598-2621
K–12th grade
Coed day school—695 students

Trafalgar Castle School
Whitby, Ontario L1N 3W9
Tel: (416) 668-3358
7th–12th grade
Girls' boarding/day—182 students

Crescent School
Willowdale, Ontario M2L 1A2
Tel: (416) 449-2556
4th–12th grade
Boys' day school—503 students

Balmoral Hall School
Winnipeg, MB R3C 3S1
Tel: (204) 786-8643
Preschool–12th grade
Girls' day/boarding—456 students

K–12th grade
Coed day school—1,307 students

Preschool–12th grade
Coed day school—895 students

K–12th grade
Coed day school—1,317 students

329 East 69th Street
New York, NY 10021

The American School in London
London NW8 0NP
Tel: 44-71-722-0101
Preschool–12th grade
Coed day school—1,316 students

Tel: (212) 570-1066
K–12th grade
Coed day/boarding—610 students

Greece

American Community Schools of
    Athens
129 Aghias Paraskevis Street
Athens College
Athens, Greece
1st–12th grade
Coed day school—3,592 students

Athens
Preschool–12th grade
Coed day school—1,309 students
TASIS Hellenic International
    School
P.O. Box 51025
Athens
K–12th grade
Coed day/boarding—380 students

Guatemala

The American School/Guatemala
Apartado Postal 83
Guatemala City

K–12th grade
Coed day school—1,520 students

Hong Kong

Hong Kong International School
Repulse Bay, Hong Kong

K–12th grade
Coed day school—1,853 students

India

American Embassy School
New Delhi 11021

Preschool–12th grade
Coed day school—700 students

Indonesia

Jakarta International School
Jakarta 12430

K–12th grade
Coed day school—2,471 students

Italy

American School of Milan
20090 Noverasco di Opera
Milan

Preschool–12th grade
Coed day school—455 students

St. Stephen's School
via Aventina 3
00153 Rome

9th–12th grade (PG)
Coed day/boarding—135 students

Japan

The American School in Japan
Chofu-Shi
Tokyo 182

Preschool–12th grade
Coed day school—1,362 students

Luxembourg

American International School of
   Luxembourg
1511 Luxembourg

Preschool–12th grade
Coed day school—440 students

Pakistan

International School of Islamabad
Islamabad, Pakistan

Preschool–12th grade
Coed day school—638 students

Philippines

Brent School
Baguio City
Preschool–12th grade
Coed boarding/day—606 students

International School
Manila
K–12th grade
Coed day school—1,810 students

Republic of Singapore

Singapore American School
Singapore 1026

Preschool–12th grade
Coed day school—1,978 students

Spain

The American School of Madrid
28080 Madrid

Preschool–12th grade
Coed day school—617 students

Switzerland

American School of Institut
   Montana
6316 Zugerburg, Zug
5th–12th grade (PG)
Coed boarding/day—66 students

The American School in
   Switzerland
CH 6926 Montagnola-Lugano
7th–12th grade (PG)
Coed boarding/day—247 students

Thailand

International School Bangkok	K–12th grade
Bangkok	Coed day school—1,770 students

NAIS Member Schools with Five-day Boarding Programs

(More complete data for each school appear in general
listing under appropriate state.)

Admiral Farragut Academy South	Florida
Belmont Hill School	Massachusetts
The Bolles School	Florida
Brenau Academy	Georgia
Castilleja School	California
Chicago Junior School	Illinois
The Doane Stuart School	New York
The Fessenden School	Massachusetts
Foxcroft School	Virginia
Gilmour Academy	Ohio
Hackley School	New York
The Harvey School	New York
Hilton Head Preparatory School	South Carolina
Interlochen Arts Academy	Michigan
Kildonan School	New York
Linden Hill School	Massachusetts
The Madeira School	Virginia
Marian Heights Academy	Indiana
McDonogh School	Maryland
Moravian Academy	Pennsylvania
Noble and Greenough School	Massachusetts
Oak Ridge Military Academy	North Carolina
Oakwood School	New York
Olney Friends School	Ohio
The Phelps School	Pennsylvania
St. Anne's-Belfield School	Virginia
Saint Mary's Academy	Illinois
St. Scholastica Academy	Colorado
St. Stephen's School in Rome	Italy
Shady Side Academy	Pennsylvania

TASIS England American School	Great Britain
TASIS Hellenic International School	Greece
Thomas Jefferson School	Missouri
TMI-Texas Military Institute	Texas
Woodward Academy	Georgia
Worcester Academy	Massachusetts

NAIS Member Schools with Junior Boarding Programs

(More complete data for each school appear in general listing under appropriate state.)

Admiral Farragut Academy North	New Jersey
Admiral Farragut Academy South	Florida
Aiken Preparatory School	South Carolina
All Saints' Episcopal School	Mississippi
The American School in Switzerland	Switzerland
American School of Institut Montana	Switzerland
The Athenian School	California
The Bement School	Massachusetts
Cardigan Mountain School	New Hampshire
Chicago Junior School	Illinois
St. Thomas Choir School	New York
Eaglebrook School	Massachusetts
Fay School	Massachusetts
The Fessenden School	Massachusetts
Fork Union Military Academy	Virginia
The Greenwood School	Vermont
Hawaii Preparatory Academy	Hawaii
Hillside School	Massachusetts
Hilton Head Preparatory School	South Carolina
Howe Military School	Indiana
Indian Mountain School	Connecticut
Indian Springs School	Alabama
The Knox School	New York
Landmark School	Massachusetts
Linden Hill School	Massachusetts
Milton Hershey School	Pennsylvania
Missouri Military Academy	Missouri

Missouri Military Academy	Missouri
North Country School	New York
Northwestern Military and Naval Academy	Wisconsin
The Oak Grove School	California
Ojai Valley School	California
The Pennington School	New Jersey
Rabun Gap-Nacoochee School	Georgia
The Rectory School	Connecticut
Ridley College	Canada
Rumsey Hall School	Connecticut
St. Andrew's School	Rhode Island
St. Scholastica Academy	Colorado
San Marcos Baptist Academy	Texas
Shady Side Academy	Pennsylvania
TASIS England American School	Great Britain
TASIS Hellenic International School	Greece
Valley Forge Military Academy	Pennsylvania
Woodward Academy	Georgia

NAIS Military Boarding Schools

(More complete data for each school appear in general listing under appropriate state. Most have day students as well as boarders. A few are coed.)

Admiral Farragut Academy North	New Jersey
Admiral Farragut Academy South	Florida
Camden Military Academy	South Carolina
Carson Long Military Institute	Pennsylvania
The Culver Academies	Indiana
Fork Union Military Academy	Virginia
Howe Military School	Indiana
Marine Military Academy	Texas
Missouri Military Academy	Missouri
New York Military Academy	New York
Northwestern Military and Naval Academy	Wisconsin
Oak Ridge Military Academy	North Carolina
Randolph-Macon Academy	Virginia
St. John's Military Academy	Wisconsin
San Marcos Baptist Academy	Texas
TMI-Texas Military Institute	Texas
Valley Forge Military Academy	Pennsylvania

APPENDIX C

FINANCIAL AID RESOURCES

*T*he following resources are designed to make paying for a private-school education easier. None offers aid in the form of scholarship grants, which are usually only available from the schools themselves. The resources listed below are of two types. One allows parents to pay costs of tuition and other school fees interest-free each month while their children attend school. Payments usually begin three to four months before the school year begins. Such "tuition payment plans" charge modest annual fees and are membership plans involving only a specific group of participating schools. Ask each school you consider whether it has any arrangements with one of the tuition payment plans. As with any comparable transactions, be certain to check on the up-to-date financial condition of any organization to which you entrust your funds. Some schools offer the option of using more than one tuition payment plan. Compare costs and benefits before choosing.

"Tuition loan programs" in the second listing below are nothing more than unsecured, long-term personal loans that allow parents to pay for their children's education over a longer period of time. In addition to the organizations listed, many banks also offer education loans. Interest on education loans, however, is exorbitantly high, and, because it is not tax deductible, it is far more advantageous to check into the availability and cost of a mortgage on your home or apartment, if you own one, or a home equity loan (second mortgage), whose interest costs are lower *and* deductible—even if the proceeds are used to pay for your child's education.

Tuition Payment Plans

Academic Management Services
50 Vision Boulevard
East Providence, RI 02914
Tel: (401) 431-1290 or (800) 635-0120

Interest-free, monthly payment plan beginning in May or June before your child
enrolls. Available only for participating schools. Parents must reapply and pay a
$45 application fee each year. Included in the application fee is a premium for
insurance for the outstanding balance of your child's education expenses for the
current school year should you die or be disabled and unable to work. AMS holds
your money for one month before disbursing it to the school.

The Education Resources Institute (TERI)
330 Stuart Street, Suite 500
Boston, MA 02116-5237
Tel: (617) 426-0681 or (800) 255-8374

Available only through participating schools, this 10-month, interest-free payment
plan costs parents an annual fee of $45, which includes insurance for the outstand-
ing balance of your child's education costs for the year, up to a maximum of $10,000.
TERI holds your money one month before disbursing it to the school.

F.A.C.T.S. Tuition Management

P.O. Box 67037	121 Floral Parkway	4630 South Kirkman Road
Lincoln, NE 68506	Floral Park, NY 11001	Orlando, FL 32811
Tel: (402) 466-1063	(516) 328-3286	(407) 296-0982
or (800) 624-7092		

Interest-free monthly payment plan for any time frame (usually 10, 11 or 12 months),
usually beginning in May or June before your child enrolls. Available only through
participating schools, which are paid twice monthly. F.A.C.T.S. charges a $35 an-
nual fee. No insurance available.

Higher Education Services, Inc.
160 South Progress Avenue, Suite 3B
Harrisburg, PA 17109
Tel: (717) 545-7998 or (800) 422-0010

Interest-free monthly payment plan for participating schools only. Application fee
of $40 to $45, depending on the school, includes insurance. HES disburses your
money to the school twice a year.

Knight Tuition Payment Plan
855 Boylston Street
Boston, MA 02116
Tel: (617) 267-1500 or (800) 225-6783

Appendix C

Insured Tuition Payment Plan: An extremely conservative financial organization, Knight sets up an account *in your name* with your payments in an FDIC-insured bank money market account that pays interest on your savings. In other words, unlike other plans in which you pay the money to the plan operator, you're actually paying money into your own bank account under the Knight plan. Knight simply manages the money and withdraws the appropriate amounts when each school bill is due. The plan, which you should begin in May or June before your child enrolls, charges a one-time $55 application fee and a $2 monthly service fee. Schools do not have to participate in the plan, because the account is in your name. Insurance is optional depending on the state where you live and costs 80 cents per $1,000. Any accrued interest on your account is paid over to you when you end the plan.

Ten-Month Payment Plan: Like most other plans, Knight's ten-month payment plan is only applicable to participating schools. Knight charges an annual fee of $35 and offers optional insurance costing 80 cents per $1,000 to cover your child's education expenses in the event of your death or disability. Interest-free monthly payments begin in May or June before your child enrolls. Knight holds your money one month before disbursing it to the school.

School Financial Management Services, Inc.
10 Woodbridge Center Drive
Woodbridge, NJ 07095
Tel: (800) 762-7808

The SMART program, as it's called, is interest free and only applicable to participating schools, which get $8 of the annual parent fee of $45. If you have more than one child, the fee is an all-inclusive $65, of which the school gets $12. SMART pays each school 10 days after the moneys are due and accumulates and holds your monthly payments until then. No insurance is available through SMART.

TADS Tuition Account Service
2305 Ford Parkway
St. Paul, MN 55115
Tel: (603) 228-1161 or (800) 258-3640

Interest-free, monthly payment plan for participating schools only. Application fee varies according to each school. No insurance available.

The Tuition Plan
57 Regional Drive
Concord, NH 03301
Tel: (603) 228-1161 or (800) 258-3640

This interest-free, 10-month payment plan is only available through participating schools. There is a $45 annual fee. Your payments are held a month, then disbursed to the school. Included in your premium costs is insurance covering the outstanding balance of your child's education costs for the year, up to a maximum of $25,000.

211

Tuition Loan Programs

Academic Management Services
50 Vision Boulevard
East Providence, RI 02914
Tel: (401) 431-1290 or (800) 637-3060

AMS offers credit lines of up to $25,000 at interest rates of 2% *a month* on the outstanding balance. That's a whopping 24% a year! Borrowers must prove their creditworthiness and have annual incomes of at least $20,000. There's a $25 annual fee, which is waived the first year. Borrowers may repay both principal and interest each month or defer repayment of the principal and only pay interest each month for two, four or six years. A credit line differs from a loan only in that it limits the maximum outstanding balance of the loan at any one time, without limiting the amount you can borrow over an extended period. Thus, if monthly repayments of principal have reduced the outstanding balance of a $25,000 loan to, say, $15,000, you'd be entitled to borrow up to $10,000 more, without making any application. AMS gives you checks, which you can use at any time to draw on your credit line if there are any funds available.

The Education Resources Institute (TERI)
330 Stuart Street, Suite 500
Boston, MA 02116-5237
Tel: (617) 426-0681 or (800) 255-8374

Called PLEASE loans (Parent Loans for Elementary and Secondary Education), these ten-year loans are only available through participating schools and only to creditworthy parents. Although the interest is set at only 2% above the prime rate, TERI charges a $45 application fee and an up-front, 6% "loan guarantee fee" deducted from the amount loaned. In other words, PLEASE is a discounted loan. Although you might, for example, borrow $10,000 "on paper," you'll only actually receive $9,400 but have to repay and pay interest on the full $10,000.

Knight Tuition Payment Plan
855 Boylston Street
Boston, MA 02116
Tel: (617) 267-1500 or (800) 225-6783

Knight has two loan plans dressed up with the fancy titles Extended Repayment Plan (ERP) and A Better Loan for Education (ABLE). Each requires a $55 application fee and is only available to creditworthy applicants. Monthly payments of both principal and interest for each loan begin immediately. ABLE loans extend for six years and ERP loans for eight. Interest on ABLE loans is adjusted quarterly to 2.5% above the prime rate, while interest on ERP loans is adjusted quarterly to 4.5% above the 13-week U.S. Treasury Bill rate, with a cap of 18%. The only limit on the amounts borrowed are the borrower's creditworthiness and the actual costs of one's children's education. Life and disability insurance are available to guarantee repayment for both types of loan.

The Tuition Plan
57 Regional Drive
Concord, NH 03301
Tel: (603) 228-1161 or (800) 258-3640

Educational Loan Program: A short-term loan program that allows creditworthy parents to borrow up to $10,000 at twice the prime rate and repay it in 12 months. Insurance is available at extra cost. All this type of loan does is allow you to pay a big tuition bill now and spread the payment over the coming year. In other words, it's the equivalent of the tuition payment plans described in the first part of this appendix, but with one big difference—interest.

Educational Line of Credit: This is a short-term line of credit of $2,500 or more, depending on the borrower's creditworthiness. Interest rates are set at 4.5% above the prime rate, and borrowers have 12 months to repay any outstanding balance.

University Support Services
205 Van Buren Street, Suite 200
Herndon, VA 22070
Tel: (703) 709-8100 or (800) 767-5626

USS offers 15-year, unsecured loans of $1,500 to $25,000 a year, with a maximum cumulative total of $100,000. Rates are adjustable monthly and range between 4% and 6% above the commercial paper rates published in *The Wall Street Journal.* USS loans also have an up-front discount fee of 4%, which is deducted in advance from your loan. There's also a $55 application fee. Borrowers must prove their creditworthiness and have annual incomes of at least $15,000 a year.

INDEX

214

Index

217